Rudolph Peters

Islam and Colonialism

The Doctrine of Jihad in Modern History

mouton

Islam and Colonialism

Religion and Society 20

MOUTON PUBLISHERS · THE HAGUE · PARIS · NEW YORK

Islam and Colonialism

The Doctrine of Jihad in Modern History

RUDOLPH PETERS
University of Amsterdam

MOUTON PUBLISHERS · THE HAGUE · PARIS · NEW YORK

ISBN: 90-279-3347-2

Printed in the Netherlands

Acknowledgements

Many friends and colleagues have contributed to the preparation of this study. Here I want to thank them all. In particular I wish to express my gratitude to the successive directors of the Dutch Institute for Archaeology and Arabic Studies in Cairo, drs. W. F. G. J. Stoetzer and Dr. F. Leemhuis, for their helpfulness and hospitality during my visits to Egypt, and to drs. G. J. H. van Gelder and drs. A. C. van den Koppel, the successive librarians of the Institute of Modern Near Eastern Studies (I.M.N.O.) of the University of Amsterdam, for their tireless efforts in providing me with literature for my research. I am greatly indebted to drs. G. J. J. de Vries for his translation of some Persian texts, and to Mr. J. de Bakker for correcting the proofs and compiling the indexes and to Dr. J. Scheffer, who kindly read the draft of this study and suggested many grammatical corrections and stylistic improvements. For her accuracy, care and patience in typing a complicated and sometimes elusive manuscript I am grateful to Miss Alice Gastkemper. Finally thanks are due to the Dutch Organization for the Advancement of Pure Science (Z.W.O.) and the Faculty of Arts of the University of Amsterdam, for their subventions that enabled me to collect the necessary material in the Middle East.

Amsterdam, September 1979 RUDOLPH PETERS

Contents

Abbreviations

BSOAS	*Bulletin of the School of Oriental and African Studies.*
EI[2]	*Encyclopaedia of Islam.* New ed., 4 vols (publ. to date). Leiden: E. J. Brill, 1960—.
GAL	C. Brockelmann. *Geschichte der arabischen Literatur.* 2nd ed., 2 vols. Leiden: E. J. Brill, 1943, 1949; 1st ed., 3 suppl. vols. Leiden: E. J. Brill, 1937, 1938, 1942.
GAS	Fuat Sezgin. *Geschichte des arabischen Schrifttums.* 5 vols (publ. to date). Leiden: E. J. Brill, 1967—.
IC	*Islamic Culture*
IJMES	*International Journal of Middle East Studies*
IQ	*Islamic Quarterly*
IS	*Islamic Studies*
MEJ	*The Middle East Journal*
MW	*The Moslem World*
OLZ	*Orientalistische Literaturzeitung*
OM	*Oriente Moderno*
PRO	Public Record Office, London
REI	*Revue des Études Islamiques*
SI	*Studia Islamica*
WI	*Die Welt des Islam*
ZDMG	*Zeitschrift der deutschen Morgenländischen Gesellschaft*

1

Introduction

This study is about the impact of Western colonialism on Islam. It will investigate the first, religiously inspired, reactions against European colonial expansion in the Islamic world. Further it will analyze modern Moslem writings on the relationship between Moslems and non-Moslems in order to establish whether the ideas on this subject have been changed under the impact of colonialism or not. The central theme will thus be the doctrine of jihad, since, of all Islamic institutions, jihad is certainly the one that offers the most admirable resources for studies on the inexhaustible and complex theme of the relationship between Islam and Western colonialism.[1]

With the rise of industrial capitalism in Europe, European expansion accelerated and assumed a different character. Hitherto, trade in luxury goods had been its major impetus. Control of the seas was more important than control of land, since the possession of small trading posts was sufficient to secure the commercial interests. However, as a result of the advent of industrial capitalism in Europe during the nineteenth century, Western nations began to expand their domination over land, either as a means of monopolizing export markets of raw material and agricultural produce and import markets for manufactured products, or in order to protect strategical interests. In some regions, such as North Africa, colonial domination was instrumental in establishing colonies of white settlers. Great Britain extended its rule over nearly all of the Indian subcontinent during the first decades of this century. By the end of the century the Dutch had subjected the entire East Indian Archipelago. The French conquered North Africa, beginning with Algeria (1830), followed by Tunisia (1881) and Morocco (1912). The Russians expanded into Central Asia during the latter half of this century. In the Middle East, the British seized Egypt in 1882 and the Sudan in 1899. Italy, a latecomer on the scene of the imperialist scramble for land, occupied Libya from 1912 onward. After the First World War, Great Britain and France got hold of the Arab provinces of the former Ottoman Empire. As a result of colonial domination, the Islamic world has experienced drastic changes, in the field of economic and social relations, as well as on the ideological level. In the initial stages of European expansion into the Islamic world, Moslems in many places forcefully resisted the new situation and appealed to the doctrine of jihad in order to mobilize the population, to justify the struggle and to define the enemy. Given the fact that the colonial rulers were non-Moslems, the doctrine of jihad was well suited for these purposes. A description of this mainly mobilizing role of jihad as illustrated by the various resistance movements against colonial domination, will be given in Chapter 3. I shall restrict this description by taking into account only Sunnite Islam. Although the Shiʿite doctrine of jihad hardly differs from the Sunnite doctrine, there is one crucial exception: according to the classical Shiʿite scholars, jihad can only be waged under the leadership of the *Imām*. Hence, modern Shiʿite authors, when referring to wars after the sad disappearance of the last *Imām*, Muḥammad al-Mahdī, in 873 A.D., generally avoid the use of the word jihad and speak of 'holy war of defence' (*ḥarb difāʿiyyah muqaddasah*).[2]

The doctrine of jihad is still a hotly debated issue in the Islamic world, although, as I shall show in this study, its practical political importance has largely decreased. As the doctrine of jihad is concerned with the relationship between Moslems and non-Moslems, these modern writings on jihad reflect the attitudes of modern Moslems towards the Western powers. Under the impact of the new circumstances created by colonial domination, many Moslem thinkers reinterpreted the doctrine of jihad. This was done within the general framework of 'modernism'.[3] In Chapter 4 I shall analyze these modern writings on jihad.

To the best of my knowledge both fields, i.e. the political role of jihad and the new interpretations of the jihad doctrine, are practically virgin territory for scientific research. H. Th. Obbink's dissertation on jihad[4] partially deals with the modernist interpretation of the Indian Cheragh Ali. With a rather modest knowledge of the Islamic sources, Obbink attempts to disprove Cheragh Ali's argument that jihad is essentially defensive. Louis Mercier in his introduction to the translation of Ibn Hudhayl's work on jihad[5] offers some interesting material on the present-day political importance of jihad. His observations, however, are outdated and written from a typically colonialist point of view. No comprehensive study on the modern significance of the doctrine of jihad has so far appeared. With regard to the classical doctrine the situation is different. Since A. Reland's treatise on the Islamic law of war[6] which gives a fairly reliable survey of the doctrine of jihad, was published in the beginning of the eighteenth century, numerous scholarly and unscholarly writings on the subject have appeared.[7] Since, however, the most comprehensive work on classical jihad, namely the one written by al-Zuḥaylī, has only been published in Arabic and is not easily accessible in the West, I shall give an exposé of the classical doctrine in Chapter 2 of this study, in order to provide a starting point for studying the significance of jihad in the modern period.

The word *djihād* in modern Arabic stands for rather a vague concept. In accordance with its original meaning, it can denote any effort towards a subjectively praiseworthy aim, which need not necessarily have anything to do with religion. Hence it has been used to mean class struggle,[8] the struggle between the old and the new[9] and even the efforts of Christian missionaries.[10] But even when it is used in an Islamic context, it does not always denote armed struggle. It may also mean a spiritual struggle for the good of Islamic society or an inner struggle against one's evil inclinations. This wide semantic spectrum of the word *djihād* has confused many a foreign visitor with a defective knowledge of the Arabic language. Hearing the word *djihād* being used in sermons, in mosques or on the radio, they were led to think that a massacre of non-Moslems was at hand. In this study, however, I shall concentrate on the notion of jihad as armed struggle as it has been defined in the classical works in Islamic law (*fiqh*).

In Western languages the word *djihād* is often rendered by 'holy war'. If we are to understand by 'holy war' a war fought exclusively for religious reasons, this translation seems *prima facie* appropriate, since the classical works on *fiqh* only mention religious aims for waging jihad. Historical research, however, has proved that the wars of the Islamic states were fought for perfectly secular reasons. In a society where politics are entirely dominated by religion, there is no articulate distinction between politics and religion and political aims will always be represented as religious aims. Therefore, if one looks upon jihad as an enterprise of the state, it is not correct to render it as 'holy war'. Moreover, this translation would presuppose the existence of 'unholy wars' besides 'holy wars'. According to classical theory, however, all wars fought by the Islamic state are jihad and subject to the same set of rules. Only on the personal level could one speak of 'holy war' in the sense that individuals were often motivated by religious reasons to volunteer for participation in wars, since this was considered a pious and meritorious act that would be rewarded in the Hereafter.[11] In modern writings on jihad one occasionally comes across the phrase '*al-djihād al-muqaddas*' (holy jihad).[12] This is probably a *calque*, coined under the influence of Western languages. At the same time it seems to reflect a growing awareness of the fact that most wars are not religious and that hence the religious character of some wars needs to be emphasized.

The Islamic doctrine of jihad has always appealed to Western imagination. The image of the dreadful Turk, clad in a long robe and brandishing his scimitar, ready to slaughter any infidel that might come his way and would refuse to be converted to the religion of Mahomet, has been a stereotype in Western literature for a long time. Nowadays this image has been replaced by that of the Arab 'terrorist' in battledress, armed with a Kalashnikov gun and prepared to murder in cold blood innocent Jewish and Christian women and children.[13] The assumption underlying these stereotypes is that Moslems, often loosely called Arabs, are innately bloodthirsty and inimical towards persons of a different persuasion, and that owing to their religion, which allegedly preaches intolerance, fanaticism and continuous warfare against unbelievers. This view of Islam and Moslems, which developed in the Middle Ages, acquired new life and vigour in the era of European imperialism. Moslems were depicted as backward, fanatic and bellicose, in order to justify colonial expansion with the argument that it served the spread of civilization, which the French called *mission civilisatrice.* At the same time, this offered a convenient pretext for the use of force against the indigenous population, for behind the outward appearance of submissiveness of the colonized Moslems, the colonizers saw the continuous danger of rebeliousness lurking, nourished by the idea of jihad and waiting for an opportunity to manifest itself. The French orientalist Louis Mercier expressed these fears in the following words:

> Cependant, tous ceux d'entre nous, qui ont vécu de longues années au contact étroit d'une population musulmane, d'orient ou d'occident, ont eu de multiples occasions de sentir, j'en suis persuadé, que l'idée du jihâd persiste à travers le temps au point de dominer, fût-ce d'une façon latente, toute la vie de cette population, d'imprégner ses aspirations profondes et d'influer sur son attitude, dans ses relations avec les *infidèles.*[14]

This Western attitude towards Islam was deeply felt and resented in the Islamic world and was the principal cause of the apologetical approach towards their own religion. As we shall see in Chapter 4, many modern writings on jihad by Moslems bear evidence of this. Moslems have become suspicious of Western publications on Islam. Since the idea of jihad played an important rôle in presenting Islam and the Moslems in an unfavourable way, some Moslem authors tend to see in the treatment of this topic by Western writers a test-case for establishing whether their feelings towards Islam are biased or not. In the words of ʿAbbās Maḥmūd al-ʿAqqād:

> Having closely followed the books on Islam that are being written in the West, I have come upon a means of promptly ascertaining the good intentions and understanding of their authors, namely a glance at their views of the theme of jihad in the Islamic religion. For this is a theme that is notorious amongst non-Moslems and they have understood it in the sense that the law of the sword and the law of Islam are identical.[15]

This remark, which expresses a general feeling amongst Moslem intellectuals, may serve as an illustration of the dominant position that the discussion of jihad occupies in modern Moslem apologetics.

Most Western authors on Islam proceeded and still proceed from the assumption that religion and religious ideas are the basic factors in moulding society. Islam, as a common religion, accounted, in their view, for a common character of the Moslems and for great similarity of political, social and economic structures all over the Islamic world. Thus they would present jihad as an independent factor that could explain the bellicosity and rebelliousness of the Moslems, especially those under colonial rule. Modern Moslem authors proceed from the same assumption when they contend that the Moslems can regain their strength in order to withstand (neo-)colonialism and zionism, by returning to and abiding by the pristine principles of Islam and especially the doctrine of jihad. Maxime Rodinson has dealt with this essentialist view[16] and has convincingly argued with regard to the Islamic world that the course of history is in last instance determined by economic and social factors and that ideology plays only a secondary role. In this study I shall take the same position. Armed conflicts between groups, be they wars or revolts, arise out of a clash of material interests. In order to secure maximal popular support, also among those who are not directly involved, the leaders will appeal to an ideology of group solidarity that may be based on e.g. tribal, religious, national or class cohesion. In a society where the ideology is entirely dominated by religion and where there is no separation between the realms of politics and that of religion, wars and revolts, regardless of their actual causes, acquire a religious dimension in that their aims, their justifications and their appeals for support are expressed in religious terms. It is precisely the doctrine of jihad that provided this dimension in Islamic history. Its basic idea, the struggle of Moslems against unbelievers, self-evidently developed when the nascent Islamic state was at constant war against the surrounding non-Moslem enemies, and was elaborated during the wars of conquest. Then it was codified as a doctrine in the works on *fiqh* and could be invoked whenever Moslems had to fight against unbelievers or heretics. Thus it is natural that the jihad doctrine played a significant part in early resistance against colonial conquest. However, it was precisely European colonial expansion that prepared the way for the transformation of this doctrine and the decline of its political significance. The ideological attacks on Islam, a corollary of colonialism, induced Moslems to reinterpret their religion, whereas the social and economic transformations and the impact of Western ideas led to a separation between religion and politics and a gradual replacement of a political ideology based on religious cohesion by one based on ethnic and cultural cohesion, viz. nationalism.

2

The Classical Doctrine of Jihad

2.1 INTRODUCTION

The classical doctrine of jihad was laid down in the works on Islamic law (*fiqh*). In this chapter I shall give an *exposé* of classical legal thought on jihad. Since one of the essential characteristics of the *fiqh* is its casuistic method,[1] I shall not try to infer general rules from the subject matter to be found in the works on law and avoid the application of modern legal categories to it. As this survey will serve as a starting point in order to establish present-day relevance of the jihad-doctrine and the extent to which modern ideas on the subject have changed, some topics that are nowadays hardly of any importance will be omitted. This applies to the division of spoils and the rules that we would consider to be pertaining to civil law, law of conflicts (i.e. private international law) and international penal law. I shall further restrict this survey by not paying attention to the rules concerning Moslem rebels, since this topic is hardly ever discussed in modern writings on jihad. In composing this *exposé* authoritative works from the four Sunnite *madhhabs* and from the Zahirite, Twelver Shiʿite and Ismaʿilite persuasion will be investigated. With regard to the three most important *madhhabs* I shall also pay due attention to the works written in their formative period, like al-Shaybānī's *Siyar*, Saḥnūn's *Mudawwanah* and al-Shāfiʿī's *Kitāb al-Umm*.[2]

2.2 DEFINITION AND PURPOSE, THE CONCEPT OF RIBĀṬ

The classical books on *fiqh* do not contain much information on the definition and purpose of jihad. Probably these subjects were considered to be of minor importance, or as lying outside the scope of a legal treatise. Only modern works devote a few lines to this question.

They give as the common meaning of the word *djihād* 'exerting oneself as much as one can', whereas they define it legally as 'fighting the unbelievers by striking them, taking their property, demolishing their places of worship, smashing their idols and the like'.[3] Some authors call jihad as defined in the *fiqh* the 'Smaller Jihad', whereas the 'Greater Jihad' denotes a more spiritual activity like fighting one's evil inclinations or studying the *fiqh*.[4] Others distinguish between the 'Jihad of the Heart', i.e. struggling against one's sinful inclinations, the 'Jihad of the Tongue', i.e. ordering what is good and forbidding what is evil (*al-amr bi-l-maʿrūf wa-l-nahy ʿan al-munkar*), the 'Jihad of the Hand', i.e. the administering of disciplinary measures such as beating, by rulers and men of authority in order to prevent people from committing abominable acts, and, finally, the 'Jihad of the Sword', i.e. fighting the unbelievers for religion's sake. This last meaning, however, is always meant when the word jihad is used without qualification.[5] The direct purpose of jihad is the strengthening of Islam, the protection of believers and voiding the earth of unbelief. The ultimate aim is the complete supremacy of Islam, as one can learn from K 2:193 and 8:39[6] (*'Fight them until there is no dissension* [*or persecution*] *and the religion is entirely Allah's . . .'*) and from K 9:33 (*'He is it who hath sent His messenger with the guidance and the religion of truth, in order that he may set it above all* [*other*] *religion, though averse are the polytheists'*).[7]

The enemies that are to be attacked are all unbelievers, with the exception of those who are entitled to protection by virtue of a special agreement (like *amān*, *dhimmah* or a truce). From Mālik it has been reported that Abyssinians and Turks may not be attacked as long as they do not attack the Moslems. Later Malikite scholars do not take this as a command but as a mere piece of advice. Because of K 9:123 (*'O ye who have believed, fight the unbelievers who are near to you . . .'*), those unbelievers must first be attacked that are near to the Moslems. There is also a rational argument for this prescription, because one can accomplish with the same strength more against a near than against a far enemy.[8]

A special way of fulfilling one's jihad duty is called *ribāṭ* after K 8:60 (*'Prepare ye for them whatsoever force and cavalry* [*ribāṭ al-khayl*] *ye are capable of . . . .*'). The legal meaning of the word *ribāṭ* became: remaining for some time at the frontiers of the Islamic territory with the intention of defending Islam against the unbelievers. Many Traditions state that this is a highly meritorious act. However, since the *sharīᶜah* does not lay down special rules for it, the word *ribāṭ*, in its legal sense, can be regarded as virtually synonymous with the word *djihād*.[9]

2.3 TERRITORY OF ISLAM AND TERRITORY OF WAR[10]

Closely connected with the concept of jihad is the division of the surface of the world into two parts: the Territory of Islam (*dār al-Islām*) and the Territory of War (*dār al-ḥarb*). As this distinction is obvious, most authors do not pay attention to it. Territory of Islam is that part of the world where there is Moslem rule and the *sharīᶜah* is applied; the rest of the world is called Territory of War.

The Shafiᶜites mention a third category: Territory of Treaty (*dār al-ṣulḥ* or *dār al-ᶜahd*). When unbelievers conclude an armistice with the Moslems on the condition that they retain the possession of their lands and pay instead a certain annual amount of money or goods to be levied on the land, their territory is called Territory of Treaty by the Shafiᶜites. The amount of money or goods to be paid is called *kharādj*. This kind of *kharādj*, however, is not like the ordinary *kharādj*, but more like poll-tax, as the obligation to pay it ceases by conversion to Islam or by selling the land to a Moslem. The Hanafites, however, who, like the other Schools, only distinguish between Territory of Islam and Territory of War, hold that this kind of territory must be considered Territory of Islam and that the non-Moslem inhabitants must pay poll-tax. For them the decisive factor is to whom the sovereignty belongs. As in the case mentioned by the Shafiᶜites the sovereignty clearly belongs to the Islamic government, this territory is Territory of Islam. If, on the other hand, unbelievers conclude an armistice with the Moslems and remain sovereign in their land, this remains Territory of War, even if the unbelievers have paid money in exchange for the conclusion of the armistice. This strict dichotomy is, however, a later development within the Hanafite School. Muḥammad al-Shaybānī (d. 189/804) still mentions Territory of Treaty (*dār al-muwādaʿah*) as a separate category, without, however, clearly defining it.

Only the Hanafites pay attention to the rules whereby Territory of War becomes Territory of Islam and *vice versa*. As a general rule, Territory of War becomes Territory of Islam when it comes under Moslem sovereignty and the rules of the *sharīʿah* are applied. Some later scholars, however, are less strict in this respect. They consider it sufficient if the Moslems are safe and some rules of the *sharīʿah*, like the holding of the Friday *ṣalāh* and the celebration of the Islamic feasts, find application. Others hold that in addition there should be a Moslem *qāḍī* judging according to the *sharīʿah*. Regarding the transformation of Territory of Islam into Territory of War, Abū Ḥanīfah (d. 150/767) has laid down three conditions:

1. Application of the laws of the unbelievers;
2. Adjacency to the Territory of War;
3. Absence of the original security of life and property for the Moslems and the protected non-Moslems (*dhimmīs*), regardless of whether the new ruler has granted them safety or not.

These conditions can be fulfilled when unbelievers conquer a part of the Territory of Islam or if a group of protected non-Moslems (*dhimmīs*) denounce their treaty of protection (*dhimmah*). Besides the opinion of Abū Ḥanīfah, which has become dominant within the Hanafite School, there is the opinion of Abū Yūsuf (d. 182/798) and Muḥammad al-Shaybānī, which is less strict. They consider it sufficient for transformation that the laws of the unbelievers are openly applied.

2.4 THE LEGAL QUALIFICATION (*ḥukm*) OF JIHAD. EXEMPTIONS FROM THE JIHAD-OBLIGATION[11]

Jihad is a collective duty (*farḍ kifāyah*). This means that it is an obligation for the community as a whole and that this obligation is fulfilled when a sufficient number of persons perform it. If nobody takes part in jihad, the whole community is guilty. At least once a year the *Imām* must raid enemy territory, preferably that part which is most dangerous to the Moslems. If there is some excuse, such as weakness of the Moslem army or the poor state of the roads leading to enemy territory, the *Imām* may delay this annual expedition. The Twelver Shiᶜites have fundamentally the same notions as the Sunnites, except that they hold that the jihad-obligation is conditional upon the manifest presence of the *Imām*. Thus the doctrine of jihad has lost its practical consequence since the last Shiᶜite *Imām* went into Concealment in the year 873 A.D. Armed defence against attacks against Moslem lives and properties, however, remains obligatory, but this is not to be called jihad.[12]

Looking for scriptural evidence for the jihad-obligation scholars were confronted with many conflicting Koranic verses regarding the Moslems' attitude towards the unbelievers. They range from orders to approach them peacefully to unconditional commands to fight them. In order to explain these differences away scholars have had recourse to the theory of abrogation (*naskh*). They held that the various verses regulating the dealings with the unbelievers contained prescriptions that had relevance only for a certain period. When the situation had changed, other verses were revealed abrogating the previous ones. This culminated in the absolute and unconditional command to fight the unbelievers, which was revealed during the last years of Mohammed's lifetime, when the Moslems had the upper hand. The first period of Islam was one of preaching, whereby Mohammed was ordered to keep aloof from polytheists and to avoid a confrontation with them. In this period K 15:94 was sent down: *'Burst forth with what thou art commanded and turn from the polytheists'*. Subsequently, Mohammed was ordered to engage himself in a discussion with the unbelievers: *'Summon to the way of thy Lord and goodly admonition, and argue against them with what is better'* (K 16:125). When after the *Hidjrah* the Islamic community was continuously being harrassed by the Meccans and some Moslems became impatient with Mohammed's passivity and wanted to strike back, the Moslems were given permission to fight: *'Permission is granted to those who are fought against in that they have suffered wrong, who have been expelled from their dwellings without justification except that they say: "Our Lord is Allah!"; verily to help them Allah is able'* (K 22:39). Fighting them was only allowed as a defence against attacks by the unbelievers, as can be learned from K 2:190: *'Fight in the way of Allah those who fight you, but do not provoke hostility. Verily Allah loveth not those who provoke hostility'*. Finally the unconditional command to fight all unbelievers was sent down, when the following verses were revealed, abrogating all earlier verses: *'Fighting is prescribed to you, though it is distasteful to you'* (K 2:216); *'Then when the sacred months have slipped away, slay the polytheists wherever ye find them, seize them, beset them, lie in ambush for them everywhere; if they repent and establish the Prayer and pay the Zakāt, then set them free; Allah is forgiving, compassionate'* (K 9:5); and *'Fight against those who do not believe in Allah nor in the Last Day and do not make forbidden what Allah and His messenger have made forbidden, and do not practise the religion of truth of those who have been given the Book, until they pay the jizya off-hand, being subdued'* (K 9:29). The last two verses are commonly called the Sword Verses (*āyāt al-sayf*).[13]

In addition to these Koranic verses several Traditions are quoted in support of the unconditional jihad-obligation. The most important of these is: *'I have been ordered to fight the people until they profess that there is no god but Allah and that Mohammed is the messenger of Allah, perform the ṣalāh and pay the zakāh. If they do so, their life and property are inviolable for me, unless when the law of Islam permits it to be taken and they will be responsible towards Allah'*.[14]

The collective character of this obligation is based on the following arguments. (1) K 4:95 (*'Those of the believers who sit still – other than those who have some injury – are not on a level with those who strive with goods and person in the way of Allah. Allah hath given preference in rank to those who strive with goods and person over those who sit still, though to all Allah hath promised the good'*); K 9:122 (*'It is not for the believers to march out altogether; so why should not a party from each section of them march out, in order that they may gain understanding in religion, and that they may warn their people when they return to them, mayhap they will beware'*); (2) The fact that the Prophet often stayed behind in Medina when he sent out patrols and raiding parties; (3) The rational argument that duties that are obligatory for a purpose other than the act itself are collective duties, because producing the intended result is important and not the act itself. Sufyān al-Thawrī (d. 161/777-8) has held that jihad is not a collective duty but merely a recommended act. Only when the enemy attacks the Moslems does it become obligatory. His arguments are K 2:190 (cited above) and K 9:36 (*'But fight the polytheists continuously, as they fight you continuously, and know that Allah is with those who act piously'*). The authoritative interpretation is, however, that these verses have been abrogated by K 9:5 and K 9:29 (both cited above).[15] Other scholars have maintained that jihad is always an individual duty. They have founded this opinion on the Tradition: *'Who dies without having taken part in a raid or without having resolved to do so, dies in a situation of hypocrisy* [*māt ʿalā shuʿbah min al-nifāq*]*'*.[16] in connection with K 2:216, K 9:36 (both cited above) and K 9:41 (*'March out light and heavy* [*hearted*], *and strive with goods and person in the way of Allah; that will be better for you, if ye have any knowledge'*). The generally accepted opinion, however, is that these verses must be interpreted in the light of K 4:95 and K 9:122 (cited above).[17] Only in some special cases can jihad become an individual obligation. This occurs when the enemy attacks Moslem territory. The duty is then incumbent upon those who are being attacked, women and slaves included, and, if they have not sufficient force to repel the enemy, upon their neighbours. Jihad also becomes an individual duty when the *Imām* appoints certain persons for participation in a raiding expedition (*istinfār*), or when someone makes a vow to do so.

There are several categories of people that are exempt from the jihad-obligation as long as it is a collective duty. When, however, the enemy attacks Moslem territory, all people that are able to fight must fight, even if they belong to those who are in general exempt from the jihad obligation. Exempt are the following categories:

1. *Minors*. This is because they are not legally capable (*mukallaf*) and also on the strength of the following Tradition about Ibn ʿUmar:

'The Messenger of Allah inspected him on the Day of Uḥud, when he was a fourteen-year-old boy and did not allow him to fight. Then, on the Day of the Trench, when he was a fifteen-year-old boy, he inspected him and allowed him to fight.'[18]

2. *The Insane*, also because they are not legally capable.

3. *Slaves*, because their masters run the risk of losing their property.

4. *Women*, since their constitution is not fit for warfare. There is also a Tradition related by ʿĀ'ishah: *'I asked the Prophet permission to take part in the jihad. He answered: "Your* [fem. plural] *jihad is the pilgrimage"'.*[19] Women are never allowed to accompany small raiding patrols (*sariyyah*). When the expeditionary army is safe old women may go with it in order to render special services like cooking, distributing drinks and nursing the wounded. It is always reprehensible that young women accompany the army, even if it is safe, for fear of temptation. When it is absolutely necessary that the army take women with them for satisfying their sexual needs, they may take slave girls but not free women.

5. *The ill and handicapped.* These must be disabled to such an extent that they cannot walk or ride a horse. The reason for this exemption is obvious. There is also Koranic support: *'No blame rests upon the frail or upon the sick or upon those who find nothing to contribute, if they are honest to Allah and His Messenger; against those who do well there is no opening* [i.e. way to the infliction of punishment]; *Allah is forgiving, compassionate'* (K 9:91) and *'There is no blame upon the blind, or upon the lame, or upon the sick – ; whosoever obeys Allah and His Messenger He will cause him to enter Gardens through which the rivers flow; but whosoever turns away, He will inflict upon him a punishment painful'* (K 48:17).

6. *Those who do not possess the necessary means for an expedition*, like equipment, provisions, a mount, subsistence for their dependents, etc. This is based on K 9.91 (cited above) and K 9:92 (*'Nor against those to whom when they came to thee that thou mightest mount them, thou saidst: "I cannot find an animal to mount thee upon"; they turned away, their eyes full of tears for grief that they found not anything to contribute'*). The Hanafites do not mention this category.

7. *The best lawyer [faqīh] of a town.* This category is only mentioned by the Hanafites, without any scriptural argument.

8. *Those who did not obtain permission of their parents to partake in jihād.* This is based on the following Traditions: *'Ibn ʿAbbās ibn Mardas said to the messenger of Allah: "I want to take part in jihad". He then asked Ibn ʿAbbās: "Have you still a mother?" When Ibn ʿAbbās answered yes, he said: "Stick to your mother, for Paradise is at your mother's feet".'*[20] *'A man came to the prophet to ask his permission to take part in jihad. Then the prophet asked him: "Are your parents still alive?" When the man answered yes, the prophet said: "So strive then on their behalf" [fa-fīhimā fa-djāhid]'.*[21] Another argument is the rule that individual duties prevail over collective duties. As devotion to parents is an individual duty and jihad a collective one, the former prevails over the latter. Scholars disagree about whether permission is also required when either or both parents is not Moslem. The Hanafites and the Malikites answer this question in the affirmative. Only if the motive of withholding permission is the desire of preventing their Moslem son to fight their co-religionists, is it not considered to be valid, and the son is entitled to march out. When their motive is a normal one, like anxiety for their son or fear that they will come into trouble when their son is away, the son is not allowed to go. The Shafiʿites and Hanbalites hold that the permission of infidel parents is never required.

9. *Debtors who did not obtain permission of their creditors to partake in jihād.* This permission is required if the debt is due and the debtor does not leave sufficient property behind, and did not give bail. According to some, permission is also not required if the debtor has no property at all. The Hanafites emphasize that, even if he obtains the permission of his creditor, it still is recommended for the debtor not to go, but to stay behind to work in order to settle the debt. The Shiʿites never require the permission of the creditor. Two arguments have been adduced for the Hanafite rule. First the Tradition: *'One day the Prophet stood up amidst them and mentioned to them that jihad on the Path of Allah and belief in Allah are the best works. Then a man rose to his feet and said: "If I were killed on the Path of Allah, will then my sins be remitted?" . . . The Prophet*

answered: "Yes, if you patiently sacrifice yourself, advancing and not retreating, your sins will be remitted but not your debts. That is what Djibrīl told me!"'[22] The second argument is analogous to the one mentioned in the preceding paragraph. As the payment of a debt is an individual duty and jihad a collective duty, the former prevails over the latter.

The Malikites, the Shafiᶜites and the Hanbalites treat the problem whether jihad remains obligatory when the head of state or the commander of the army is an unjust tyrant. They answer this question in the affirmative, because good orders should be obeyed, without regard to who gives them.

2.5 THE SUMMONS (*daᶜwah*)[23]

Before the Moslems attack their enemies, they must summon them to conversion to Islam or to submission and payment of poll-tax (*djizyah*) if they belong to those of whom this can be accepted (cf. par. 2.15). This duty is founded on K 17:15 (*'We have not been accustomed to punish until we have sent a messenger'*), K 16:125 (*'Summon to the way of thy Lord with wisdom and goodly admonition and argue against them with what is better'*), and finally a saying of the Prophet: *'When you meet your heathen enemies, summon them to three things. Accept whatsoever they agree to and refrain then from fighting them. Summon them to become Moslems. If they agree, accept their conversion. In that case summon them to move from their territory to the Abode of the Emigrants* [i.e. Medina]. *If they refuse that, let them know that then they are like the Moslem bedouins and that they share only in the booty* [*ghanīmah* and *fay'*] *when they fight with the Moslems. If they refuse conversion, then ask them to pay poll-tax* [*djizyah*]. *If they agree, accept their submission. But if they refuse, then ask Allah for assistance and fight them.'*[24] The function of the summons is to inform the enemy that the Moslems do not fight them for worldly reasons, like subjecting them and taking their property, but that their motive is a religious one, the strengthening of Islam.

The wording of the summons may be general, but if the enemy wants more detailed information, e.g. about the prescriptions of Islam or about the amount of the poll-tax, such information must be given. Only the Malikites give detailed prescriptions about the procedure of summoning: On three subsequent days the enemy must be summoned to conversion. If he still refuses, he must be summoned to pay poll-tax on the beginning of the fourth day. If he refuses again, he may be attacked immediately. All scholars agree that a summons is not required if this is impossible, for instance when the enemy attacks the Moslems by surprise, or if it would endanger the Moslem position. This last situation arises for instance when it is suspected that the enemy will take advantage of the delay by strengthening his forces, or when the Moslem force is so weak that it can only win by a surprise attack. However, if this is not the case and the Moslems do attack without a summons, most schools do not hold these Moslems responsible for manslaughter or murder. Only the Shafiᶜites do so and consider it obligatory for them to pay blood money (*diyah*) to the relatives of the killed enemies and to perform expiation (*kaffārah*). The other scholars argue that the life of an unbeliever is not protected, except in special cases, none of which are applicable here.

There is controversy about the necessity of summoning peoples who have been summoned before, or whom the summons has reached before. The Malikites consider it obligatory also in this case, the Hanafites think it recommended and the Shafiᶜites and Hanbalites hold that it is legally indifferent (*djā'iz*). The inhabitants of the lands adjacent to Moslem territory are considered to be well-informed about the summons to Islam. Only 'peoples behind the Byzantines and the Turks' may not have heard of it. They should be summoned before being attacked.

2.6 RULES CONCERNING THE METHODS OF WARFARE[25]

It is allowed to kill the enemy using all possible weapons, like arrows, lances, swords and mangonels (which nowadays have been replaced by guns and bombs as Ibn ᶜĀbidīn remarks: III, 308), and means, like drowning them by diverting the course of a river, starving them by cutting off the supply of food and water, by poisoning the water, by throwing boiling oil and by setting them on fire. With regard to some methods there are certain reservations. Drowning or burning the enemy is only allowed if the Moslems cannot obtain victory by any other method. The Malikites consider the use of poisoned arrows forbidden because of the danger to the Moslems themselves, since the arrows may be cast back.

The use of mangonels is allowed, even if there are women and children in the besieged fortress, for the Prophet erected mangonels during the siege of al-Ṭā'if. Further evidence can be found in the following Tradition: *'Once the Prophet was asked about the children of the polytheists. Could they* [the polytheists] *be attacked at night with the possible result that they* [the Moslems] *would hit some of their women and children? He then answered: "They belong to them".'*[26] Finally it has been argued that only intentional killing of women and children is forbidden and not unintentional killing. Most scholars hold that Moslems may continue the struggle and shoot when the enemy shelters behind women and children, provided the Moslems do not aim at these women and children. The Malikites, the Shafiʿites and the Shiʿites show some hesitation in this case: they only allow it when there is no other way of conquering them. The reason for this hesitation is that killing these women and children infringes the rights of those who have a share in the booty.

When there are Moslem prisoners or merchants within the enemy fortress, or when the enemy shelters behind them, only Awzāʿī (d. 157/774) and Abū Thawr (d. 240/854) consider it forbidden under any circumstance to attack. In support of their opinion they cite K 48:25 (*'Had it not been for men and women who were believers, whom ye did not know, lest ye should have trampled them and disgrace fallen upon you unwittingly on their account – in order that Allah may cause to enter into His mercy whomsoever He willeth – had they been separated out, We should have inflicted upon those of them who have disbelieved a punishment painful'*). The other Schools consider it permissible in cases where there is no way for the Moslems to gain the victory other than by attacking the enemy with the risk of killing their co-religionists. This rule is based upon practical necessity, because there are Moslem prisoners and merchants in nearly every enemy town or fortress. In this case, however, the utmost caution is required and everything possible must be done to save their lives. The Malikites consider it in this situation forbidden to drown the fortress or to set it on fire. If during the fighting Moslems within the enemy fortress are killed by the Moslem army, the Shafiʿites and Hanbalites hold that the one who caused the death is obliged to pay blood money (*diyah*) and to perform expiation (*kaffārah*). The Shiʿites hold that in this case only expiation is obligatory.

Carrying the severed heads of the defeated enemies to Moslem territory or shooting them with catapults into the besieged fortress is considered reprehensible (and even forbidden by the Malikites), unless the Moslems may derive some profit from it, e.g. because it vexes the enemy or reassures the Moslem civilians.

2.7 ENEMY PERSONS WHO MAY NOT BE KILLED[27]

All Schools agree that minors and women may not be killed, unless they actually fight against the Moslems. According to several authentic traditions the Prophet has forbidden this. An additional argument is that by killing them, the Moslems destroy their own property, since women and children become slaves merely by being captured.

There is no unanimity about the prohibition of killing other categories of persons, like the aged, the insane, monks, the chronically ill, the handicapped, the blind, farmers and serfs. According to the opinion of the Hanafites, the Malikites and Hanbalites, these persons may not be killed. In their opinion only people that are able to fight may be killed, regardless of whether they actually fight or not. As people belonging to the categories mentioned usually do not fight, they may not be killed. However, if they do fight, or if they assist their warriors in any other way, e.g. by giving money or advice, then they may be killed. This opinion is founded on K 2:190 (*'Fight in the way of Allah those who fight you'*) and on several Traditions, e.g.: *'Once, when Rabāḥ ibn Rabīʿah rode out with the Messenger of*

Allah, he and the companions of the Messenger of Allah passed by a woman who had been slain. The Messenger of Allah halted and said: "She was not one who would have fought". Then he looked at the faces of the men and said to one of them: "Catch up with Khālid ibn al-Walīd and tell him that he must not slay children, serfs and women"'.[28] Another Tradition to the same effect: *'Once Mohammed said: 'Do not kill a decrepit old man, nor a small child, nor a woman"'.*[29]

The Shafiʿites and Ibn Ḥazm consider it permissible to kill persons belonging to these categories. They argue that K 9:5: *'Then when the sacred months have slipped away, slay the polytheists wherever ye find them, seize them, beset them, lie in ambush for them everywhere; if they repent and establish the Prayer and pay the Zakāt, then set them free; Allah is forgiving, compassionate.'* has abrogated K 2:190 (quoted above). Further they adduce the following Tradition: *'The Messenger of Allah has said: "Kill the old men of the polytheists and save the lives of their children"',*[30] and the fact that the Messenger of Allah gave orders for Durayd ibn al-Ṣimmah, who was a very old and blind man, to be killed. The Shafiʿites and Ibn Ḥazm regard unbelief as the justification for killing them, rather than their ability to fight. As these Schools only recognize the Traditions relating to the prohibition of killing women and children as authentic, they allow the killing of all other categories of unbelievers.

If a Moslem kills an unbeliever belonging to one of the categories mentioned, only the Shafiʿites oblige him to pay blood money (*diyah*) to the relatives of the victim and to perform expiation (*kaffārah*). The Hanafites and the Malikites – the other Schools do not treat this problem – consider it reprehensible that a Moslem kills his heathen father in a battle. If he meets him in the battle, he should wait until another Moslem can finish him off, unless he has to kill him in self-defence. Their opinion is founded on K 31:15 (*'Bear them* [parents] *kindly company in this world'*) and on the rule that one is obliged to maintain one's parents, even if they are unbelievers. Killing them is not compatible with this injunction.

Those who may not be killed should be taken captive. Only those who cannot contribute to the enemy force, like very old men –

except when the Moslems expect that the enemy will ransom him – or monks may be left behind. The Malikites state explicitly that enough food and other necessities must be left with them, so that they will not die of hunger or cold. If this obligation cannot be fulfilled from seized enemy property, then the Moslem treasury [*bayt al-māl*) must provide for this.

2.8 ENEMY PROPERTY[31]

By seizure and conquest all enemy property becomes Moslem property. Besides this general rule, there are certain specific rules about what damage may be inflicted upon enemy property. Awzāʿī (and the Ismaʿilis) considered burning and destruction of vegetation forbidden. Their arguments are a Tradition that Abū Bakr has said, when he sent out an expedition: *'I order you ten things, so remember them well: . . . (4) Do not cut trees with fruit on them. . . .'*[32] and K 2:205 (*'And when they turn away, they run about in the land to cause corruption therein, and to destroy the tillage and the stock; Allah loveth not the causing of corruption'*). The other Schools allow this as well as burning and demolishing buildings. They found their opinion on the Tradition that the Prophet burnt and cut the palmtrees of the Banū al-Naḍīr[33] on K 59:5 (*'The first palmtrees which ye cut down or left standing on their roots – it was by the permission of Allah, and that He might humiliate the reprobate'*), which refers to the cutting and burning of the palmtrees of the Banū al-Naḍīr, and finally on K 9:120 (*'Nor do they make any invasion which rouses the anger of the unbelievers, nor do they wreak any stroke on an enemy, but a good deed is thereby written down to their credit'*). The prohibition that can be inferred from Abū Bakr's words, addressed to the Moslem army setting out for Syria, is explained away by the interpretation that Abū Bakr only forbade this as the Prophet had predicted that Syria would fall into Moslem hands, so that destruction of the vegetation would be detrimental to Moslem interests. Other scholars use a more methodological argument: deeds of the companions can never abrogate deeds of the Prophet. The

Hanafites adduce a logical argument: since killing people is permitted in wartime, destruction of vegetation is *a fortiori* allowed.

All Scholars agree that movable property that cannot be taken to Moslem territory, must be burnt or destroyed so that the enemy cannot take advantage of it anymore. There is, however, some controversy concerning animals. The aforementioned Tradition from Abū Bakr also contains the following instructions: *'(6) Do not slaughter a sheep or a camel except for eating'* and *'(7) Do not burn bees'*. There are other Traditions with the same purport. Therefore the Shafiʿites and Hanbalites do not allow enemy animals to be killed, except during the battle or for eating. The Hanafites and the Malikites regard it as permissible to kill enemy animals if the Moslems cannot take these with them to Moslem territory and if the enemy would otherwise profit from them. The Malikites also allow enemy animals to be hamstrung, an operation which the Hanafites consider forbidden.

2.9 FLEEING FROM THE BATTLEFIELD[34]

As a rule Moslems are not allowed to flee from the enemy because of K 8:15 (*'O ye who have believed, when ye meet those who have disbelieved moving into battle, turn them not your backs'*) and K 8:45 (*'O ye who have believed, when ye meet a [hostile] party, stand firm and call Allah frequently to mind, mayhap ye will succeed'*). There are three exceptions to this rule. In the first place, a Moslem may flee from the enemy if his intention is to find a better tactical position or to lure the enemy into an ambush or if he wants to join another group of Moslems in order to strengthen their or his position. This is based on K 8:16 (*'Whosoever turns his back to them, unless it be swerving to a fight or wriggling round to a company, has become liable to anger from Allah, and his resort is Gehenna – a bad destination'*). Secondly, Moslems may flee if the number of the enemy force is more than twice that of the Moslems. This is on the strength of K 8:66 (*'Now Allah hath made it lighter for you and knoweth that there is weakness among you; so if there be a hundred of you who endure, they will overcome two hundred, and if there be a thousand of you, they will overcome two thousand, by the permission of Allah; Allah is with those who endure'*). This verse has been revealed to abrogate K 8:65 (*'If there be twenty of you who endure, they will overcome two hundred, and if there be a hundred of you, they will overcome a thousand of those who have disbelieved, because they are a people of no intelligence'*). The Malikites and Hanbalites take K 8:66 literally: for them the number is the relevant factor. The Hanafites and Shafiʿites, however, also take the relative strength (arms, equipment, mounts etc.) into account. The Hanafites and the Malikites hold that when the Moslem army numbers more than 12,000, they never may flee, regardless of the strength of the enemy. Ibn Ḥazm has a different opinion in this matter. According to him Moslems may never flee. K 8:66, he argues, only establishes that Moslems can overcome an enemy force twice as great as their own: it says nothing about the permissibility of fleeing. Finally, the Malikites and Shafiʿites hold that Moslems must flee, even if the number of the enemy force is less than twice that of the Moslems, when the Moslems are convinced that they will be defeated. They found their opinion on K 2:195 (*'Contribute in the way of Allah; hand not yourselves over to destruction, but do well; Allah loveth those who do well'*).

2.10 ASSISTANCE OF UNBELIEVERS[35]

If necessary, Moslems may ask for the assistance of unbelievers, since the Prophet asked the help of the Jewish tribe of Qaynuqāʿ in the Battle of Ḥunayn, and the help of the Meccans in the Battle of Khaybar. Before the aid is sought, it must be certain that the unbelievers concerned are well disposed towards the Moslems. The Malikites, however, regard this as forbidden. Military help of unbelievers may, in their view, only be accepted when they offer it spontaneously. Non-military assistance, like the services of sailors, diggers, tailors etc. may be asked for. The Malikites found their opinion on the following Tradition: *'On the day of the Battle of Badr the*

Prophet said to a man who followed him: "Go back, for I shall never ask for the assistance of an unbeliever".[36] Scholars of the other *madhhabs* explain this Tradition by the fact that at the time of the Battle of Badr, the Moslems were not in need of help from unbelievers.

2.11 TRADE WITH THE ENEMY[37]

Only the Hanafites and Ibn Ḥazm pay attention to the problem of trade with the enemy. They regard as forbidden the export of the following goods: slaves, riding animals, arms and materials that can be used for the fabrication of arms. The reason why the export of other goods is permitted, though the enemy may become stronger by obtaining them, is the fact that the Moslems profit from commodities that can only be obtained in enemy territory. In order to get them, barter is necessary. As for food, the permissibility of exporting it to the enemy is supported by the fact that the Prophet ordered Thamāmah to provide the Meccans with food, though the latter were still at war with the Moslems.

2.12 CAPTIVES AND PRISONERS OF WAR[38]

Upon being captured, women and children of the enemy (*saby*) become property of the Moslems and are part of the booty. The Malikites hold that the *Imām* may return them to the unbelievers, with or without payment of ransom. The other Schools, however, hold that the *Imām* has no such right. Adult male enemies who have not been killed in fighting, must be taken to Moslem territory as prisoners of war (*asārā*). The Hanafites exclude from this rule those enemies that cannot contribute to the fighting power and that will not be able to do so in the future. Hence, the aged and monks that cannot fight and are no longer fit for procreation, may be left behind, unless the Moslems expect the enemy to be willing to pay ransom for them. The Malikites hold the same view, with, however, the proviso that a sufficient amount of food, clothing etc. be left to them so that they will not die. If these goods cannot be provided for out of captured property, the Moslem treasury (*bayt al-māl*) must pay for it.

With regard to the fate of prisoners of war, the *Imām* has the choice between several policies: he may kill them, set them free in return for ransom or otherwise or he may enslave them. The Malikites hold that, in addition, the *Imām* may set them free with the status of protected non-Moslem subjects (*dhimmīs*), liable to pay poll-tax (*djizyah*). The *Imām* must take this decision according to the best interest of the Moslems. Until he has taken this decision, the prisoners must be treated well.

Prisoners that are converted to Islam after being captured may not be killed. The same applies to those categories of persons that may not be killed during the actual fighting. If the *Imām* decides that the prisoners be killed, this may not take place by torture, nor may the prisoners be mutilated. This prescription is founded on the following Tradition: *'Whensoever the Prophet sent out a raiding party, he used to say: "Raid in the name of Allah and on the path of Allah. Fight those who do not believe in Allah. Raid, do not embezzle spoils, do not act treacherously, do not mutilate and do not kill children"'.*[39] The Shafiʿites and the Hanbalites regard it as forbidden to burn prisoners of war, since the Prophet has said, referring to a certain enemy: *'If you catch him, kill him, but do not burn him; for the only one to punish by the fire is the Lord of the Fire* [i.e. Allah]'.[40] The other Schools hold that this Tradition has been abrogated by the unconditional command to fight the unbelievers as laid down in e.g. K 9:5.

Some of the earlier scholars (like al-Ḥasan al-Baṣrī, d. 110/728-9; Ḥammād ibn Abī Sulaymān, d. 120/738, and ʿAṭā' ibn Abī Rabāḥ, d. 114-5/734) have held that killing prisoners of war is forbidden, or, at least, reprehensible. Their main argument is K 47:4 (*'So when ye meet those who have disbelieved,* [*let there be*] *slaughter until when ye have made havoc of them, bind* [*them*] *fast* [i.e. make prisoners], *then either freely or by ransom* [i.e. liberate them out of kindness or in return for ransom]'). In support of their view they have further adduced K 2:191 ('. . . *but if they fight you, slay them* . . .') and a Tradition according to which Ibn ᶜUmar has said when a prisoner was brought before him: *'By Allah, as for someone who is trussed up, I shall not kill him'.*[41] The generally accepted opinion, however, is that the *Imām* has the right to kill prisoners. This is based upon the unconditional command to fight the unbelievers, which has abrogated K 2:191 and enlarged the possibilities enumerated in K 47:4. Further evidence is to be found in the example of the Prophet, since he had some prisoners killed after the Battle of Badr and had the Banū Qurayẓah put to death after their defeat. As to the Tradition of Ibn ᶜUmar, this must be interpreted as containing an interdiction to kill prisoners when they are trussed up. A more general argument is that, according to Islamic law, a non-Moslem can only obtain protection of life by conversion to Islam or by virtue of a special contract of protection (*dhimmah* or *amān*), not by mere captivity.[42]

As to the *Imām*'s right to set prisoners free, in return for ransom or otherwise, this is founded on K 47:4 (quoted above) and on the example of the Prophet, who liberated some prisoners after the Battle of Badr. The Hanafites, however, hold that the *Imām* has no such right, except in case of necessity, e.g. in order to redeem Moslem prisoners. They argue that K 47:4 has entirely been abrogated by the unconditional command to fight the unbelievers. For further evidence they cite K 8:67 (*'It was not for a prophet to have prisoners so as to cause havoc in the land; ye intend the chance gains of this world but Allah intends the Hereafter; Allah is sublime, wise'*),which was revealed after the Battle of Badr and is interpreted as a reproof against Mohammed for setting free some of his prisoners.[43] Finally they reason that if the *Imām* liberates prisoners in return for ransom, his policy is incompatible with the objective of jihad, since jihad aims at strengthening Islam, not at amassing wealth. If, however, he were to set them free without ransom, he would infringe the rights of the Moslems to their shares in the booty.

Not all prisoners may be enslaved, but only those who qualify for becoming protected non-Moslem subjects of the Islamic state (*dhimmīs*) according to the rules laid down by the various Schools (cf. par. 2.15).

2.13 SAFE-CONDUCT AND QUARTER (*amān*)[44]

Amān is the temporary protection of a non-Moslem's life, freedom and property, which is binding upon all Moslems. Two different situations are envisaged in which *amān* can be granted. One form of *amān* is quarter, granted during a period of actual warfare to one, several or all persons of a hostile fortress, town or region. The other form is safe-conduct, granted to individual non-Moslems at the borders of the Territory of Islam. The first form of *amān* does not include protection of property and, if it is granted after their defeat – a possibility held to be legal by all Schools except the Shafiʿites and Twelver Shiʿites – it does not even entail protection of freedom. In other words, despite the *amān*, they may be enslaved in this case. Individual *amān* accords protection of life, freedom and property. The *Imām* is bound to protect the *musta'min* (the non-Moslem who has been granted *amān*) against all those who are under his authority, Moslems and non-Moslems alike and, if expressly stipulated, even against non-Moslems that do not fall under his authority. If *amān* is violated by a Moslem or a non-Moslem subject of the Islamic state (*dhimmī*), the offender is liable to pay blood money (*diyah*) in the case of manslaughter or wounding, or to make good the damage inflicted upon the *musta'min* in his property.

Collective *amān*, i.e. *amān* granted to a fortress, an army, a town or a region, can only be granted by the *Imām* and in special cases by the army commander. In accordance with the rules concerning prisoners of war, it is also the *Imām*'s prerogative to accord *amān* after the defeat and capture of the enemy. If a Moslem grants a collective *amān*, he only binds himself, not the other Moslems. Individual *amān*, on the other hand, may also be granted by any adult and sane Moslem man, and according to most Schools, even by women, slaves and minors endowed with discernment. The validity of an *amān* accorded by a woman is only disputed by some Malikites, who hold that such an *amān* is subject to the *Imām*'s authorization. The prevailing opinion is founded upon the Tradition according to which the Prophet has said: '*We bestow protection upon those to whom you have granted protection, Umm Hānī*'',[45] upon the words of

ʿĀ'ishah: *'If a woman grants someone protection against the Moslems, this is valid'*[46] and finally upon the words of ʿAbd Allāh ibn ʿUmar: *'The amān of a woman, a slave or a minor is valid'.*[47] Those who hold that a woman's *amān* is not valid, argue that the aforementioned Tradition with regard to Umm Hāni' points at the fact that the Prophet expressly authorized Umm Hāni''s act, not that he accepted its validity. The validity of the *amān* granted by a slave is only contested by the Hanafites and some Malikites. The arguments in favour of its validity are the Tradition: *'The protection [dhimmah] of all Moslems is indivisible. Even the lowliest [adnāhum] of them strives for it'*,[48] and the words of ʿAbd Allāh ibn ʿUmar, that have been quoted above. The Hanafites, however, argue that the *amān* of a slave is only valid if his master has permitted him to fight. They hold that the word '*adnāhum*' in the aforementioned Tradition means 'the smallest number of them, i.e. one' and not 'the lowliest'. Finally they argue that a slave, who cannot bind himself by civil or commercial transactions, is *a fortiori* incapable of binding all Moslems by granting *amān*. Most Malikites hold that the *amān* accorded by a minor endowed with discernment is valid. The Hanafites make this conditional upon his parents' permitting him to take part in fighting. With regard to *amān* granted by Moslem prisoners of war or merchants within enemy territory, the Hanafites hold that this is never valid, since *amān* is generally obtained under duress in these circumstances. The other Schools, however, consider this kind of *amān* as valid unless duress is proved. If *amān* is granted by an unqualified Moslem and the non-Moslem is not aware of this fact, he may not be killed instantaneously, but must be safely conducted to enemy territory. *Amān* obtained from a Moslem who is in general qualified to grant it, but has been forbidden to do so by the *Imām*, is still valid. The Moslem, however, is in this case liable to be punished for disobedience.

Amān can be given by words in any language or by gestures. If the words or the signs are not clear, the outward appearance is decisive, not the intention. The Hanafites and the Shafiʿites emphasize that granting *amān* is a bilateral legal act and they require that the *musta'min* show his acceptance. Foreign envoys and messengers are automatically protected by *amān*. This is founded upon the Tradition: *'Were it not that envoys are not to be killed, I would behead you'*.[49] The Hanafites, however, do not accept the declarations of the envoy or messenger at face value and require that there be circumstantial evidence, such as letters written by the king he represents. *Amān* is also automatically accorded to merchants and to those who come to the territory of Islam in order to instruct themselves about the Islamic religion, on the strength of K 9:6 (*'If one of the polytheists asks thy protection, grant him protection until he hear the word of Allah, then see that he reaches a place of security; that is because they are people who have no knowledge'*).

If a non-Moslem and a Moslem are found together within the Territory of Islam and the non-Moslem claims that the Moslem has granted him *amān*, whereas the Moslem denies this, the non-Moslem's claim is accepted, unless there be circumstantial evidence to the contrary, e.g. when the non-Moslem is fettered. If a non-Moslem is found alone within the Territory of Islam, his *amān* can only be established by the testimony of two Moslem witnesses, not including the Moslem who granted him *amān*, since, as a general rule, one cannot testify to one's own acts.

Amān is accorded for a certain period, not exceeding one year. The Shafiᶜites and the Hanbalites consider it recommended that this period be no longer than four months because of K 9:2 (*'So go about in the land for four months and know that ye cannot frustrate Allah and that Allah is the humiliator of the unbelievers'*). *Amān* ends by return to enemy territory, by expiration of the stipulated time or by revocation by the *Imām*. If a *musta'min* returns to enemy territory but leaves property behind in the Territory of Islam, the *amān* remains in force with regard to his property. If a *musta'min* does not return to enemy territory within the stipulated period, the *Imām* must conduct him safely to enemy territory or fix a period after which the *musta'min* becomes a protected non-Moslem subject and must pay poll-tax. The Hanafites hold that the *musta'min* automatically becomes a protected non-Moslem subject and has to pay poll-tax in case he buys land and begins tilling and sowing it. *Amān* can be revoked by the *Imām* if the *amān* turns out to be against the interests of the Moslems. The revocation must be formally conveyed to the *musta'min*, who then has the right to be safely conducted to enemy territory. The mere fact that the *musta'min* commits crimes does not *per se* terminate the *amān*. Only the Malikites consider an *amān* causing damage to the Moslems, e.g. if the *musta'min* is a spy, as null and void *ab initio*.

The Hanafites hold that a non-Moslem who enters the *ḥaram* in Mecca may not be killed or taken prisoner. The Moslems are even obliged to provide him with food and water, since otherwise they would indirectly kill him. They found their opinion on K 29:67 (*'Have they not considered that we have appointed a secure ḥaram while all around them the people are plundered?'*), on K 3:97 (*'In it there are signs, Evidences – the station of Abraham, and the security of him who enters it'*), and finally on K 2:191 (*'Do not fight them, however, in the precincts of the Sacred Mosque, until they fight you therein, but if they fight you, slay them'*). The other Schools regard these verses as having been abrogated by the unconditional command to fight the unbelievers.

A Moslem who enters enemy territory with an *amān* granted to him by the non-Moslems, is considered to have implicitly accorded *amān* to them. This *amān*, then, is only binding upon himself. On the strength of it he is not allowed to kill the non-Moslems or take their property.

2.14 ARMISTICE[50]

Armistice (*muʿāhadah*, *ṣulḥ*, *muṣālaḥah*, *hudnah*, *muhādanah*, *muwādaʿah*) is a treaty of peaceful coexistence with the enemy, who remains independent and not subjected to Islamic rule. For individual enemies it entails protection of life, freedom and property (*amān*). They may travel freely in Islamic territory, without, however, being allowed to settle there permanently. The *Imām* guarantees their safety against attacks from those who are under his authority, but not against attacks from other enemies, unless expressly stipulated. Concluding an armistice, which may only be done by the

Imām or his representative, is allowed if it serves the interests of the Moslems, e.g. if the Islamic State suffers from internal strife (*fitnah*) or if the Moslem army is weak, or if it is to be expected that the enemy will be converted to Islam or offer to pay poll-tax (*djizyah*). This is founded on K 47:35 (*'So do not grow faint and call for peace, seeing ye have the upper hand, and Allah is with you, and will not defraud you of your works'*).

Conclusion of armistices is legal on the strength of K 8:61 (*'If they incline to peace, incline thou to it'*), of the example of the Prophet since he concluded an armistice with the Meccans at Ḥudaybiyyah and finally on the strength of the argument that conclusion of an armistice, since it is restricted to situations where it is favourable for the Moslems, must be regarded as a continuation of the jihad-duty with different means. That treaties of armistice are binding upon the Moslems is usually argued with reference to verses like K 5:1 (*'O ye who have believed, fulfil contracts'*) and K 9:4 (*'Fulfil their covenants up to* [*the end of*] *its period'*). Only Ibn Ḥazm holds that the conclusion of armistices is forbidden. The Prophet's example of Ḥudaybiyyah has, he argues, been abrogated by *sūrat al-Tawbah*, especially by verses like K 9:1 (*'Renunciation by Allah and his Messenger of the polytheists with whom ye have made covenants'*); K 9:5 (*'Then when the sacred months have slipped away, slay the polytheists wherever ye find them'*); K 9:29 (*'Fight against those who do not believe in Allah, nor in the Last Day* [etc.]'), and finally K 9:7-8 (*'How shall the polytheists have a covenant with Allah and with His messenger? . . . How? If they get the upper hand of you they will not regard bond or agreement'*).

All Schools except the Hanafites agree that an armistice must be concluded for a specified period of time. The Shafiʿites and Shiʿites, however, allow an armistice for an undefined length of time on the condition that the *Imām* stipulate the right to resume war whenever he wishes to do so. As the Treaty of Ḥudaybiyyah was concluded for ten years and exceptions to a general rule (i.e. the obligation to fight) should be restrictively interpreted, Shafiʿite, Hanbalite and Ismaʿilite scholars do not allow armistices for periods longer than ten years. If an armistice has been conluded for a longer period, they hold that it expires automatically and becomes null and void after ten years have elapsed. Renewal of the treaty after this period is perfectly legal according to them. All Schools stipulate that, except in cases of absolute necessity, it is recommendable for the *Imām* not to conclude an armistice for a period longer than four months, because of K 9:2 (*'So go about in the land four months and know that ye cannot frustrate Allah and that Allah is the humiliator of the unbelievers'*).

Certain stipulations cannot be included in a treaty of armistice. Some of these stipulations render the treaty null and void, others are themselves null and void, without affecting the validity of the treaty. As usual, the works on *fiqh* do not give a general rule in order to determine to what category a certain stipulation belongs. They merely give a few examples. The following stipulations are generally considered as rendering the treaty null and void:

1. The stipulation that Moslems will remain as prisoners in the hands of the enemy or that the enemy keeps Islamic territory occupied.

2. The stipulation that the Moslems pay money in return for the conclusion of the armistice. This stipulation, however, is valid if the Moslems are being threatened with extermination. In this situation it is permitted because the Prophet, when surrounded by hostile tribes, considered offering one-third of the date harvest of Medina to the enemy in return for willingness to conclude an armistice. Though nothing came of it as the enemy demanded one half of the harvest and the Medinans did not agree, the fact that the Prophet was prepared to follow that course of action proves that it is allowed. A second argument for the permissibility can be found by analogical reasoning: if the Moslems are being threatened with extermination, they can be compared with Moslem prisoners in the hands of the enemy, who may be ransomed.

3. The stipulation that the *Imām* or both parties may terminate the armistice unilaterally and resume fighting whenever they wish. The Shafiʿites and the Shiʿites, however, allow that, in the case of an armistice for an undefined length of time, the *Imām* makes such a stipulation.

The following stipulations are generally considered as being null and void without affecting the validity of the rest of the treaty:

1. The stipulation that hostages, kept for securing fulfilment of the treaty, will be killed if the enemy fails to fulfil his obligations. Hostages have a right to protection of life and property (*amān*) and this right is not nullified by treachery of their own people. Therefore Muʿāwiyah did not kill his Byzantine hostages when the Byzantines broke their pledges.

2. The stipulation that women of the enemy who have been converted to Islam and come to the Moslems, will be sent back. This rule is based on K 60:10 (*'O ye who have believed when believing women come to you as emigrants, examine them – Allah best knoweth their belief – then if ye know them to be believers, do not send them back to the unbelievers – such women are not allowable for them* [*in marriage*], *nor are they allowable for such women – so pay them what they have expended* [*as dowry*]*'*). A similar stipulation with regard to men is considered to be valid by all Schools, with the exception of the Hanafites and some Malikites.

As a general rule, an armistice is terminated when the agreed term expires or when the enemy fails to fulfil his obligations or denounces the armistice. That in this case the Moslems are not bound anymore by the treaty can be inferred from K 9:7 (*'As long as they act straight with you, act straight with them'*) and K 9:12 (*'But if they violate their oaths after they have made a covenant and attack your religion, fight the leaders of unbelief'*). It must, however, be clear that the acts constituting the breach of the armistice have been performed by the enemy ruler or his representative, or, anyway, with his knowledge and consent. An armistice can also be terminated when the *Imām* of the Moslems denounces it. On the strength of K 8:58 (*'If thou fearest treachery at all from any people, cast back to them* [*thy covenant*] *equally'*), he may do so when there is evidence to the effect that the enemy is planning to break the armistice. The Hanafites, however, hold that the *Imām* may denounce the armistice whenever the continuation of warfare is more favourable for the Moslems than the continuation of peace. They base their opinion on the fact that the Prophet denounced his treaty with the Meccans, when it became more profitable for him to do so. If the enemy originally paid money in return for the conclusion of the armistice, the *Imām*, in this case must pay back the remainder, in proportion to the duration of the armistice and of the period for which it had been concluded. All Schools agree that after denunciation the enemy should be allowed some time in order to divulge the news in all parts of his realm.

2.15 TERMINATION OF JIHAD[51]

The aim of jihad is the subjection of the unbelievers. This can be attained by two means. In the first place, unbelievers can be converted to Islam. They then become subjects of the *Imām* of the Moslems and have the same rights and obligations as the other Moslems. In the second place they can submit themselves to Islamic government, without, however, being converted. They then obtain a special status with a certain autonomy, are subjected to special discriminative measures and must pay poll-tax (*djizyah*). The treaty whereby they submit themselves to Islamic government in exchange for protection, is called *dhimmah* and these non-Moslem subjects of the Islamic state are named *dhimmīs*.

A *dhimmah*-treaty cannot be concluded with all unbelievers. All Schools agree that apostates are to be excluded, as they should be killed. The Hanafites also exclude Arab idolaters. The criterion in deciding who is an Arab is to be found in the mother tongue. The Malikites only exclude the idolaters of the Quraysh tribe. Their argument is that during Mohammed's lifetime all Qurayshites had been converted to Islam, so that afterwards Qurayshite idolaters could not be but apostates. For practical reasons they also exclude tribes and peoples who live in remote parts of the world where Islamic rule cannot be effectively established. The other Schools are more exclusive and hold that a *dhimmah* treaty can only be concluded with Christians, Jews and Zoroastrians (*madjūs*). Their argument is that the command to fight the unbelievers is general and that exceptions to it must be interpreted restrictively. These exceptions can be found in K 9:29 (*'Fight against those who do not believe in Allah nor in the*

Last Day and do not make forbidden what Allah and his messenger have made forbidden, and do not practise the religion of truth of those who have been given the Book, until they pay the jizya off-hand, being subdued') and in the saying of the Prophet, referring to the Zoroastrians: *'Follow with regard to them the custom with regard to the People of the Book'*.[52] Those who are excluded from the possibility of concluding a *dhimmah*-treaty, have the choice between Islam and the sword, i.e. between conversion or being slain.

3

Jihad and Resistance Against Colonialism

3.1 INTRODUCTION

The classical doctrine of jihad, as expounded in Chapter 2, has inspired many movements that have waged armed struggles against Western colonial domination. In this Chapter I shall describe a number of these movements. In each case a succinct exposé will be given of the economic, social and political developments that made the Moslem population revolt against Western domination and a survey of how these struggles were ideologically conceived by those who took part in them. Historians specialized in the regions and periods I shall deal with, will not find new facts in this study, except, perhaps, with regard to the religious aspect. As for the historical background, I have drawn chiefly on secondary sources pertinent to the periods and regions under discussion. In describing the religious aspects of these movements, however, I have tried to avail myself, where possible, of primary sources in order to let the leaders of these movements, or their propagandists and contemporary partisans speak themselves.

The Islamic world covers a vast area inhabited by a great number of peoples of different cultures and languages. With the rise and expansion of Western industrial capitalism in the nineteenth and the beginning of the twentieth century, most of these peoples were subjected to Western colonial rule. In the great majority of the regions brought under Western domination, resistance amongst the local population in the initial stages of colonization organized itself in politico-religious movements that fought the foreign rulers under the banner of jihad. In this part I shall not deal with all of these movements. For practical purposes I have confined myself to the central lands of Islam, including the Indian subcontinent. Thus I have excluded the jihad-movements in Indonesia (e.g. the revolt of Dipå Negårå, 1825-1830, the Atjeh-war, 1873-1904),[1] in Central Asia (the resistance against Russian expansion in the second half of the nineteenth century)[2] and in Somalia (the Mahdist movement led by Muḥammad ibn ᶜAbd Allāh against British and Italian conquest, 1899-1920).[3] For the same reasons I shall not deal with the various jihad-movements in Black Africa, the more so as most of these movements were not directed against Western domination and thus fall outside the scope of this study.[4] For reasons that I have expounded in Chapter 1, I have also restricted this study to movements whose religious character derived from Sunnite Islam. Hence, I have excluded the various wars and revolts against Western influence in Iran (e.g the war with Russia in 1826-28, the Tobacco-revolt of 1891) and the anti-British Iraqi revolt of 1920, since all of these were, with regard to religious propaganda, ideologically inspired by concepts from Shiᶜite Islam.

The choice of the topics needs further elucidation on some points with regard to their classification as being anti-colonial. It may cause some surprise that I have included the Mahdist revolt in the Sudan in this study, since formal colonization only took place after the defeat of this movement, when, in 1899, the Anglo-Egyptian condominium was established. I felt, however, justified in doing so, as the Turco-Egyptian conquest, from its inception in 1821, gradually assumed characteristics that made it very similar to European colonization. From the 1870s onwards it can be labelled as Western colonization at a remove, since the Egyptian expansion into Africa was conditioned by Western, mainly British, interests. Moreover, the Egyptian government employed an increasing number of Western administrators and military men in the Sudan. This Western character was very clearly perceived by the *Mahdī* and his followers and was in fact one of their main grievances. About a year after the beginning of the Mahdist movement Egypt was occupied by the British. The Mahdist state was then drawn into a direct confrontation with British power. Another point concerns the treatment of the Ottoman jihad-proclamation of 1914 in this framework. It may well be argued that the Turkish participation in World War I can hardly be regarded as anti-colonial struggle. However, as this jihad-proclamation was part of war-propaganda addressing Moslem peoples outside the Ottoman

Empire and inciting them to rise against their colonial rulers, there are good reasons to include the subject in the scope of this study.

In view of the above-mentioned considerations, I shall deal in chronological order with the following topics:

1. Moslem resistance against British colonialism in India;
2. Algerian resistance, led by ʿAbd al-Qādir, against French colonialism;
3. The Mahdist movement in the Sudan;
4. Egyptian resistance, led by Aḥmad ʿUrābī, against the British occupation of Egypt;
5. Sanūsī resistance against Italian colonialism in Libya;
6. The Ottoman jihad-declaration of 1914;
7. Religious opposition against British colonialism and zionism in Palestine.

In the resistance against Western colonialism, the doctrine of jihad was of paramount importance. However, it was not the only doctrine that was invoked by the leaders of these movements. Just as in Mohammed's lifetime, the call for jihad was often accompanied by the call for emigration, *hidjrah*, from territory ruled by unbelievers, *dār al-ḥarb*, to Islamic territory, *dār al-Islām*. According to the works on *fiqh* the obligation for Moslems residing in the *dār al-ḥarb* to emigrate to the *dār al-Islām* holds for those who are prevented from performing their religious duties and are capable of emigrating. In other cases, emigration is recommended as it will strengthen the Islamic state and put an end to intercourse with unbelievers. The obligation of *hidjrah* derives from K 4:97-100 and from some of the Prophet's sayings, such as: *'I have nothing to do with any Moslem that resides amongst the polytheists'*.[5] The Hanafites, however, do not mention this duty, regarding it as having been abrogated on the strength of the tradition: *'No emigration after the Conquest* [*of Mecca*]*'*.[6] After Mohammed's death, the doctrine was of no practical significance. Therefore it is omitted in most works on *fiqh*. Not until the Christians recaptured Sicily and Spain, was the discussion renewed and were *fatwās* asked with regard to the question whether Moslems could remain under Christian rule.[7] Since many jihad movements saw as their principal aim the establishment of a purely

Islamic state, ruled by the *Sharīʿah*, the doctrine of *hidjrah* came in useful in order to induce the Moslems living under colonial rule to join the territory where the new state was to be established or had already begun to take shape. Later, when active resistance was not possible anymore, the obligation to emigrate, in some cases, played an independent role, when large numbers of Moslems collectively emigrated from colonized territories. The most famous of these religiously inspired movements of passive resistance were the exodus from Tlemcen in 1911[8] and the *Hijrat-Movement* in India in 1920, when tens of thousands of Indian Moslems set out for Afghanistan, following a *fatwā* to this effect.[9]

Another concept that we meet quite frequently in Islamic anti-colonial resistance does not derive from the *Sharīʿah* but belongs to the realm of Islamic eschatology. This is the belief in the coming of the *Mahdī* (the rightly guided one). According to this belief, the *Mahdī* will appear shortly before the End of Time. He will restore justice on earth and put an end to corruption and oppression. Obviously such a belief can have two opposite effects. It may lead to resignation and fatalism *vis-à-vis* injustice and oppression. Those who suffer, will patiently endure all wrongs and passively await the coming of the *Mahdī*. In some cases this belief has been consciously used in order to produce this effect and to keep the population quiet. Thus, during ʿAbd al-Qādir's war against the French in Algeria, the leaders of a rival order, the Ṭayyibiyyah *ṭarīqah*, who wanted to undermine ʿAbd al-Qādir's position, employed the *Mahdī* belief in this sense and issued the following proclamation:

> Patientez, musulmans, patientez car le jour de la délivrance approche . . . Attendez avec calme l'arrivée de celui auquel rien ne pourra résister et qui rejettera les escadrons des impies dans la mer qui les a vomis contre nous. Patientez car le Sultan régénerateur et vengeur, le Moule Saa[10] s'avance vers vous pour assurer votre triomphe. Patientez car ses étendards flottent déjà au couchant et portent dans ses plis votre résurrection. Patientez, patientez.[11]

Some orientalists regarded this as the essential aspect of the *Mahdī* belief and hence opposed this belief to the doctrine of jihad:

> The way the jihad-doctrine is being explained by Mohammedan scholars and is being professed, in a less systematic fashion, by the popular masses, offers an excellent criterion of the progress of Islam in the direction in which the political circumstances of our days increasingly force it. Finally it will have to yield: it must abandon the doctrine of jihad and partly transfer it to the practically harmless doctrine regarding the end of the world, the Messianic or Mahdist expectations. . . . Before it comes to that, however, the last political centre of Islam will probably have been brought under European influence, and all less civilized Mohammedan peoples must have learnt to submit to a strong European rule.[12]

On the other hand, the belief in the coming of the *Mahdī* could provide a powerful mobilizing force, whenever a *Mahdī* claimant rose and assumed command in a struggle against oppression and injustice. This has happened several times in the course of Islamic history. ʿUbayd Allāh (d. 934), founder of the Fatimid dynasty, and Ibn Tūmart (1077-1130), founder of the Almohad dynasty, both declared themselves to be the expected *Mahdī* and could thus acquire a large following in order to overthrow the existing governments. The rise of Western colonial expansion with its concomittant social and economic changes, provided a fertile soil for Mahdist movements, the more so as the spread of non-Moslem rule over the territory of Islam was, according to the *Mahdī*-belief, one of the signs that would precede the coming of the *Mahdī*. In many parts of the Islamic world, *Mahdīs* rose and fought against colonial domination. In Algeria, several *Mahdī* revolts took place during the latter half of the nineteenth century.[13] In India, a man called ʿAbd al-Raḥmān proclaimed himself *Mahdī* in Surat in 1810,[14] whereas after the death of Aḥmad Shahīd, the leader of the *Ṭarīqa-i Muḥammadī*, in 1831, rumour had it that he would return as the *Mahdī* and that the Moslems should in the meantime continue their struggle against the British until he would reappear to lead them to final victory.[15] In Upper Egypt, a *Mahdī* revolt broke out in 1865.[16] Generally, these revolts were only short-lived and of little lasting effect. There were, however, exceptions like the *Mahdī* revolt in the Sudan and the struggle of Muḥammad ibn ʿAbd Allāh against the British and the Italians in Somalia.

In this historical survey of the most important religiously inspired movements of resistance against colonialism in the Islamic world, I shall concentrate upon the study of jihad without, however, neglecting the part played by other Islamic ideological concepts.

3.2 MOSLEM RESISTANCE AGAINST BRITISH COLONIALISM IN INDIA

The second half of the eighteenth and the first decades of the nineteenth century saw the rapid expansion of British domination in India. In 1765 the East India Company had acquired by contract the right to collect the tax revenues of Bengal from the Mogul Emperor Shāh ʿĀlam II. Thenceforth the British extended their rule by means of treaties of protection, annexation and conquest. By 1820 British supremacy had been firmly established. Although the Mogul court lingered on until 1857, the Emperors had gradually lost their power and had been reduced to mere puppets in the hands of the British. The new rulers introduced many administrative measures that had enormous economic and social consequences for the country. In 1793 they enacted a series of financial reforms, the *Permanent Settlement*, in Bengal, which deeply disturbed the existing social order. The introduction of the Sales Law which authorized the auction of the holdings of an owner who did not pay his dues, whereas previously he would have been fined or imprisoned, the demand of documentary proof for rent-free tenures, which in many cases could not be produced and high assessments brought the class of Moslem landowners to ruin. Their place was taken by Hindu tradesmen and moneylenders from the towns.[17] The higher tax burden led to a greater oppression of the peasants, to whom this burden was passed on, whereas, on the other hand, the patronage relations that had previously existed between the landlords and their tenants and had mitigated the hardships of the latter, were severed when the holdings came into other hands. The enactment of the Permanent Settlement also affected the *waqf*-holdings, which were exempt from taxation.

The new laws required that their deeds of foundation be produced. As these had often been lost, many of these holdings could not retain their privileged status. This entailed a reduction of the financial contributions for instruction and the maintenance of mosques. The ruin of the Moslem landed aristocracy, finally, dealt a severe blow to the local handicraft industries, which used to produce luxury goods like fine textiles, jewellery, decorative swords, etc. The decline of these handicrafts was accelerated by the introduction of machine-produced goods from England.[18]

Discontent amongst the Moslems was, in the sphere of religion, reflected in the discussion about the status of India under British rule. Was it to be considered *dār Islām* or *dār ḥarb*?[19] This was not entirely a theoretical discussion, since the outcome would affect the application of certain rules of the *sharīʿah*.[20] The discussion, however, was not a completely novel one. When the Hindu dynasty of the Marathas had overrun great parts of Moslem India in the eighteenth century, the same question had been posed. At that time, most scholars had been of the opinion that India had not lost its status of *dār Islām*.[21] However, as the British occupation of India, contrary to Maratha rule, which had left the social order more or less intact, had a deeply felt impact upon the Indian society, the growing discontent and frustration amongst the Moslems, expressed itself in *fatwās* stating that India had become *dār ḥarb*. Thus Shāh ʿAbd al-ʿAzīz (1746-1824), the son of the famous theologian and reformer Shāh Walī Allāh, issued the following *fatwā* in 1803:

> *Question*: Does *dār Islām* become *dār ḥarb* or not? *Answer*: In the authoritative books generally the opinion is preferred that *dār Islām* becomes *dār ḥarb* under three conditions. In *al-Durr al-Mukhtār* it is written that *dār Islām* can only become *dār ḥarb* by three things: by the enforcement of the rules of the polytheists, by being contingent to *dār ḥarb* and by the fact that no Moslem or *dhimmī* remains protected on the strength of his original *amān*. *Dār ḥarb* becomes *dār Islām* by the application of the rules of the Moslems. In the *Kāfī* it is written that by *dār Islām* a region is understood where the *Imām al-Muslimīn* wields authority and which is under his sway, and that by *dār ḥarb* a region is

> understood where the commands of its ruler are applied and which is under his sway. In this city [sc. Delhi], the *Imām al-Muslimīn* wields no authority at all whereas the authority of the leaders of the Christians is enforced without any trouble. By the enforcement of the rules of unbelief is meant that unbelievers can act on their own authority in governing and dealing with the subjects, in collecting land-tax, tolls, tithes, customs and excises, in punishing highway robbers and thieves, in settling disputes and in punishing crimes. It is true that certain Islamic rules like those regarding the congregational prayers of Friday and the festivals, the call for prayer and the slaughter of cows are not being interfered with. This, however, is because the essence of these things is of no value to them, for they demolish mosques without any scruples and Moslems or *dhimmīs* can only enter this city or its surroundings by asking *amān* from them. It is only for their own sake that they do not interfere with the traffic of travellers and merchants. On the other hand notables like Shudjāᶜ al-Mulk and Wilāyatī Begam cannot enter these regions without their permission. The rule of the Christians extends from this city to Calcutta. Admittedly, they have not enforced their authority to the left and to the right, like in Hyderabad, Lucknow and Rampur, but this is because of peace treaties and because the rulers of those territories obey them. From the Traditions and the study of the lives of the noble companions and the great Caliphs the same conclusion presents itself.[22]

Before long the opposition against British rule developed into armed resistance. This struggle was waged under the banner of Islam and the doctrine of jihad played a significant part in it. The most important of these opposition movements was the *Ṭarīqa-i Muḥammadī*, led by Sayyid Aḥmad Barēlwī (1786-1831) and actively supported by two learned scions of the Shāh Walī Allāh family, viz. Shāh Ismāᶜīl (1779-1831) and Shāh ᶜAbd al-Ḥayy (d. 1828), the one a son-in-law and the other a nephew of Shāh ᶜAbd al-ᶜAzīz.[23] The *Ṭarīqa-i Muḥammadī* started in Delhi, in Northern India in 1821. It was both a revivalist religious movement, striving for reforms in order to ban all pernicious religious innovations (*bidaᶜ*) and to achieve an amelioration of the present corrupt society, and a political and social organization, working for the liberation of the country from the unbelievers. The distinction between pure monotheism (*tawḥīd*) and polytheism (*shirk*) was one of its principal doctrinal elements. Because of the striking ideological resemblances to the Wahhābī movement in Arabia, the British used to call the followers of the *Ṭarīqa-i Muḥammadī* Wahhabites, but it has not been established that there existed organizational ties between the two movements. As the name reveals, the organizational structure of the *Ṭarīqa-i Muḥammadī* was modelled after that of the mystical orders (*ṭuruq*), with strong personal bonds between the leader of his lieutenants and the followers. The latter had to pledge allegiance (*bayʿah*) to the leader. Sayyid Aḥmad's teachings have been recorded by Shāh Ismāʿīl in the *Ṣirāṭ-i Mustaqīm*. This work was written before he set out to fight the unbelievers. Yet the book contains a paragraph on jihad, the only paragraph where the existing political situation is expressly referred to:

> One should know that jihad is an advantageous and beneficial institution. Mankind derives benefit from its advantages in various ways, just like rain, the advantages of which are imparted upon both plants, animals and men. The benefits of this great institution are of two kinds: a general benefit in which obedient believers, stubborn unbelievers, sinners, hypocrites and even *djinnīs*, human beings, animals and plants collectively partake, and specific benefits for special groups, i.e. some persons derive some sort of benefit from it and other persons other benefits. The general benefit, as accurate experience has established, consists in the fact that, because of the justice of the rulers, the piety of the merchants, the generosity and liberality of the rich and the good intentions of the common people, the blessings of heaven, such as timely downpour of rain, abundant vegetation, growth of profits and trade, absence of calamities and pestilences, growth of wealth and presence of men of learning and perfection, will increasingly manifest themselves. [These blessings] will likewise and in the same manner materialize, even a hundredfold more, when the majesty of the Religion of Truth [is upheld], when pious rulers govern in

> the different regions of the earth, when the righteous community [gains] military strength and when the principles of the *sharī'ah* are being propagated in villages and towns. One should judge the situation of India in comparison with Turkey (Rūm) and Turkestan (*Tūrān*) as far as the descent of the blessings of heaven is concerned. Or one should compare present-day India, in the year 1233 [H = 1817-18 A.D.], now that the greater part of it has become *dār ḥarb*, with previous periods, two or three hundred years ago, with regard to the descent of the blessings of heaven, and the number of pious men and venerated scholars.[24]

At first, Sayyid Aḥmad organized the *Ṭarīqa-i Muḥammadī* as a religious movement. After his return from pilgrimage in Mecca (1824) he began to prepare for jihad. By that time his movement had acquired a large following, mainly from the oppressed Moslem peasants and craftsmen in Bengal and Northern India, who had suffered from the recent social and economic changes, caused by the introduction of foreign rule. Sayyid Aḥmad's strategical aim was to liberate the country from British domination. Tactically the most effective way to achieve this was in his view to occupy some territory out of reach of the British, in order to establish a righteous Islamic government that could conduct the struggle for the liberation of India. Thus he combined the Islamic precepts of *hidjrah* (emigration), that enjoin Moslems living in a region that has become *dār ḥarb* to emigrate to *dār al-Islām*, with those of jihad. As the most suitable region for his plans, he saw the North Western frontier area near the Afghan border. This region was inhabited by Moslems, who were being ruled by the Sikhs. Therefore, in 1826, Sayyid Aḥmad called for *hidjrah* and jihad against the Sikhs. In this struggle he had to rely heavily upon the help of local Moslem tribesmen. However, as these unruly warriors were not inclined to submit to his strict and rigid application of the *sharī'ah*, especially in fiscal matters, many of them deserted. Thereupon Sayyid Aḥmad was defeated and killed by the Sikhs at Balakot in 1831. After his death, it became a widespread belief that he had been the expected *Mahdī* and that he had temporarily disappeared. In the meantime Moslems should unite and fight the English unbelievers. Then he would return to lead them to ultimate victory.[25] In about the same period as Sayyid Aḥmad was engaged in fighting the Sikhs, another leader of the *Ṭarīqa-i Muḥammadī*, Titu Mir (d. 1831) was active in West Bengal. He had assembled a large following of local peasants and artisans and conducted a struggle, under the banner of jihad, against the oppression of the Hindu *zamindars* and the British indigo planters. In a battle with the British army in 1831, his forces were defeated, and he was killed. The *Ṭarīqa-i Muḥammadī*, however, did not stop its anti-British activities. The successors of Sayyid Aḥmad continued warfare against the British from Sittana, at the North Western Frontier. Their organizational headquarters, however, were at Patna in North East India. Emissaries were sent all over India to recruit followers and to preach jihad. In this period many tracts, extolling the virtues of jihad against unbelievers were written and distributed.[26] It was not until 1883 before the British could completely suppress this movement.

Another revivalist movement that became active in this period was the *Farā'iḍī*-movement, founded in 1804 by Ḥadjdjī Sharīʿat Allāh (1781-1840).[27] Just as the *Ṭarīqa-i Muḥammadī*, it was originally a purely religious movement, striving for spiritual aims like the propagation of pure monotheism and the prohibition of un-Islamic innovations. Under the leadership of Ḥadjdjī Sharīʿat Allāh's son, Muḥammad Muḥsin, better known as Dudu Miyan (1819-1861), it acquired a definite social dimension, as it began to organize the Moslem peasants and artisans in their struggle against the *zamindars* and the British indigo-planters. Although its leaders held India under British rule to be *dār ḥarb* and therefore did not permit congregational Friday and festival prayers to be held,[28] they did not draw the conclusion that jihad against the British was obligatory. Therefore, the doctrine of jihad did not play any role in the doctrine of this movement.[29]

In 1857, India revolted against the British. The revolt had started as a mutiny of Indian soldiers in the British army, but before long it spread among the civil population all over North and Central India. It seems that at the local level, adherants of the *Ṭarīqa-i Muḥammadī* played a certain role and that in many places *fatwās* were proclaimed.[30] This rising, however, cannot be regarded as a jihad-movement, as in many places, Hindus and Moslems fought side-by-side and saw this struggle as a common one. Religion, nevertheless, played a great part in the justification of the revolt, as both communities accused the British of interfering with their religious practices and of making serious attempts to convert the Indians to Christianity. Several proclamations, among them one of the last Mogul Emperor Bahādur Shāh Zafar II, who as a pensionary of the East India Company still held court at Delhi, voiced the grievances of Moslems and Hindus alike.[31]

Despite the participation of both communities alike, for the first decade or so after the Mutiny the British singled out the Moslems for deliberate repression, since they saw the revolt as an attempt of the Moslem landed and military aristocracy that derived its power from Mogul rule, to restore the *ancien régime*. This oppression mainly affected the Moslem upper and middle classes.[32] Before the revolt they had already been in a sorry plight. The introduction of English instead of Persian as the official language and the replacement of the *sharīʿah* by English law had broken the monopoly of the Moslems in the civil service, the administration of justice and in the police forces. Their places were increasingly taken by Hindus, who showed more inclination to adapt themselves to the new circumstances.[33] To the inimical attitude of the British, these Moslem middle and upper classes responded by offering proof of their loyalty to the British Empire. From about 1870 many *fatwās* and articles were published in which it was stated that the Indian Moslems were not obliged by their religion to rebel against the British.[34] The most important of these were a *fatwā* of the *ʿulamā'* of Northern India,[35] a decision of the Muhammadan Literary Society of Calcutta[36] and a number of articles by the well-known reformer Sayyid Aḥmad Khān.[37] The reasoning of these *fatwās* is of interest, because they arrive at the same conclusions, departing from different assumptions. The *ʿulamā'* of Northern India have argued on the tacit premise that India under British rule is *dār ḥarb*, that jihad against the British is unlawful:

> The Musalmans here are protected by the Christians, and there is no Jihad in a country where protection is afforded, as the absence

> of protection and liberty between Musalmans and Infidels is essential in a religious war and that condition does not exist here. Besides it is necessary that there should be a probability of victory to Musalman and glory to the Indian. If there be no such probability, the Jihad is unlawful.[38]

The Muhammadan Literary Society of Calcutta, by the mouth of Maulavi Karāmat ʿAlī, declared India to be *dār Islām* and held, on the strength of this argument, that jihad against the colonial power was not allowed:

> The second question is, 'Whether it is lawful in this country to make Jihad or not'. This has been solved with the first. For Jihad can by no means be lawfully made in Dar-ul-Islam. This is so evident that it requires no argument or authority to support it. Now, if anyone were to wage war against the Ruling Powers of this Country, British India, such war would be rightly pronounced rebellion; and rebellion is strictly forbidden by the Muhammadan Law. Therefore such war will likewise be unlawful; and in case any one should wage war, the Muhammadan subjects would be bound to assist their Rulers, and, in conjunction with their Rulers, to fight with such rebels.[39]

Sayyid Aḥmad Khān offers a third interpretation and is of the opinion that jihad is only allowed in case of positive oppression or obstruction of the Moslems in the exercise of their faith, impairing the foundation of some of the pillars of Islam. As religious liberty is guaranteed by the British, there are no terms that would justify jihad against them.[40] As to the question whether India is to be considered *dār Islām* or *dār ḥarb*, he contends that both terms can be applied to the Indian situation, and that India had better be called *dār amān*:

> It will thus be seen, that an Infidel Government in which the Mahomedans enjoy every sort of peace and security, discharge their religious duties with perfect freedom, and which is connected with a Mahomedan Government by a treaty, is not Dar-ul-Islam, because it is a Non-Mahomedan Government, but we may call it so as regards the peace and religious freedom which the Moslems enjoy under its protection; nor is it Dar-ul-Harb, because the treaty existing between it and the Moslem Government makes Jihad

> against it unlawful. It may however be called Dar-ul-Harb as it is not a Mahomedan Government. The position of Hindustan is exactly such as described in the last two sentences.[41]
>
> Now the Dar-ul-harb is essentially and absolutely a country in which these conditions [= religious oppression] exist, and in which jihad is lawful. It cannot be according to the natural meaning of the term, and so long as words are used in their primary sense, a country where jihad is illegal. . . . If a land is the 'home of war', war must be waged, or the Faithful remove therefrom. It is mere abuse of language to apply the name Dar-ul-harb to a country with which it is lawful for true believers to maintain any friendly relations whatever; it is a mere legal subtlety to declare that a country is 'home of war', and yet to allow that Moslems therein enjoy 'amàn', whether the greater or lesser. We do not deny that the title Dar-ul-harb has been applied, even by Moslem doctors of authority and weight, to a country in which jihad is not lawful; but we contend that this is a misapplication of the term: Dar-ul-harb *cannot* mean a country where war cannot lawfully be waged in defence of the faith. . . . The proper term would under these conditions rather be Dar-ul-amàn, or 'land of security', in which the Moslem may lawfully reside as moostámin, or seeker of amàn.[42]

In order to have their opinions endorsed, Indian *ʿulamā'* asked for *fatwas* on this subject from the Meccan *muftīs*.[43] The scope of the question, however, was restricted to the status of India, so that the Meccan *muftīs* could content themselves with stating that India under the present circumstances was to be regarded as *dār Islām* and ignore the problem of whether jihad against the British rulers was obligatory upon the Indian Moslems or not. They must have been the happier about this limitation, as a request to answer this last question would have put them in a quandary. According to the orthodox legal texts, the answer is clear. A *fatwā* to this effect, however, would have brought them into conflict with their overlord, the Ottoman sultan, since it would endanger the friendly Anglo-Ottoman relations. With an irenic interpretation of the *sharīʿah* in this matter, they would have clashed with the establishment of orthodox *ʿulamā'*, that could not condone any novel interpretation of the law.[44] Such an interpretation, therefore, had to be brought forward by the Indian Moslems themselves. As we shall see in Chapter 4, such scholars as Sayyid Aḥmad Khān and Chirāgh ʿAlī have transformed the doctrine of jihad, in order to convince the British that Islam was a basically peaceful religion and that the Indian Moslems could be loyal subjects of the British Empire. Thus the Moslem middle and higher classes, who, for their livelihood depended to a great extent on government employment, hoped to achieve a better relationship with the British. The rise of Hindu nationalism strengthened their pro-British attitude, since they were convinced that only British rule could protect them against Hindu domination. Their intellectual centre was the Mohammadan Anglo-Oriental College at Aligarh, founded by Sayyid Aḥmad Khān. Among the Moslems of the lower, mainly peasant classes, however, revivalist Islam as propagated by the *Ṭarīqa-i Muḥammadī* and the *Farā'iḍī*-movement still had a large following and represented the spirit of the disgruntled Moslems opposed to foreign rule in India. Deoband College, founded in 1867, became their ideological stronghold.[45] However, in view of the unassailable position of the British, backed by superior military strength, a new jihad movement did not arise.

3.3 ALGERIAN RESISTANCE, LED BY ʿABD AL-QĀDIR, AGAINST FRENCH COLONIALISM

On the 14th of June, 1830, a French army set foot on the shore of Sīdī Farrūsh, near the town of Algiers. It was not long before the French had occupied most littoral regions, formerly held by the Turkish rulers of Algiers. After the defeat of the Turkish army and the occupation of the main coastal towns, resistance came from the Arab and Berber tribes in the hinterland, which feared further French expansion. In the East the French were fought under the leadership of Aḥmad Bey, the ruler of Constantine. He could continue his struggle until 1837, when a French army chased him to Biskra. In the West revolting tribes had the backing of the Moroccan sultan ʿAbd al-Raḥmān (1823-1859). Under French pressure, however, he was forced to withdraw his support. Resistance then came from the religious brotherhoods, the *ṭuruq*. They offered the organizational framework necessary for waging a struggle against a superior enemy. Amongst the several orders that existed in Algeria at the time, the *Qādiriyyah*, an order with reformist and revivalist leanings, played a most important part.[46] Its *shaykh*, Muḥyī al-Dīn, succeeded in forming a large confederation of tribes and took command of the struggle against the French. In view of his age, however, his son, ʿAbd al-Qādir (1808-1883), was the actual military commander. In 1832 the leaders of the tribal confederation and the *ʿulamāʾ* pledged allegiance (*bayʿah*) to him[47] and recognized him as their commander (*amīr*). During the two years that followed, he continued the war against the French and was able to bring more tribes into the confederation.

During the first years of the occupation, the French were not able to make up their minds and decide on their future role in Algeria. They were in command of the coastal towns and followed a policy of *occupation restreinte* with the aim of keeping the interior under control by means of indirect rule. In 1834 they concluded an agreement with ʿAbd al-Qādir, recognizing his authority in the Western Algerian hinterland. This gave him respite to organize his affairs. He set up an army with a nucleus of regularly paid and well-trained soldiers instead of relying solely upon tribal levies that used to be raised in time of war.[48] Further, he secured himself of regular revenues by collecting taxes according to the Koranic prescriptions, i.e. *zakāh*, *ʿushr* and a special war tax, *muʿūnah*. In order to collect those taxes and to administer justice according to the *sharīʿah* he appointed paid officials, called *khalīfah* or *āghā*, in the different provinces of his territory. By taking Islam as a unifying force, he tried to overcome the particularism inherent in Algerian tribal society. But simultaneously the seeds of discord were sown since the centralization of public functions in his hands brought him into conflict with vested interests. Previously, the administration of justice and the collection of the *zakāh* had been in the hands of the various religious brotherhoods, the *ṭuruq*, whereas the collection of the other taxes and tributes and the maintenance of public security had been performed by the *makhzan*-tribes, i.e. tribes that had special bonds with the central Turkish government.[49]

The first treaty with the French did not last long. Soon fighting was resumed. In 1837 a new agreement was signed. During the years of relative calm that followed, ʿAbd al-Qādir managed to extend his control over the Eastern regions of Algeria. In 1839 a conflict arose between ʿAbd al-Qādir and the French over the exact extent of their respective zones of influence, that had been delimited by the 1837 treaty. When a French army invaded territory that ʿAbd al-Qādir claimed to be his according to the terms of this treaty, he dispatched letters to the French King Louis Philippe, to his cabinet and to the French military commander, to the effect that, as they had violated the provisions of the peace treaty concluded between them, he saw no way but to resume jihad against them as prescribed by Islam.[50] The French then gave up their policy of *occupation restreinte* and began to conquer the rest of the country. The army under marshal Bugeaud waged a ruthless war of scorched earth and in 1843 ʿAbd al-Qādir had to seek refuge with the Moroccan sultan. Thereupon the French attacked Morocco and forced the Sultan to sign a treaty to the effect that he would treat ʿAbd al-Qādir as an outlaw and expel him from his territory. A tribal revolt against the French, led by a religious chief, called Bū Maʿzah, who claimed to be the expected *Mahdī*,[51] kept the French army busy and gave ʿAbd al-Qādir a chance to return with his men and to continue the struggle, but only for a short period. In 1847, hunted by Moroccan and French troops, he was forced to surrender. The French took him to Paris where he was confined until 1852. After his release he settled in Damascus, where he died in 1882.

When he was in power, he tried as much as possible to act in agreement with the prescriptions of the *sharīʿah*. He preached a fundamentalist Islam, emphasizing monotheism (*tawḥīd*) and violently denouncing polytheism (*shirk*). He strongly condemned innovations (*bidaʿ*) and especially worship of saints.[52] The struggle against the French was logically perceived as jihad. His zeal in complying with the rules of the *sharīʿah* in every respect induced him to write treatises on certain topics that had a bearing on his military and administrative practice. Whenever he was in doubt as to the permissibility of certain measures, he consulted scholars of renown in other countries and asked for *fatwās* on these points. These documents reflect the political and economical difficulties with which ʿAbd al-Qādir had to cope. His main problem was in keeping his state together. The centrifugal forces that were inherent in his attempts to centralize the state apparatus and to do away with the privileges of the *makhzan*-tribes and the *ṭuruq*, showed themselves in the defection of some tribes and in individual or collective collaboration with the enemy. Rivalling *ṭuruq* either cooperated with the French or denounced ʿAbd al-Qādir for having concluded treaties with the enemy. The second problem, closely connected with the first, was the unwillingness of the tribes to pay the Koranic taxes. The only way to deal with these difficulties was the use of force. In order to know whether the *sharīʿah* allowed him to take a firm line with the defecting and obstinate tribes, he, in 1837, asked a *fatwā* from the Moroccan *Shaykh al-Islām* ʿAlī ʿAbd al-Salām al-Tasūlī (d. *c.* 1843) in the following words:

> [Please give us] your answer – may Allah preserve you –, with regard to the serious and distressed situation in the land of Algiers, that has become a place where the crows of unbelief slaughter [the believers], since the enemy of the Religion attemots to subject and to enslave the Moslems, sometimes by means of the sword and sometimes by means of political intrigues. There are Moslems that join them, cooperate with them and bring them cattle, good horses and other kinds of riding animals. Sometimes they even point out the weak spots of the [defence of the] Moslems to them. There are also tribes that act in this manner. When they are requested to denounce the culprits, they explode in anger and make common cause in telling lies and denying everything, although they know exactly who have committed those acts. What is Allah's decree concerning these two groups, [with regard to] their person and their wealth? What is [Allah's] decree with regard to those that fail to take part in the defence when the *Imām* or his representative has proclaimed a general mobilization in order to defend the Religion and the country? Do they deserve punishment for that and of what

> can this punishment consist? As punishment can only be administered by fighting them, can in that case their wealth and property be seized? What is Allah's decree concerning those that wholly or partly refuse to pay the *zakāh*, claiming that they do not possess the minimum amount of property for being assessed, although it is beyond doubt that they do possess this amount on the spot. Must their claim be accepted, despite the weakness of the Religion in these times, or is there room for independent judgement (*idjtihād*)? From where must the army that is defending the Moslems and protecting the frontiers against attacks by the enemy, be fed? At the moment there is no regular treasury and what has been collected from the *zakāh* is not even sufficient to feed them, let alone to pay for their uniforms, weapons, horses and other equipment. Must events be left to take their course so that the enemy can take possession of the country, or must the Moslem community provide for what the army stands in need of? If the latter is the case, is it then an obligation upon all Moslems or only upon the rich? Are those who refuse to pay the war tax (*muʿūnah*) to be regarded as rebels or not? What is [Allah's] decree concerning the property of rebels? Is it allowed to act in accordance with the opinion that it is not necessary to return it to them [after the fighting] or not?[53]

In reply to these questions, al-Tasūlī wrote an elaborate treatise,[54] in which he dealt in detail with all the problems mentioned in ʿAbd al-Qādir's letter. He even went further and treated of connected subjects, such as the permissibility of concluding treaties with the enemy,[55] and the obligation of the Moslems residing within enemy territory to emigrate to Islamic territory. For strategical reasons, this last issue was of the utmost importance for ʿAbd al-Qādir. His position would be strengthened if the Moslems from the territories administered by the French would fly *en masse* to his camp. Therefore, in the same year, he asked a *fatwā* on this point from the Egyptian *ʿulamā'*. It appears that in Algeria there was a discussion between *ʿulamā* that had remained under French domination and did not deem emigration obligatory and *ʿulamā'* that had sided with ʿAbd al-Qādir and insisted upon the necessity of leaving occupied territory.

The former no doubt belonged to the Hanafite *madhhab* that was followed by the Turkish ruling class and that regarded emigration only obligatory in extreme cases of religious oppression. In his letter, ʿAbd al-Qādir set forth the positions of both groups:

> What is your opinion on a Moslem region that has been attacked and conquered by infidel enemies. Some mountainous areas on the border of the said region have not yet been reached and subdued by them. These areas are being protected by their inhabitants. Some inhabitants of the said region have emigrated to them with their families, their property and their children. Others have remained under the rule of the unbelievers as their subjects. The unbelievers have imposed a tax (*kharādj*) upon them, similar to the well-known *djizyah*, which they collect from the believers. Amongst those who have emigrated as well as amongst those who have remained there are *ʿulamā'*. Those who have emigrated with the Moslems to the said mountains hold that emigration is obligatory and have issued *fatwās* to the effect that those Moslems that have remained under [the domination of] the unbelievers may lawfully be killed and that their property, their families and their children may be captured. Their main argument is that those who have remained with the unbelievers although they were able to emigrate, help them in fighting the Moslems and in plundering their property and strive for the domination of the unbelievers over the Moslems. The *ʿulamā'* amongst those who have remained under [the rule of] the unbelievers and have not emigrated, assert that emigration is not obligatory. Their principal arguments are: '[*Let not the Believers take the Unbelievers as friends in preference of the Believers. If anyone does that, he is not of Allah's party at all;*] *unless it be that ye are in some measure afraid of them*' [K 3:28], and the Tradition: '*There is no emigration after the Conquest* [*of Mecca*]'.[56]

ʿAbd al-Qādir's request was answered by the Egyptian scholar Muḥammad ʿIllaysh (1802-1883),[57] who composed a long *fatwā* in which he extensively quoted older *fatwās* regarding the Moslem retreat from Sicily and Spain and showed that emigration was obligatory.[58] The problem of the obligation to emigrate kept occupying ʿAbd al-Qādir's mind, for in 1843 he himself wrote a treatise on the subject,[59] in which he vehemently attacked his learned opponents:

> As we have learned, these ignoramuses that issue *fatwās* without knowledge and thus err and lead people astray, and who fit [the description of] the tradition: *'Once there will come a time for the people, in which their scholars stink more than the carrion of a donkey'*, have adduced as a proof [for their opinion that emigration is not obligatory] the Tradition: *'No emigration after the Conquest [of Mecca]'*. This Tradition, however, which is to be found in the *Ṣaḥīḥ* of al-Bukhārī, cannot serve as evidence for their opinion. For when someone asked the Prophet about [the obligation of] emigrating from Mecca to Medina after the Conquest [of Mecca], he replied that the obligation of emigrating from Mecca to Medina had come to an end because of the Conquest and that it had been abrogated just as the prohibition for the emigrant to return to his country had been abrogated when it had become *dār Islām*. But [the obligation] to emigrate from *dār al-kufr* to *dār al-Islam* [, he continued,] will remain in force until the sun rises from the West.[60]

In order to have a justification for treating collaborators harshly, ʿAbd al-Qādir sent a letter to the chief *qāḍı* (*qāḍı l-quḍāh*) of Fes, ʿAbd al-Hādī l-ʿAlawī al-Ḥasanī, asking him to declare that these collaborators were apostates, who might legally by killed. In the same letter he sought to obtain a clear and unambiguous statement as to the legal obligation of helping him in his struggle against the French:

> What is Allāh's decree concerning those who have entered the service of the infidel enemies, have made friends of them and have become their helpers? They fight on their side against the Moslems and receive pay as soldiers of their army. If one shows courage in fighting the Moslems, the unbelievers give him a badge on his breast, which they call *'l'honneur'* and which shows the portrait of their king. Are they apostates or not? And if you are of the opinion that they are, must they then be made to repent or not? . . . Is the established [rule] that when the enemy attacks people that are incapable of pushing him back, the obligation [to defend Moslem territory] is passed on to those who live near to them, a general [rule], binding upon the entire Moslem community, or is it a

> special [rule] only binding upon Sultans, since they have authority over their subjects? Can the obligation of defending and helping [the Moslems under attack] only by fulfilled in person or can it be fulfilled either in person or by [sending] money?[61]

The answer cannot have been very satisfactory for ʿAbd al-Qādir, for ʿAbd al-Hādī did not give a clear reply to the first question. He contented himself with enumerating the different opinions within the Mālikite *madhhab* on the matter. The answer to the second question, however, was clear, as the texts did not leave any room for interpretation: helping Moslems that are unable to defend themselves against an enemy attack is a general obligation incumbent upon all Moslems that are near to them. They can perform this duty either in person or by giving financial support.[62]

In 1846, betrayed by the Moroccan Sultan ʿAbd al-Raḥmān, he sent a letter to Egypt to ask the judgment of the Egyptian scholars on the acts committed by ʿAbd al-Raḥmān, and, probably, in the hope of obtaining help from them:

> Please give us your answer concerning the legally abominable deeds of the Moroccan Sultan, deeds that one does not expect from any person, let alone from notables. . . . The Sultan of Morocco has acted towards us in such a manner as to strengthen the Party of Unbelief and to weaken us, and he has caused us great damage.

He then goes on to specify those acts, mentioning that the Sultan had provided the French with cattle when ʿAbd al-Qādir was blockading them, that the Sultan had confiscated the money of ʿAbd al-Qādir's representatives in Morocco and had prevented Moroccans to support ʿAbd al-Qādir's cause, that the Sultan had agreed with the French to extradite ʿAbd al-Qādir to them and that he had ordered ʿAbd al-Qādir to stop waging jihad against the French.[63] The first lines of the answer, written by Muḥammad ʿIllaysh, clearly condemn these acts but also evidence a certain hesitation:

> Yes, everything you have mentioned is forbidden for the said Sultan (may Allah adjust his position). These prohibitions are axiomatic articles of faith and nobody who has but a grain of faith left in his heart, can entertain any doubts about it. We would never

have expected that our Lord Sultan ʿAbd al Raḥmān (may Allah grant him success) would promulgate such orders with regard to a man like you. But we belong to Allāh and to Him we shall return. What Allāh has decreed, will necessarily be.[64]

The Sultan's refusal to support him, the cruel war of extermination conducted by the numerically and technically superior French army and the defection of a number of Algerian tribes, were the direct causes of ʿAbd al-Qādir's defeat. The collapse of his movement opened the road for large-scale expropriation and colonization of vast areas. The spirit of resistance and jihad, however, was not completely extinguished. Famine and epidemics, the aftermath of marshal Bugeaud's ruthless military operation, aggravated by the expulsion of large groups from their lands, made the Algerian people revolt repeatedly against French colonial rule. These revolts, however, often led by self-styled *Mahdīs* and accompanied by apocalyptic visions[65] were always regionally limited and never became general.[66] Thus, they could easily be crushed by the French. Not until the suppression of the Kabyle rebellion under Sīdī Muqrānī in 1871, did French colonial rule become firmly established. The Algerian Moslems were compelled to live in a country where the political and legal structure mainly served the French *colons* and where education tended to suppress the Arab-Islamic identity of the population. The military superiority made all effective resistance impossible. In this period the phenomenon of collective emigration gained importance. Economic crises and the climate of political and cultural oppression made many Moslems respond to the Islamic command to emigrate from the *dār al-ḥarb* to the *dār al-Islām*.[67] The emigrants went to Morocco, Tunisia and also to Syria, where ʿAbd al-Qādir had settled after his release from captivity. When in 1893 the region around Constantine was struck by famine, the number of emigrants alarmed the colonial administrators. They, however, regarded this emigration merely as a result of Ottoman, pan-Islamic propaganda and acted accordingly by trying to obtain *fatwās* that were favourable for the French administration and would appease religious opposition to French rule. Thus, the Governor-General, Jules Cambon, approached the Meccan *muftīs* and asked them to issue a *fatwā* on the position of Moslems residing in territory conquered by unbelievers, that govern them without, however, hindering them in the exercise of their religious practices, that appoint for them one of their co-religionists as a *qāḍī* to apply the injunctions of the *sharīʿah* and that pay him a regular salary. What then, the question goes on, is the duty of these Moslems in the mentioned circumstances: (1) Are they obliged to emigrate or not? (2) Are they obliged to fight the unbelievers in order to regain authority, even if they are not convinced that they have sufficient power to achieve this? (3) Is the region where the Moslems live *dār ḥarb* or *dār Islām*? The Hanafite *muftī* only answered the first and the third question, remaining silent on the obligation of waging jihad. As to the emigration, he cited some classical texts to the effect that emigration is only compulsory when the Moslems cannot openly perform their religious duties and when they have sufficient means for the journey. The reply to the last question was that such a region is to be considered *dār Islām* as long as the *sharīʿah* is being applied. The Shafiʿite *muftī* answered the question concerning the emigration in the same fashion as his Hanafite colleague. As to the status of the region, he asserted that it had become *dār ḥarb* as the unbelievers had conquered it. Jihad, however, was not obligatory in his opinion, since these Moslems were not capable of successfully waging it.[68] The French administration distributed these *fatwās* amongst the population. Presently the number of emigrants declined, but this was probably due to the improvement of the economic situation. Another manifestation of this kind of religiously motivated protest occurred in Tlemcen around 1911. Several hundreds of Moslems emigrated to Moslem countries. Besides by economic grievances connected with the introduction of land registration, they were motivated by the fear of being drafted into the French army and having to fight against their fellow-Moslems, the Moroccans.[69] This was to be the last instance of typically religious resistance against French colonial domination in Algeria.

3.4 THE MAHDIST MOVEMENT IN THE SUDAN

In 1821 Egypt conquered the Sudan. This conquest was mainly motivated by financial considerations as the ruler of Egypt, Mehmet ʿAli, wanted to increase his revenues and saw in southward expansion a means of achieving this aim. His exaggerated expectations with regard to the presence of gold proved to be illusory and the principal sources of income were to be slave trade and taxation of the population of the newly conquered territories. Since this taxation was so much higher than under previous rulers, it disrupted the economic life in the region. In 1823-24 the population of the Sudan revolted against the Egyptian administration. This revolt was smothered in blood.[70] Already during the first years after the conquest, Mehmet ʿAli developed schemes for improving Sudanese agriculture in the prospect of tapping new sources of income by promoting the growth of cash-crops and monopolizing their export. Although not all of these schemes turned out to be successful, yet the agricultural area increased owing to the introduction of new techniques and better irrigation. Several nomadic tribes settled down in these areas in order to satisfy the growing demand for agricultural labour. When in 1859 the Egyptian state monopoly on trade was abolished and transport facilities improved, Sudan was gradually opened up for foreign trade. Besides the traditional trade in slaves, which found eager markets in Egypt, the Hejaz and Turkey, European commercial houses bought gum Arabic, ivory and ostrich feathers, which were wanted commodities in the West. European industrial goods were being sold by petty traders, mainly Syrian Christians, Greeks and Copts. Owing to these developments, many foreigners settled in the Sudan, in addition to the Turco-Egyptian and Western administrators and military men. Thus foreign influence in the Sudan increased, whereas the power of the local leaders declined. The tribal leaders had, for all practical purposes, become dependent on the Egyptian administration. They were responsible for the collection of taxes and could be disposed of at will.

In the wake of the Turco-Egyptian administration, orthodox Islam entered the Sudan. Although the Northern parts of the region had already been arabicized and islamicized, the prevailing form of Islam was to a great extent mixed with pagan superstitions and strongly influenced by mystical tendencies.[71] The carrier of this local blend of Islam was the *fakī*, a word that, typically, seems to derive from both *faqīh* (specialist in the field of the *sharīʿah*, and, colloquially, schoolmaster) and *faqīr* (adherent of a religious order, derwish), as its plural *fukara* indicates.[72] The position of these *fakīs* was now threatened by the orthodox religious functionaries, who were state officials and had received formal education at the Azhar University. The latter represented official Islam as understood by the ruling classes of the Ottoman Empire. This confrontation caused mistrust and enmity among the *fakīs* against the newly arrived religious dignitaries that formed part of the Turco-Egyptian administration.[73]

The situation of the Sudanese population deteriorated during the 1870s. Under pressure of his foreign creditors, the Khedive was forced to seek additional sources of revenue. One of these was heavier taxation of the Sudan, a burden that mainly fell upon the shoulders of the cultivators. This resulted in the emigration of large groups of peasants and, consequently, in famine. Due to the economic crisis, trade slackened. The net result of the new fiscal measures was a decrease in tax income for the Egyptian state. Discontent amongst the Sudanese increased when the European Powers compelled the Egyptian government to suppress the slave trade. This greatly affected the economy of the country, which relied heavily on the use of slaves for menial labour, and aroused the enmity of the slave traders. The measures of the Egyptian government were not only resented for material reasons, but also for religious considerations. As Islam permits slavery, most Moslems did not see any harm in it. Suppression of it, especially as it was actually carried out by Europeans employed by the Egyptian government, was seen as an affront against Islam.

In this explosive situation, Muḥammad Aḥmad (1844-1885), a *shaykh* of a religious order, proclaimed himself to be the expected *Mahdī* in 1881 and challenged the authority of the Egyptian administration. In the beginning he hardly met any serious resistance on the part of the Egyptians, as the Egyptian government was in financial difficulties due to the enormous foreign debt and further incapacitated by the ʿUrābī-revolt. Thus the *Mahdī* could organize his movement and recruit followers, who came mainly from the social groups that had suffered most from the Egyptian domination: tribes that had lost their autonomy, like the Fur, slavetraders with their private armies and the *fakīs*. After his first success, peasants joined his movement in great numbers. From 1881 until his death in 1885, the *Mahdī* conquered most of the Sudan, including its capital, Khartoum. After his death the leadership of the newly formed state passed into the hands of his successor (*khalīfah*) ʿAbd Allāh ibn Muḥammad al-Taʿāyishī, whose reign lasted till 1898 when a British army brought the country under combined Anglo-Egyptian rule.

Mahdist expectations were not unknown in the Sudan, with its rich *ṣūfī* tradition.[74] They became more widespread by the end of the 1870s as the year 1300 A.H. (= 1882/3 A.D.) was approaching. Hence it is accountable that discontent with the prevailing situation and opposition against the alien rulers, who were held responsible for this situation, took the shape of a politico-religious movement led by a *mahdī*. The aim of this movement was the establishment of a state, ruled in accordance with the prescriptions of the Koran and the *Sunnah*. In his teachings the *Mahdī* emphasized the unity of Allah (*tawḥīd*), attacked polytheism (*shirk*) and rejected innovations (*bidaʿ*). The gist of his message was that he wanted to restore Islam to the state it was in during the first period of its existence, to fill the earth with equity and justice and to ban injustice and oppression. He organized his movement along the lines of a religious order (*ṭarīqah*) with a strong personal bond between the leader and his followers. The latter had to pledge allegiance (*bayʿah*) to him with the following words:

> We pledge allegiance to Allah and to His prophet. We pledge allegiance to thee in that we assert the unity of Allah, do not associate anyone to Him, that we will not steal, nor commit adultery, nor bring false accusations and in that we will not disobey thee in what is lawful. We pledge allegiance to thee in renouncing and abandoning this world and contenting ourselves with

> what is with Allah out of desire for what is with Allah and for the world to come. We pledge allegiance to thee in that we will not flee from the jihad.[75]

The central concepts in the *Mahdī*'s more practical teachings were emigration (*hidjrah*) and jihad. He urged his followers to emigrate to him, thereby consciously following the example of the prophet Mohammed, and stressed the duty of jihad. Contrary to orthodox doctrine he forbade his followers to perform pilgrimage to Mecca with the argument that performing jihad was at that moment of greater importance.[76] Immediately after having proclaimed himself the expected *Mahdī*, he began sending letters to religious dignitaries and tribal leaders, describing the visions in which the prophet Mohammed had revealed to him that he was the expected *Mahdī* and inviting them to join his movement by emigrating to him and taking part in jihad:

> It is evident that times have changed and that the *Sunnah* has been abandoned. No one with faith and intelligence will approve of that. Therefore, it would be better that he leave his affairs and his country in order to establish the Religion and the *Sunnah*. . . . Emigrating with the Religion is obligatory on the strength of the Book and the *Sunnah*. Allah has said: *'Oh ye who have believed, respond to Allah and to the messenger when He calls you to what will give you life'* [K 8:24]. The prophet has said: *'He who flees with his religion from one territory to another, even if it is* [only the distance of] *an inch, will be worthy of Paradise and be the companion of his father Ibrahim, Allah's bosom friend, and of His prophet Mohammed'*. And [there are] similar Koranic verses and Traditions. . . . If you understand this, [know then that] I have ordered all those [of you] who are legally capable, to emigrate to us for the sake of jihad in the way of Allah, or to the country that is nearest to you, on the strength of Allah's words: *'Oh ye who have believed, fight the unbelievers who are near to you'* [K 9:123]. Those who fail to fulfil this [duty], fall under the threat of Allah's words: *'Say: "If your fathers and your sons* [*and your brethren and your wives and your clan, and properties which ye have acquired, and trade which ye fear may go slack, and dwellings which*

> *please you are dearer to you than Allah and His messenger and striving in His cause, then wait until Allah cometh with His affair; Allah guideth not the people who are reprobates"* (K 9:24)]', and: *'O ye who have believed, what is the matter with you? When one says to you: "March out in the way of Allah", ye are weighed down to the ground; are ye so satisfied with the nearer life as to neglect the Hereafter?* [*The enjoyment of the nearer life is in comparison with the Hereafter only a little thing. If ye do not march out, He will inflict upon you a painful punishment, and will substitute* (for you) *another people* (K 9:38-39)]'. If you understand this, then: onwards to the jihad in His way. Do not fear anyone but Allah, since the fear of a creature for something else than Allah makes his faith null and void, which Allah may forbid.[77]

As his principal enemies the *Mahdī* saw the Turks, by which name he referred to the Egyptian administrators and military men, that, indeed, were mainly of Turco-Circassian stock, and the 'evil *ʿulamā*'' (*ʿulamā' al-sū'*), the orthodox religious functionaries that were loyal to the Egyptian administration. Behind these he saw, not without justification, the machinations of the Europeans:

> Well-being with Allah can only be achieved by following the Religion, by reviving the *Sunnah* of His prophet and His community, by suppressing these recent innovations (*bidaʿ*) and errors and by turning repentantly to the Exalted One in all situations. This has become imperative, especially now that corruption has spread over all countries. For as a result of the machinations of the unbelievers against the Moslems and the errors they have introduced into the hearts of the people, the Religion has vanished and the prescriptions of the Book and the *Sunnah* are not being applied anymore. Injustice is rife, innovations are widespread and what Islam has forbidden is now allowed. The faithful are in serious distress.[78]

The sectarian character of the *Mahdī*'s movement is apparent from his assertion that those who denied his Mahdī-ship were unbelievers (*kuffār*).[79] Thus he could appeal to the doctrine of jihad in his struggle against Egyptian domination. When the Egyptian army commander Yūsuf Ḥasan al-Shalālī wrote a letter to the *Mahdī* asking him to surrender and accusing him of having illegally killed fellow-Moslems, the *Mahdī* answered:

Your contention that we have unjustly and wrongly killed a group of Moslems that had settled in this region, is untenable since we have only killed the inhabitants of the [Djabal] al-Djarādah after they had called us a liar and attacked us. The Prophet and all possessors of gnosis (*ahl al-kashf*) have informed me that those who question my Mahdī-ship and deny and contradict it, are unbelievers who can lawfully be killed and whose property is booty. For this reason we have fought and killed them. . . . Equally untenable is your assertion that the soldiers that we have killed were Moslems and followers of what the messenger has brought [to us] and that we shall be held responsible for their lives in the presence of Allah. Al-Quṭb al-Dardīr has laid down in the chapter of robbery that the rulers (*umarā'*) of Egypt and all their soldiers and followers may [lawfully] be attacked, because they have taken the property of the Moslems against their will.[80] Therefore, it is permitted to kill them. As Allah has said: *'The recompense of those who make war on Allah and His messenger and exert themselves to cause corruption in the land is that they should be killed'* [K 5:33]. On the other hand, the prophet has expressly ordered us to fight the Turks and has informed us that they are unbelievers since they have acted against the commands of the messenger to follow us and want to extinguish Allah's light [cf. K 9:32], with which He wanted to make His justice visible. How then can we be held responsible after all this [evidence]. Moreover, a group of brethren [i.e. followers of the *Mahdī*] have witnessed that the limbs of the Egyptian soldiers that were killed, very clearly blazed in anticipation of their punishment, so as to expose their true condition.[81]

At another occasion, the *Mahdī* combined his religious arguments for fighting the 'Turks' with social and political grievances:

The Turks used to drag your men away in fetters and keep them imprisoned in chains. They used to capture your wives and children and unlawfully kill persons, which Allah has declared forbidden. All this [they did] because of [the collection of] taxes

> (*djizyah*)[82] that are not in conformity to the commands of Allah or His messenger. Moreover, they did not have mercy with the humble people amongst you, nor did they respect the notables amongst you. How could you forget this and fail to take part in the jihad? Why were you not overcome by the zeal for Allah's Religion and for the extirpation of what He has forbidden? What will your answer be in the presence of Allah, in view of the fact that you have not responded to Allah's summoner and that despite your humiliation by the Turks and despite their contempt for you, you were submissively obeying their commands wherever they gave orders.[83]

In pursuance of his belief that his message was a universal one, the *Mahdī*, imitating the example of the prophet, who had sent letters to the kings of Byzantium and Persia, approached the rulers of other countries, elucidating his claims and requesting them to recognize them. Thus, he sent letters to the Sultan of Wādāy, to Muḥammad al-Mahdī al-Sanūsī, head of the powerful Sanūsiyyah-order in Cyrenaica and to Ḥayātū ibn Saʿīd, a disaffected member of the ruling house of the Sokoto Caliphate.[84] Not confining himself to the Islamic world, he also wrote to the Negus of Abyssinia, Yuḥannā IV inviting him to embrace Islam and to accept his Mahdī-ship.[85] After the capture of Khartoum, at the zenith of his power, he wrote to the Khedive, warning him of the unbelievers and the evil *ʿulamā'*.

> You were not right in taking the unbelievers as patrons in preference to Allah and asking their assistance while they were shedding the blood of the community of Mohammed. Have you not heard Allah's words: *'O ye who have believed, do not choose Jews and Christians as patrons, they are patrons to each other; whoever makes patrons of them is one of them'* [K 5:51], and: *'One does not find a people who believe in Allah and the Last Day in friendly relations with any who obstruct Allah and His messenger even though they were their fathers* [*or their sons or their brethren or their clan'* K 58:22], and *'O ye who have believed, do not take My enemy and your enemy as patrons, offering them love, though they have disbelieved in the truth which has come to you'* [K 60:1], and: *'O ye who have believed, take not as your patrons those who take your religion as a butt of ridicule and fun,*

> *from amongst those who have been given the Book before you and the unbelievers'* [K 5:57]. Why do you obey the enemies of Allah, whereas Allah says: *'O ye who have believed, if ye obey a part of those to whom the Book has been given, they will render you unbelievers again after your having believed. And how can ye disbelieve when ye have the signs of Allah recited to you* [*and His messenger is amongst you? He who seeks defence in Allah, has been guided to a straight path.*] *O ye who have believed, fear Allah, which is due to Him, and die not except as Moslems'* [K 3:100-3]. If you are amongst those who can see things in their true light and do not prefer the contemptible goods of this world to the bliss of the Hereafter, then do take this as a warning and hasten to be saved and to obtain real success, which is the success of the faith. Declare yourself above being permanently the captive of Allah's enemies and do not lead to perdition those of the community of Mohammed that are with you. . . . Beware of relying upon the evil *ʿulamā'* that are intoxicated with love for glory and wealth, to such an extent that they have bought the present life in exchange for the Hereafter [cf. K 2:86], for they will ruin you like they have ruined others before you. In the *ḥadīth al-qudsī*[86] it is related: *'Do not hold me responsible for a scholar who is intoxicated with love for this world, for he will turn you away from my path. They are waylaying my worshippers'.*[87]

After this admonition, he urges the Khedive to accept his claims and join hands with him in expelling the unbelievers. Should he, however, fail to do so, the Mahdī threatened him that he would come with his army to Egypt and defeat him.[88]

As the tenets of the Mahdist movement on many points clearly contradicted orthodox Islam, it was an easy target for counter-propaganda from the side of the religious establishment. The Ottoman Sultan Abdülhamid promulgated an official proclamation against the *Mahdī*, which was widely published.[89] A *fatwā* to the same effect was issued by the *ʿulamā'* of the Azhar University.[90] Also some Sudanese *ʿulamā'* composed treatises in order to refute the *Mahdī*'s claims.[91] Aḥmad al-Azharī ibn Ismāʿīl, *muftī* of the Western Sudan published a tract in 1882 under the title: *Al-Naṣīḥah al-*

ʿāmmah li-ahl al-Islām ʿan mukhālafat al-ḥukkām wa-l-khurūdj ʿan ṭāʿat al-Imām [*Advice to the people of Islam not to oppose the rulers and not to rebel against the Imām*],[92] which is chiefly concerned with disproving Muḥammad Aḥmad's pretension to be the expected *Mahdī*. Adducing Traditions with regard to the *Mahdī* and comparing them with the course of Muḥammad Aḥmads life, he concludes that he cannot possibly be identified with the *Mahdī* that is mentioned in the Traditions. A similar tract was published by the *muftī* of the Eastern Sudan, Amīn al-Ḍarīr, entitled: *Hady al-mustahdī ilā bayān al-Mahdī wa-l-mutamahdī* [Guidance for him who needs it to the explanation of the difference between the true and the false *Mahdī*]. In the same year Shakīr al-Ghazzī, *muftī* of the court of appeal in Khartoum wrote a treatise called *Risālah fī buṭlān daʿwā Muḥammad Aḥmad al-Mutamahdī* [Treatise on the invalidity of the claim of Muḥammad Aḥmad, the false *Mahdī*],[93] of which the main concern was to prove that the *Mahdī* and his followers were rebels against the legitimate authority of the Ottoman Sultan and that fighting them was allowed.

> Know, o brethren, that Allah has arranged things for me and you in such a way that Religion and authority are two inseparable brothers. Religion, then, is the foundation, whereas authority protects it and keeps it erect. Now, that which is not protected will perish and lack support. Therefore, Religion can only exist through authority. . . . Allah has said: *'O ye who have believed, obey Allah and obey the messenger and those of you who have the command'* [K 4:59]. The prophet has said: *'Obedience is obligatory on you, even if an Abyssinian slave with a head like a raisin has taken command over you'*, and: *'You shall obey* [your ruler], *even if he beats your back and seizes your money'*. If you know all this and also that these glorious verses of the Koran and these magnificent Traditions imply that it is obligatory to obey those who have the command and that it is forbidden to fight them and to rebel against them, then you will no doubt be satisfied that he who withdraws from obedience, even if it is only an inch, is rebellious against Allah and will die a heathen. And if you

> moreover know that the consequence of dissension, strife and enmity is destruction and ruin, then you will no doubt be convinced that it is your duty to return to harmony and agreement.

He then elaborately sets out his arguments against Muḥammad Aḥmad's pretensions to be the expected *Mahdī* and continues:

> Now we have indicated the correct path for you and we have adduced strong arguments that leave no room for doubt as to the fact that Muḥammad Aḥmad is not the *Mahdī*. His followers are only people who are deeply imbued with barbaric practices, who have fallen into the darkness of ignorance and greediness for the possession of [other] men and who have sold their Religion in exchange for the present world. They are a bunch of stupid bedouins and foolish derwishes whose sole aims are robbery, plunder and slaughter. They are more astray from the right path than cattle and they possess neither understanding, knowledge nor religion. . . . Beware, O Brethren, of emulating these fools and their practices. They must submit again to the government and stop following Satan, their leader. For if they are exposed and hit by bombs, guns, rifles and bullets, they will look for rescue, but then it will be too late for them. Nobody can deny that the government has 100,000 troops at its disposal and that it is at any time capable of bringing millions of new troops and equipping them with sufficient war materials. . . . This is what has been prepared for them in this world. However, Allah has prepared for them Gehenna, a bad place to go to [cf. K 4:97], as a punishment for their rebellion against Allah, His messenger and those who have the command, and for killing what Allah has forbidden to kill. *'If anyone kills a believer intentionally, his recompense is Gehenna, to abide therein'* [K 4:93]. O servants of Allah, you must fear Allah and act in accordance with Allah's book and the *Sunnah* of His messenger. Submit to Allah again and to the government. Do not follow these diabolical fancies nor these superstitious insinuations. . . . Know, O Brethren that the founders of the different *madhhabs* are of one opinion about that rebellion is one of the greatest sins, even if the Sultan is unjust. One may not rebel against him, whereas he may fight [the rebels]. You must fight the rebels together with him and

> help him against them, for they have severed their ties with Islam. The prophet has said: *'Whoever departs from the community, even if it is only an inch, has severed his ties with Islam'*. . . . O Moslems, you must help Allah through helping your Sultan. Allah has said: *'O ye who have believed, if ye help Allah He will help you, and set firm your feet'* [K 47:7]. In order to protect your religion and safeguard your wealth, you must fight these rebellious charlatans and slay them wherever ye find them [cf. K 9:5]. You must stop all those who want to rebel with them, scatter their community and prevent them from increasing in number. It is forbidden for you to bring them weapons, or anything that may make them stronger or more numerous, until they return to the Truth and announce their submission.

The author then addresses the followers of the *Mahdī* and urges them to repent and show their sincerity by following the orders of the government. He concludes his treatise with a fine piece of governmental propaganda, enumerating the benefits that the government has conferred upon the Sudanese. The picture he presents of the situation in Egypt is rather optimistic and not quite accurate. Especially his reference to the 'amply provided treasury' makes an ironical impression if one knows that the Egyptian state was totally bankrupt at the time:

> Refrain from these evil deeds, for how many splendid benefits has the government bestowed upon you and how much forgiveness has it showed towards you. It has raised you in the cradle of its justice and has lavishly bestowed its favours on you. It has rescued you from your earlier kings that used to seize you as slaves and servants. Your country has become prosperous and safe and your agriculture has increased, whereas previously your country was in a state of extreme ruin and destruction. Your wealth and your families were exposed to plunder and captivity and you could not keep anybody in control, be it people of importance or not. Now – praise be to Allah – you are in a state of extreme security, prosperity and wealth, thanks to the favours and the fine policy of the government. With all this the government spends large sums from its amply provided treasury for the sake of the prosperity of your

> country and protection of your lives, whereas it does not make you pay for anything of this. It spends the taxes collected from you plus an additional amount from the [treasury] on the welfare and the necessities of your country. Despite all this, the assessment is not half as high as that of anyone of the [Egyptian] districts, although Allah has imposed on you to pay to the government the *zakāh* from your livestock, such as camels, cows and sheep and the *kharādj* from your lands. If the government would assess you on the basis of what you must pay it according to the *sharīʿah* and if it would collect the taxes from you in conformity with it, then you would pay many times more than the present taxes.[94]

The *Mahdī*'s only response to these propagandistic attacks is to be found in a letter in which he reacts against the treatise written by Amīn al-Ḍarīr. His basic thesis is that rational arguments against his claims and doctrine are pointless, as his beliefs and his knowledge are the result of a revelation from Allah and His messenger.[95] The propaganda of the *ʿulamā'* seems to have had little effect. The *Mahdī* was able to recruit a large following from among the Sudanese population. He found even supporters outside the Sudan[96] and among Moslem intellectuals like Djamāl al-Dīn al-Afghānī and the young Muḥammad ʿAbduh, who were impressed by his strength in resisting the semi-colonial Anglo-Egyptian domination.[97] After his death, the Mahdist state, ruled by his successor, the *Khalīfah*, continued to exist until it was eventually overthrown by the British in 1898. Notwithstanding its relatively short-lived existence, it has exerted great influence upon the later developments in the Sudan, mainly because it has laid the foundations for a genuine Arab Sudanese national feeling. After the overthrow of the Mahdist state, Mahdism in connexion with the doctrine of jihad continued to play a role in local anti-British insurrections, which broke out several times during the Anglo-Egyptian rule.[98]

3.5 EGYPTIAN RESISTANCE, LED BY AḤMAD ʿURĀBĪ', AGAINST BRITISH OCCUPATION

During the second half of the nineteenth century, Egyptian society underwent profound social and economic transformations. One of these affected the position of the Turco-Circassian ruling class. Thanks to the grants of large tracts of land by Mehmet ʿAlī, the Turco-Circassians were the most important landowners in Egypt. Gradually, however, they lost this position, as Arabic-speaking Egyptians also acquired large holdings. At the same time, the latter were admitted to the provincial administration and the officer corps. Tensions arose from the fact that these newly emerging Arabic-speaking classes did not have access to the central government, where the Turco-Circassians retained their dominating position. Another important change in Egyptian society was the increasing foreign influence, accompanied by immigration of foreigners. Foreign interest in Egypt was the result of the great financial and economic opportunities connected with the cotton-boom and the manifold projects of the Khedives Saʿīd (1854-1863) and Ismāʿīl (1863-1879). The extravagant loans they contracted with foreign bankers led ultimately to bankruptcy of the Egyptian State in 1876 and to the institution of an international *Caisse de la Dette Publique*, through which Great Britain and France could control the revenues – and the affairs – of the Egyptian State. The public debt was so large that in 1877 out of the total budget of the State of 9.5 million pounds, 7.5 million pounds had to be paid as interest and repayments.[99] In order to meet the demands of the creditors, state expenses were cut – with the exception, however, of the high salaries of foreign officials – and taxes were raised beyond the limit of what was tolerable. The situation in the countryside became still worse due to drought and cattle epidemics during the years 1878 until 1881. Part of the financial policy imposed by the foreign powers was a plan to reduce the army, which would, conveniently enough, also curtail the power of the Khedive. When it appeared that especially the Arab army officers would be the victims of this reduction and not the Turco-Circassians, who still held the positions of command in the army and as a group enjoyed considerable privileges, the majority of the army revolted. Aḥmad ʿUrābī (1841-1911) then became the spokesman of the disaffected officers.

When the action of the Egyptian army officers had some initial success, many Egyptian landlords and provincial notables, who resented not having a share in or, at least, access to the state power, saw an opportunity for achieving their aims by joining the movement of the officers. From 1881 onward, the political demands of both groups were voiced by the National Party, *al-Ḥizb al-Waṭanī*.[100] Its main demand was the convocation of the Council of Delegates (*Madjlis al-Nuwwāb*), which had been established by Ismāʿīl with the aim of strengthening his position *vis-à-vis* the Western powers. The National Party wanted the Council to prepare a constitution that would confer more authority on the delegates. The officers hoped that a stronger Council would be able to protect them against the highhandedness of Ismāʿīl's successor Tawfīq (1879-1892) and his Turco-Circassian environment. The provincial notables expected such a Council to give them access to the central government, so that they could better further their interests. During September, 1881, the army revolted again in support of the National Party. The specific demands were: dismissal of Riyāḍ as prime-minister, since he represented the interests of the Turco-Circassians, convocation of the Council of Delegates and raising the army to a strength of 18,000 men. Tawfīq was forced to accept these demands. ʿUrābī, who had acted as a mouthpiece of the officers and had thereby risked his neck, was then celebrated as Egypt's national leader and spokesman for the National Party.

On the whole, the National Party was hardly revolutionary. Its adherents were inspired by a liberal ideology of constitutionalism, of freedom and equality for all men regardless of race and religion and of progress by education. They did not want to overthrow the existing social and political order, but only to reform it, recognizing the Khedive and the Ottoman Sultan as their legitimate rulers. As to the position of the foreigners, their demands can barely be called radical: they accepted the necessity of foreign financial control, but criticized the way it operated. They objected especially against the employment of an increasing number of foreign officials with exorbitant salaries, and against the fiscal and legal privileges of the foreigners.[101] The Egyptians saw how the riches of the country flowed into the pockets of the foreign creditors and could not be used in the interest of the country. They resented the influence and the position of the well-paid foreign officials in the Egyptian administration.[102] Finally, there were fears lest England would occupy Egypt, fears that were strengthened by the French occupation of Tunisia in 1881.[103]

As a result of the army revolt of September, 1881, Tawfiq appointed a new cabinet in February, 1882. In this cabinet, the Arab-Egyptian element was for the first time well represented. ʿUrābī held the post of Minister of War. At about the same time, a new constitution replaced the old law concerning the Council of Delegates. This new constitution gave the Council some limited powers *vis-à-vis* the cabinet, but hardly curtailed the Khedive's prerogatives. However, despite its narrow scope, it was important in that it provided the provincial notables with a platform from where they could voice their opinions and exert a certain influence upon the central government. Thus their self-confidence grew and they began criticizing the government and especialy the administrative services run by foreigners. The latter, who saw their lucrative and influential jobs endangered, reacted by launching a vehement propaganda campaign against the Council, which they claimed, had come completely under the influence of ʿUrābī and his radical fellow-officers. ʿUrābī, on his part, had also incurred the fierce hatred of the Turco-Circassian military establishment, since, in his position as Minister of War, he had broken their monopoly of the higher military ranks.

It was clear that the Khedive looked upon these developments with disfavour and feared to lose control over the events. He must have realized that the foreign powers were as much opposed to ʿUrābī and the National Party as he was. Therefore, he decided that foreign intervention might help him escape from his predicament. A favourable opportunity presented itself when a number of Turco-Circassian officers, who had hatched a plot to assassinate ʿUrābī, were tried by a court-martial. The verdict had to be ratified by the Khedive, but he refused to do so and, at the same time, perfidiously told the foreign consuls that the cabinet had threatened with a general massacre of foreigners, should he fail to accept the proposals of the court-martial. Actually, the cabinet wanted to solve the conflict and to convoke the Council so that it could mediate between the cabinet and the Khedive. The consuls, however, strongly objected to this proposal, alleging that the delegates would certainly dethrone Tawfiq, send the exponents of the ruling dynasty into exile and appoint ʿUrābī or the prime minister Maḥmūd Sāmī as governor-general of Egypt. Their actual motives, however, were that they wanted to prevent a settlement between the cabinet and the Khedive, so as to prepare the way for military intervention. In order to emphasize their opposition to the convocation of the Council, the British and the French governments sent a fleet to Alexandria. This, however, did not produce the intended effect, as the display of strength did not intimidate the officers and the National Party. The Egyptian population rallied around ʿUrābī and petitions from all over the country entreated him to take upon him the defence of Islam and the country. The Khedive, wanting to dismiss ʿUrābī as Minister of War, could not assert his will against the opposition of the military. In June, 1882, after anti-European disturbances had broken out,[104] the Khedive put himself under the protection of the British fleet hoping thus to be able to maintain his position in the face of the domestic opposition.

A month later, the British fleet bombed Alexandria and the British army invaded the country. All this happened under the pretext that the Egyptians were reinforcing the ramparts of Alexandria against the outspoken wish of the British. The true reasons, however, were of an economic and strategical nature, viz. protection of the British financial and commercial interests and control over the Suez Canal.[105] Immediately after the invasion, ʿUrābī organized the struggle against the British, a struggle that was to last two months and end with ʿUrābī's surrender on September 14th. Although the Khedive had issued proclamations to the effect that the British army had only come to restore law and order and was acting on his command[106] and although he had formally dismissed ʿUrābī as Minister of War, the latter knew that he had the support of the majority of the

Egyptian population and issued a proclamation that he would take command of the armed forces. At the same time he convoked a meeting of notables. This meeting endorsed his position and declared that the orders of the Khedive or his ministers were to be considered null and void, without, however, deposing him and without severing the ties with the Ottoman Sultan. In fact ʿUrābī and his partisans hoped that the Sultan would depose Tawfiq and appoint another Khedive. Their expectations, however, were frustrated when the Sultan proclaimed ʿUrābī a rebel against the legitimate government.[107] Nevertheless, ʿUrābī continued his military preparations for the defence of Egypt, raising 25,000 troops and requesting the population to contribute money for the equipment of the army. Many responded to his appeals, but the badly trained and insufficiently equipped army was no match for the British. After a series of bloody battles, ʿUrābī was forced to surrender to them. The Egyptian army was disbanded and the leaders of the anti-British resistance were tried and sentenced, mostly to banishment.

When events had developed into an armed struggle against the European invaders, the doctrine of jihad offered the most appropriate ideology for mobilizing the people.[108] On 11 July, the day Alexandria was bombed by the British fleet, a jihad proclamation was published in *al-Waqāʾiʿ al-Miṣriyyah*, the Official Gazette of Egypt.[109] All over the country, *ʿulamāʾ* preached jihad and exhorted the Egyptians to support the army in its struggle against the unbelievers:

> Everyone is familiar with the duty of contributing his share for the support of the Religion. Thus the rich must help the army according to their capabilities with provisions and they shall protect it against starvations and feed it. For the army is the fortified stronghold for the defence against the enemy and against the despicable traitor [i.e. the Khedive]. Those who sacrifice themselves in support of their Religion will attain success and acceptance [with Allah]. Those who rush forward to protect their honour and dignity will achieve what they have desired and hoped for. So be determined, o people of religious zeal! Make haste, o people of Islamic ardour! Offer your assistance, o community of

the Guide, the Announcer, the Warner [i.e. Mohammed]! *'Fight the unbelievers who are near to you and let them feel a rough temper in you and know that Allah is with those who show piety'* [K 9:123]. Think but of the victory that Allah has promised to us and be patient, for patience makes difficult things easy.[110]

O servants of Allah! . . . It has become manifest that the English have come to wage war in order to plunder our property and to rape our women (which Allah may prevent). They have treacherously and perfidiously come in order to trap the country in the snares of their stratagems without fighting and [being met with] resistance, as is their disgusting practice everywhere. But now intelligent and brave people have been alerted and have begun defending their honour and their country and have prepared a hearty welcome for them. May Allah assist the Moslems by means of the Egyptian troops and may He help them with His divine providence. May the noble Lord bestow firmness upon them. Some ignoramuses have been misled by their guiles and have spread foul words, thus deviating from the straight path. Wake up from your heedlessness, o sons of this land, and free yourselves from shame and ignominy. Cause the English to taste a painful punishment and prepare for them whatsoever force and cavalry ye are capable of gathering [cf. K 8:60]. . . . Allah is the patron and helper of those who fight in the way of Allah. Victory comes from Allah, the Mighty One, the Wise One.[111]

Many *ʿulamā'* attributed the British invasion to the un-Islamic behaviour of the rulers, that had taken unbelievers as patrons and had imitated their behaviour, paying no heed to the injunctions of Islam:

It is quite evident that of late the Moslems have passed through troubled times. This was entirely due to the rulers' lack of Islamic zeal. They were like the dark night, being wholly engaged in the domain of worldly fortune and paying no heed to the Religion. But now propitious signs of the power and strength of the Moslems have appeared, since the present rulers – may Allah support them – have adopted the right course by firmly adhering to the Religion and restoring the power that the Moslems have lost. They are now exerting themselves to keep the Community away from disturbances and to achieve safety, since the leader of the *mudjāhids*, who is being supported by the assistance of his Lord, has begun to expel those who were the principal cause of the disturbed state of the Community. He has sold himself and his army to the jihad in the way of Allah, not caring about hardship and fatigue. [He does] all this so as to safeguard the country and to raise the word of Allah [cf. K 9:40][112]

The same line of argumentation can be found in a pamphlet written during the war, which incites the believers to partake in the jihad against the foreign aggressors or to give financial support to the army:[113]

As everyone knows, the unbelievers have for the past years attacked the Moslems, especially in Egypt. This is caused by the fact that the Moslems have joined [them], cooperated with them and attempted to ingratiate themselves with them, to such an extent that they have affected their manners in language and conduct. As a result their hearts have become imbued with attachment to these [manners]. This is the substantiation of what the prophet has said: *'You are certainly going to follow the practice of those who were before you* [i.e. the non-Moslems], *inch after inch, yard after yard, to the extent that if one of them enters a lizard's lair, you will enter it too'.* This development continued and sin increased and spread amongst them. They even openly indulged in it. Usury became general and was being practised by almost everybody. Thereupon Allah became exasperated with them and gave their foes authority over them [cf. K 4:90]. These humiliated them and employed them in all kinds of degrading activities. This went so far that unbelievers would ride horses or carriages with Moslems running in front of them, or that those cursed [unbelievers] would extend their feet with those black shoes to Moslems in order to have them polished by them. Thus they were in a position of extreme humiliation and contempt. In the eyes of the unbelievers, Moslems were even more contemptible than Jews, of whom Allah has said: *'Humiliation and poverty were stamped upon them'* [K 2:61]. Then the unbelievers, by cooperating with our rulers and presenting their affairs in a favourable light to them,

> were able to instruct them to compose laws that are in conflict with the *sharīʿah* and with our rules, in order that these laws would be applied in court and that people would follow them. [Our rulers] adopted [these laws] from them and ordered the presidents of the courts to apply them. They have discarded Allah's book, as if they did not know [how grave a sin this is]. Religion has become exceptional, just like the Prophet has said: *'Islam has begun as something exceptional and it will be again as it has begun'*. There is no strength nor power but through Allah, the High One, the Magnificent One. However, in the year 1299 [H = 1881-2 A.D.], Allah has conferred His blessing and His favour upon us in order to strengthen the religion of Islam, by sending a person with a strong faith and great force. He seriously and energetically set out to raise the Word of Truth and Religion.[114]

Whereas all over the country ʿUrābī's propagandists incited the people to lend support to the struggle against the foreign invaders, Alexandria, firmly in the hands of the English and the Khedive, became the centre of counterpropaganda. Besides relating tales of horror about the conduct of ʿUrābī's soldiers,[115] his adversaries kept playing on the argument that he was to be considered a rebel since he disobeyed the orders of the legitimate rulers and that therefore ʿUrābī's struggle had nothing to do with religion and could not possibly be called jihad. Furthermore they upheld the fiction that the British army had invaded Egypt on the Khedive's request to restore law and order:

> O Lord, do not lead us to perdition [as a punishment] for what some fools amongst us have done. O servants of Allah, you surely know how often I have emphasized with conclusive arguments that the Islamic community will only attain success by activating the Religion, which is based upon high moral principles and enjoins that *dhimmis*, *musta'mins* and unbelievers with whom a pact or peace treaty has been concluded be treated well and friendly. These are the four categories to which – as we have previously stated – all foreigners in Islamic countries without exception belong. Another [Islamic] prescription is to prepare whatsoever force and cavalry one is capable of gathering [cf. K 8:60]. There is no doubt

that 'force' includes guns and all sorts of modern equipment that can be used at any time and at any place, and also any conceivable contraption that is fit to inflict damage upon the adversary. But, unfortunately, it seems that this noble verse, ordering to prepare what has been mentioned, has been especially revealed for the benefit of the foreigners, since they have followed it, whereas we have not. We have rejected it as well as other religious practices and injunctions of our Lord. The result has been that the proficiency of these ignorant rebels in the military arts and their experience in inflicting damage to the enemy was such that they faced the modern English military equipment, which had been produced only a few months or even weeks before, with antique armaments that for generations had been eaten by rust, covering it in thick layers. But [as the poet says]:

It is ignorance when a dog bays at his master
And pebbles are cast at a comet when it falls.

If we assume – which is absurd – that this war in this situation is a religious war and that it is being fought by the order of the supreme Caliph or his representative, the eminent Khedive, then one should, according to the *sharīʿah*, oppose their orders, since it amounts to emperilling the country and the people. Allah has forbidden us to hand ourselves over to destruction [cf. K 2:195] and why should we, now that this war, as we have said before, is occasioned by self-love, by personal interests, as we shall explain later, and by madness, which ʿUrābī now feigns in order to escape the evil outcome [of his actions], although all his deeds, from the beginning to the end, were sheer madness. . . . I shall not stop telling you that the only aim the English have in mind is to restore order and to subdue the army to its legitimate ruler, the representative of the Commander of the Faithful, and that His Majesty the Khedive is very pious and religious. You must be aware of the fact that sometimes our Mohammedan Religion must get its support from others [i.e. non-Moslems], and also that His Majesty the Khedive is not the first to become victorious through the assistance of others. On the contrary, this used to happen frequently and some

> of the most outstanding men of the Islamic community have been involved in it.[116]

After the suppression of the ʿUrābī revolt, the British were to rule Egypt with a firm hand. It was not until 1919 that the Egyptian people rebelled again. But then the prevailing ideology was nationalism and the doctrine of jihad did not play a significant part.

3.6 SANŪSĪ RESISTANCE AGAINST ITALIAN COLONIALISM IN LIBYA

In order to check further European expansion, the Ottoman Empire, in 1835, recaptured Libya which, although formally falling under Ottoman authority, had enjoyed a high degree of autonomy under the dynasty of the Qaramanlis. Henceforth, Libya was to be governed by Turkish governors, sent to the country for a limited period of office, as it was customary in the other provinces of the Ottoman Empire. Turkish authority, however, hardly extended beyond the few coastal towns. The hinterland was the realm of independent nomad tribes that did not recognize any government and revolted whenever the Ottomans tried to extend their sway over them. The separation between town and country life was great, greater than in the rest of North Africa, owing to the absence of settled agriculturists, who are usually bound to the towns by economic ties of landownership, taxation and usury. The interior of the country, however, was not completely ruled by anarchy. Some typical governmental functions were performed by the Sanūsiyyah order, a religious brotherhood established in Cyrenaica in the 1840s by Muḥammad al-Sanūsī (1791-1859). The Sanūsiyyah strictly adhered to orthodox Islam and had strong revivalist leanings, striving for the purification of Islam from later innovations. This order had managed to win over the nomad and semi-nomad tribes of Libya, Egypt and the Southern Saharan regions. Its *shaykhs* provided the population with education in its *zāwiyahs*, administered justice and maintained to a certain extent public security. The position of the order was strengthened as it served as a kind of buffer between the Ottoman administration and the tribes. Through the order, the

Ottomans dealt with the tribes. Thus, with their support the order could resist any encroachments upon its prerogatives by the Ottoman administration. On the other hand, it could in combination with the administration prevent the tribes from becoming too powerful. In this way, the Sanūsiyyah developed into some sort of a 'proto-state with an embryonic government of its own'.[117]

By the end of the nineteenth century, Italy, unlike many other European states, had not yet taken its share from Asia or Africa. It had had designs upon Tunisia, but these had been thwarted by the French occupation of 1881. Italy then looked eastward to Libya, where it had already certain economic interests. There were Italian traders, there was a branch of the Banco di Roma, a medical and postal service was being operated by the Italians and Italian companies had purchased land for agricultural schemes. Hence, in the jubilant atmosphere of colonial expansion prevailing in Europe during that epoch, it was logical that Italy would attempt to occupy Libya, the more so as it expected to meet hardly any resistance from the local population. The Italians thought that the Libyan Arabs would remain neutral or even side with them against the Turks. They had been led to believe this, as a certain animosity between both groups had come into existence, due to the Young Turk revolution of 1908. The Libyans were opposed to liberal and secular reforms, to the strong Turkish nationalist tendencies and, finally, to the deposition of Sultan Abdülhamit II in 1909. When the new Ottoman government began to take measures to curb further Italian penetration and the Germans, simultaneously tried to obtain an economic foothold in Libya, the Italians deemed the time ripe for military intervention with the aim of subjecting the country to colonial domination. In October, 1911, an Italian expeditionary army of more than 60,000 troops occupied the coastal towns. However, despite their overwhelming numerical superiority – the Turkish army consisted of no more than 7,000 men – the Italians could not advance beyond the littoral, as the Turks, contrary to the Italian expectations, were being assisted by local bedouin warriors under the command of the Sanūsiyyah. Just as they had done when around the turn of the century they had tried to check French expansion into the Sahara, they saw this struggle as jihad against the unbelievers. The head of the Sanūsiyyah at the time, al-Sayyid Aḥmad al-Sharīf (1873-1933), grandson of its founder, issued a jihad proclamation which was published in an Egyptian magazine in January, 1912.[118] It addresses 'all Moslems especially in such countries as have been occupied by the enemies of the Religion' and contains the conventional exhortatory Koranic verses and prophetic Traditions. The author argues that those who fail to take part in the jihad are apostates (and, consequently, may legally be killed):

> [Among the Traditions that threaten the believers not to abandon jihad is the following Tradition:] *'If you traffic the best part of your herd, if you hold on tightly to the tails of your cattle, if you content yourselves with tilling the land and if you abandon the jihad, then Allah will impose a humiliation upon you that will only be taken away when you return to your Religion',* i.e. to what is incumbent upon you, namely jihad against the enemies, giving them a rough time, establishing Islam, assisting the Religion and its adherents, raising Allah's Word and subjugating unbelief and the unbelievers. This implies that abandoning jihad means leaving the Religion, since one can only return to something if one has left it. This goes for the jihad that is a collective duty and therefore *a fortiori* for the jihad that has become an individual duty because of an attack by the enemy. If one who refrains from partaking in the jihad, does not anymore belong to the Religion, [the same holds true] *a fortiori* for those that side with the enemy for the sake of wordly goods in order to fight the Moslems and that enroll themselves in their army.[119]

The jihad of the Sanūsiyyah raised echoes all over the Islamic world. Substantial assistance, however, was not given, except for some medical aid.[120] In Egypt the Sanusī call for jihad, which was as usual indiscriminately proclaimed against all unbelievers aroused some anxiety amongst the Christian population. Moslem authors, however, wrote articles to allay these fears, demonstrating that this particular jihad was only directed against the Italian aggressors.[121]

In October, 1912, the Ottoman Empire, being harrassed by the Balkan War, was forced to accept a treaty of peace with the Italians (the Treaty of Lausanne) and to cede Libya to them. The wording of this treaty, however, was not wholly unambiguous, as the Sultan retained his spiritual authority over the Libyan Moslems and the right to appoint the Grand *Qāḍī* of Tripoli.[122] Despite this treaty the commander of the Ottoman army in Libya, Enver Bey (who was later to become Minister of War) requested al-Sayyid Aḥmad al-Sharīf to continue the war against the Italians in the name of Sultan Mehmet V. Some Turkish troops were left behind in Cyrenaica to support the bedouins. Thus, the guerilla war lingered on, preventing the Italians from occupying the Cyrenaican hinterland. Around the beginning of 1914 the remnants of the Turkish army left Cyrenaica after a disagreement with al-Sayyid Aḥmad al-Sharīf and the bedouins had to fend for themselves. Actually, because of the resistance of the local population, which had become manifest from the very beginning, the war could not be regarded as one in which a foreign power tried to wrest a colony from a tired empire, but became a real colonial war with the aim of depriving a native people from its liberty and land.[123] The common struggle against the Italian aggressors had a unifying effect upon the segmentary tribal society of Libya. The tribes, in their opposition against a European state, were forged together into a similar statelike structure, which was provided by the Sanūsiyyah, that had also previously performed governmental functions and could give the tribes a common symbol which stood for their common interests.[124]

In this period a treatise on jihad, written by the Sanūsī leader al-Sayyid Aḥmad al-Sharīf, was published in Cairo.[125] Contrary to the proclamation of 1912, this treatise especially addressed the Libyan Moslems, from the Tunisian border to Sallūm:[126]

> How can you live with vipers and scorpions and with those who openly profess polytheism and the Trinity [of God] and who destroy the *miḥrābs*. How can the light of the sun of Islam shine over you when the Banner of the Cross and the Darkness flutters amongst you[127]

The treatise exhorts the Libyans to partake in the jihad or to support the war effort, quoting the appropriate Koranic verses and prophetic Traditions. The author warns his followers not to listen to defeatists that call for terminating the jihad and surrendering to the enemy. He asserts that these are to be regarded as apostates:

> Beware, o Moslems, of the delusory words of those who have the appearance of being Moslems, but do not at all belong to Islam. Beware that you do not listen to their idle and foolish talk. Beware of the venom they squirt out. Beware of their call for surrender and submission to the enemy, for they are hypocrites who will satisfy you with their mouths but whose hearts will refuse; the most of them are reprobates [cf. K 9:8]. They have submitted to the enemy and have traded their religion for worldly goods. They have become their helpers and show them the way to enable them to take possession of the country of their brethren. *'These are they who have bartered the guidance for error; their trade has not turned out profitable and they have not been rightly guided'* [K 2:16]. *'Upon them is the curse of Allah, and the angels, and the people as a whole'* [K 3:87]. They exert themselves for them [the enemies] with the aim of making the country accessible and enslaving its inhabitants, so that the latter cease to fight them and so that their [the enemies'] word will be the highest. Allah forbid that we yield to the enemy as long as our veins are pulsating and our blood is running through them. Those who incite us to conclude peace and to submit to the enemy must be fought. *'Their resort is Gehenna – a bad place to stay'* [K 9:73]. There is no doubt as to the unbelief and the apostasy of people that support the unbelievers against the believers and fight the believers. May Allah save us from people that strive for humiliating Islam and its adherents. What kind of unbelief is worse than this kind? If they are not apostates, who are then the apostates?[128]

The treatise is illustrative of the practical problems that confronted the Sanūsiyyah in performing its governmental functions in its struggle against the Italians. It deals with topics like the collection of extra taxes above those prescribed by the *sharīʿah*,[129] the obligation to emigrate from regions occupied by the enemy[130] and the treatment of spies.[131] Basically these were the same difficulties as faced ʿAbd al-Qādir eighty years before, so it is not surprising that al-Sayyid Aḥmad al-Sharīf quoted extensively from the *fatwā* issued by the Moroccan *Shaykh al-Islām* al-Tasūlī.

Despite the problems of guerilla warfare and the lack of discipline among the bedouin tribes, the Sanūsī forces were able to defeat an Italian army corps in April, 1915. After this victory, the Sanūsiyyah controlled not only the Cyrenaican hinterland, but also that of Tripoli. When the First World War broke out and Italy joined the Allied Powers in May, 1915, the military situation in Libya changed. The Sanūsī troops received help from the Turks and the Germans, who broke the Italian blockade with submarines. Under the influence of his Turkish and German advisors, on whose assistance he became more and more dependent, and obeying the Sultan's call for jihad against the British, al-Sayyid Aḥmad al-Sharīf boldly attacked Egypt. The Sanūsī army could advance as far as Mersa Matruḥ, but was then defeated by the British. After this defeat, al-Sayyid Aḥmad al-Sharīf, feeling that the Libyans were too exhausted to carry on the unequal struggle, especially as they had been suffering from a serious shortage of food supplies during the last two years, decided that negotiations with the British and the Italians would have to be entered into. Therefore, he handed his political power over to his cousin, al-Sayyid Muḥammad Idrīs (later to become King of Libya). He himself remained the spiritual head of the Sanūsiyyah. The period from 1917 till 1923 was relatively quiet. The Italians had to a certain extent recognized the sovereignty of the Sanūsiyyah over the interior of Cyrenaica and both sides had worked out a way of living together. This situation, however, changed when the fascists took over in Italy. The new regime considered the situation in Libya as inconsistent with Italy's 'honour' and resumed the war against the Libyan bedouins in order to gain possession of the entire country. Despite the numerical and material superiority of the Italians, it took them nine years of bitter fighting to overcome the resistance of the local population. During this new war, the Sanūsiyyah again gave evidence of its organizational strength. Whereas the Sanūsī family hardly played any role, the local leaders, *ikhwān*, did. The actual commander of the struggle was the Sanūsī *Shaykh* ʿUmar al-Mukhtār (1862-1931), who after being captured by the Italians, was publicly hanged in 1931. In the beginning of 1932 the Italians had crushed the resistance of the last bedouin bands. The armed struggle of the Sanūsiyyah had come to an end.

3.7 THE OTTOMAN JIHAD DECLARATION OF 1914

On 11 November, 1914, the Ottoman Sultan Mehmet V declared war on Russia, France and Great Britain. Following the customary practice in the Ottoman Empire, this declaration was accompanied by a *fatwā* to the effect that war under the circumstances was legal according to the *sharīʿah* and that jihad had become an individual duty on the strength of the general mobilization (*istinfār ʿāmm*) by the Sultan. The *fatwā*, or rather the five connected *fatwās*, are composed in the ordinary manner and cast in the form of an elaborate question enumerating all relevant details and circumstances, on which a simple affirmative or negative answer suffices:

> *Question:* When it occurs that enemies attack the Islamic world, when it has been established that they seize and pillage Islamic countries and capture Moslem persons and when His Majesty the Padishah of Islam thereupon orders the jihad in the form of a general mobilization, has jihad then, according to the illustrious Koranic verse: *'March out light and heavy* [*hearted*], *and strive with goods and persons* [*in the way of Allah; that will be better for you'* (K 9:41)], become incumbent upon all Moslems and has it become an individual duty for all Moslems in all parts of the world, be they young or old, on foot or mounted, to hasten to partake in the jihad with their goods and money?
>
> *Answer:* Yes.
>
> *Question:* Now that it has been established that Russia, England, France and the governments that support them and are allied to them, are hostile to the Islamic Caliphate, since their warships and armies attack the Seat of the Islamic Caliphate and the Imperial Dominions and strive (Allah forbid) for extinguishing and annihilating the exalted light of Islam [cf. K 9:32], is it, in this case, also incumbent upon all Moslems that are being ruled by these governments, to proclaim jihad against them and to actually attack them?
>
> *Answer:* Yes.
>
> *Question:* If some Moslems, now that the attainment of the aim [viz. the protection of the Ottoman Empire] depends on the fact

that all Moslems hasten to partake in the jihad, refrain from doing so (which Allah forbid), is this then, in this case, a great sin and do they deserve Divine wrath and punishment for their horrible sin?

Answer: Yes.

Question: If the states mentioned that are fighting against the Islamic government compel and force their Moslem population by [threatening them] to kill them and even to exterminate all members of their families, is it even in this case according to the *sharīʿah* absolutely forbidden for them to fight against the troops of the Islamic countries and do they [by transgressing this prohibition] deserve the hell-fire, having become murderers?

Answer: Yes.

Question: Is it in this case for the Moslems that are in the present war under the rule of England, France, Russia, Serbia, Montenegro and their allies, since it is detrimental to the Islamic Caliphate, a great sin to fight against Germany and Austria which are the allies of the Supreme Islamic Government and do they deserve [by acting so] a painful punishment [in the Here-after]?

Answer: Yes.[132]

In comparison with earlier *fatwās* this one introduced a novel element as it was expressly addressed to all Moslems, especially those under the colonial rule of Turkey's adversaries, and not only to the Ottoman subjects.[133] Consequently, it was translated into other Islamic languages, viz. Arabic, Persian, Urdu and Tataric.[134] In order to enhance the effect, several proclamations directly addressing the Moslem peoples outside the Ottoman Empire were issued in connexion with this *fatwā*:

Thus all Moslems living in the countries ruled by the aforementioned aggressive governments, like the Crimea, Kazan, Turkestan, Bukhara, Khiva, India, or in China, Afghanistan, Persia, Africa and other countries of the world, hastened together with the Osmanli in accordance with the Illustrious *Fatwās* that have been issued on the subject, to partake in the Great Jihad; they have all considered in their hearts the glorious Koranic verses: *'O ye who have believed, what is the matter with you? When one says to you: "March out in the way of Allah", ye are weighed down to the*

> *ground; are ye so satisfied with this nearer life as to neglect the Hereafter? The enjoyment of this nearer life is in comparison with the Hereafter only a little thing. If ye do not march out He will inflict upon you a painful punishment, and will substitute [for you] another people; ye will not injure Him at all; Allah over everything has power'* [K 9:38-39]. And: *'Say: "If your fathers and your sons and your brethren and your wives and your clan, and properties which ye have acquired, and trade which ye fear may go slack, and dwellings which please you are dearer to you than Allah and His messenger and striving in His cause, then wait until Allah cometh with His affair; Allah guideth not the people who are reprobates"'* [K 9:26]. It is now one of the greatest religious duties of the Moslems, that those who consider these Koranic verses in their hearts, save themselves from the painful punishment that they would meet in this or in the other world, and attain eternal bliss. Those enemies call up their Moslem subjects, lead them against the Caliph of the Moslems or his helpers and allies and expose them to annihilation in the hottest parts of the Western and Eastern battlefields. Or rather, they employ thousands of ignominious guiles in order to have their crimes against the religion of Islam carried out by the hands of the Moslems themselves. Hence, it is one of the most important duties and one of the main religious obligations to make all kinds of sacrifices in order to heal as quickly as possible the heart rending pain that the believers cannot suffer anymore.[135]

The attempt to incite the Moslems outside the Ottoman Empire to join the Ottoman jihad[136] was a logical outcome of the Pan-Islamic policy initiated by Abdülhamid II. As a reaction against the claims of some Western powers to the right of protection of Christian minorities within the Ottoman Empire, he stressed the universal character of his Caliphate and strived for his recognition as the spiritual head of all Moslems, those under colonial rule included. Many Moslem intellectuals who were apprehensive of the increasing Western economic and political influence in the Islamic world, tended to see the unification of all Moslems under the leadership of the Ottoman Sultan as the only means of resisting Western domination. About three decades before the outbreak of the First World

War, Djamāl al-Dīn al-Afghānī had written in his magazine *al-ʿUrwah al-Wuthqā*:

> By Allah, if the Ottomans would be aware of their moral authority over the Moslem subjects of England, and would employ this authority in an intelligent manner, then they would not have to swallow passively with bitterness the domination and the unjust acts of the English and their encroachments upon the rights of the Sultan, like in the Egyptian question, which is actually an Ottoman or Islamic question.[137]

In the provinces of the Ottoman Empire, the jihad *fatwā* met with some response from local religious dignitaries, who composed, in their turn, *fatwās* and tracts supporting the Sultan's cause.[138] In the Hejaz, however, the call for jihad was received with a certain reservation. This was an unpleasant surprise for the Ottoman government, as an endorsement by the religious dignitaries of Mecca would greatly enhance the prestige of the jihad-*fatwā*. The Sharīf Ḥusayn of Mecca, who had already been approached by the British with plans for an Arab revolt against the Turks, refused to associate himself openly with the Ottoman jihad, under the pretext that by doing so he would risk a blockade and perhaps bombardment of the Hejazi ports, since the British navy was supreme in the Red Sea.[139]

In pursuance of the religious war propaganda initiated by the jihad-declaration, the Ottoman and German governments set up committees of pro-Turkish *ʿulama'* and Islamic personalities (e.g. Shakīb Arslān and ʿAbbās II Ḥilmī, the former Khedive of Egypt, who had been deposed by the British in 1914, and the Tunisian *ʿulamā'* Ṣāliḥ al-Sharīf and Bāsh Ḥanbah ʿAlī), in Istanbul, Berlin and Switzerland. These committees published propagandistic magazines and pamphlets that appealed to pan-Islamic feelings and incited the Moslem population of the British and French colonies to revolt against their oppressors.[140] In the Halbmond Lager (Crescent Camp) at Wünsdorf, Germany, a P.O.W.-camp especially destined for Moslem prisoners, *ʿulamā'* were employed to win the prisoners over to the side of the Central Powers and to persuade them to defect with an appeal to religious feelings and the loyalty to the Ottoman Sultan due by all Moslems.[141] Although it appears that this propaganda was mainly directed to the North African Moslems, there were also contacts between the Ottoman authorities and Indian Moslem nationalists.[142] As an antidote against the Ottoman pan-Islamic propaganda the colonial powers prevailed on the local *ʿulamā'* to publicly endorse their cause. In Algeria the heads of the *ṭuruq* and the *muftīs* issued declarations denouncing the folly of the Turks in proclaiming jihad and enjoining the Algerian Moslems to remain loyal to the legitimate authorities.[143] In India and Egypt, *fatwās* were published to the effect that it was legally obligatory to obey the English.[144]

Despite the efforts of the Central Powers, the effect of the Ottoman jihad-proclamation and the subsequent stream of religious propaganda was minimal. Here and there religious leaders expressed pro-Ottoman feelings in their sermons and preached on the theme of jihad,[145] but nowhere did anti-colonial revolts break out in support of the Turks. This was partly due to the repression of the colonial authorities that arrested pro-Turkish leaders and suppressed pro-Turkish literature.[147] The main reason, however, was that Pan-Islamism lacked any form of political mass organization. Despite the exaggerated notions with regard to its force and impact prevalent in Europe, it was no more than an idea espoused by some intellectuals as a reaction against the rapid spread of Western domination during the last quarter of the nineteenth century.

3.8 RELIGIOUS OPPOSITION AGAINST BRITISH COLONIALISM AND ZIONISM IN PALESTINE

After the First World War, Britain and France remained in possession of the Arab provinces of the former Ottoman Empire. The League of Nations legitimized their rule by assigning the mandates over these regions to them. An Arab government set up in Damascus by Fayṣal, the son of Sharīf Ḥusayn of Mecca was only short-lived. In 1920 the French army took Damascus and put an end to Fayṣal's kingdom. The disappointment among the Arabs was great, the more so as Great Britain had promised them independence as a reward for their participation on the side of the British in the war against the Turks. In the year 1920, the disappointment resulted in disturbances and revolts in almost all parts of the Fertile Crescent. These, however, did not assume the character of jihad-movements. In Syria, the revolts were regional and sectarian, mainly Druze and Alawite. Shiʿite *ʿulamāʾ* played a major part in the Iraqi revolt by fomenting religious feelings against the British, but owing to the peculiarities of the Shiʿite doctrine on this point, one cannot call it a jihad-movement.[148]

In Palestine the disturbances of 1920 and 1921 were spontaneous popular outbursts in which both Moslems and Christians participated. Although religious feelings played a certain role, the main motor behind these disturbances and demonstrations was nationalist fervour and no jihad-declarations were issued. When the nationalist movement, both in Syria and in Palestine, gained strength during the first half of the 1920s, the doctrine of jihad was not invoked to justify the struggle against the foreign rule, nor was it employed to mobilize the population. The nationalist leaders, who were without exception recruited from the upper classes, wanted to achieve their aims by means of negotiations and diplomacy more than through popular action, let alone armed struggle. Another factor that prevented the doctrine of jihad being used was the foremost part played by Christians in the Palestinian national movement. Moreover, the ideology of Arab nationalism, which was the driving force behind the Palestinian national movement, had developed in opposition to centralizing tendencies in the Ottoman Empire and hence had a distinctly secular character, since Islam was identified with the ruling institutions of the Empire.

Although in the outset the Palestinian National movement formed part of the national movement in the whole region of Greater Syria, it gradually acquired specific traits of its own. For Palestine was not only a country under foreign domination, such as e.g. Syria, but also subject to colonization by foreign settlers, the zionists. During the first decade of the Mandate the Palestinian nationalists saw the zionist movement as their main enemy, and not the British. Of course they were opposed to the Balfour Declaration of 1917 which stated that H. M. government viewed with favour the establishment of a Jewish national home in Palestine and to the preamble and article 2 of the Mandate Charter in which the Balfour Declaration had been incorporated. However, they did not regard this pledge as an essential part of British policy in Palestine, but rather as an unfortunate but accidental feature. They overrated Jewish influence on British politics and regarded Great Britain as a friend that was in principle willing to grant them independence, but had been led astray by bad counsels. Consequently, the efforts of the Palestinian political leaders were engaged in convincing Great Britain that its policy in Palestine was unjust and wrong. They tried to do so by negotiations and other legal methods, avoiding to antagonize the British. In times of popular unrest they made attempts to assuage and appease the masses. Although the national leadership could count on popular support, they never fully exploited the potential strength of mass action.[149] It is evident that such an attitude is not compatible with the notion of jihad, which implies armed struggle.

However, this cooperative stand towards the British Mandatory Power changed during the 1930s. Besides the Arab Executive, elected by the successive Palestine Arab Congresses organized by the Moslem Christian Associations, more political parties came into existence and gained influence. Many of these advocated a more radical position against the Government, as they began to realize that the root of the zionist evil was the British domination. This radicalization, however, did not have as a consequence that these nationalist parties resorted to the doctrine of jihad. Whereas during the 1920s the political leaders sometimes employed the religious feelings of the population for political aims,[150] the new generation of politicians, many of whom had studied in the West, espoused radical liberal ideas and were in general totally averse of mixing religion with politics. A major cause of this political radicalization was the deplorable economic situation of the country and the impoverishment of the peasants – about two-thirds of the Arab population – and the workers. The British governmental reports are revealing in this respect.[151] The peasants were up to their necks in debt and were heavily taxed. Many of them left for the cities because they could not support themselves on the land or because their landlords had sold their land to the zionists. The influx of villagers into the cities caused large-scale unemployment and a decrease of wages, a development which was aggravated by the fact that the expanding Jewish industry and Jewish agricultural enterprises were practically closed for Arab labour. At the same time many traditional handicrafts declined due to the competition of the technically advanced Jewish industries, which increased the number of unemployed. The wretched situation of the majority of the Arab population was, not entirely without reason, ascribed to Jewish immigration. Popular discontent had found outlets in large-scale disturbances like those of 1929 and 1933. Sometimes peasants, driven to despair by their situation, formed armed gangs that practised a mixture of Robin Hood-like brigandage and guerilla warfare. In 1929 and 1930 the Band of the Green Hand (*ᶜAṣābat al-Kaff al-Akhḍar*) was active in Northern Galilee and in 1933 and 1934 the band of Abū Djildah operated in the hills of Nābulus.[152] These groups, however, were doomed to failure by lack of organization and of a clear political and military strategy.

The movement of *shaykh* ᶜIzz al-Dīn al-Qassām[153] was different in this respect. Although it also gave expression to the discontent amongst the masses, it did have clear political and military aims. It opposed the Mandate and zionist colonization, because it regarded these as an infringement of the integrity of the *dār al-Islām* which made jihad an individual duty. Consequently, this struggle was viewed as purely religious. Al-Qassām was a *ᶜālim* who had studied at the Azhar University in Cairo. He was born in the north-west of Syria in 1882, but fled to Palestine in 1922, having been condemned to death by the French for his participation in an anti-French revolt. He then settled in Haifa and became *imām* in one of its mosques. In 1928 he was elected president of the Haifa branch of the Young Men's Moslem Association (*Djamᶜiyyat al-Shubbān al-Muslimīn*). Convinced that the political leaders of the country would never achieve any tangible results by peaceful means, he decided in 1929 to form an organization consisting of small cells of not more than five men in order to wage a guerilla warfare against the British and the zionists. In the same year he was appointed marriage registrar (*ma'dhūn*) for the villages around Haifa. By virtue of this office he had many contacts among all strata of the population. This enabled him to set up his organization and secure financial support. It seems that he recruited most of his followers from the lower classes in the streets of Haifa and from the minor religious dignitaries in the villages. He was well known for his fiery Friday sermons which were larded with Koranic verses and Traditions that urged on the believers to partake in jihad in person or by means of their wealth. A famous story relates that he once proposed to the *Muftī* (the highest religious authority in the country and also one of the most important political leaders) to give him an appointment as an itinerant preacher (*wāʿiẓ ʿāmm*), so that he could prepare revolution in Northern Palestine. The *Muftī*, however, did not accept this proposal for fear of popular movements. Although there is some doubt as to the authenticity of this story, it is illustrative of the differences that existed between al-Qassām's movement and the nationalist politicians. Al-Qassām wanted to achieve his aims by means of armed combat supported by a thoroughly prepared mobilization among the masses, whereas the nationalist leadership tried to attain their ends by means of political negotiations, reinforced from time to time by peaceful demonstrations. Al-Qassām was critical of the politicians and especially of the religious establishment, as the leading *ʿulamā'* did not preach jihad and spent large sums on the restoration of the al-Aqṣā Mosque, money that in his opinion would be better employed in arming the people in preparation for rebellion. In 1935, after six years of preliminary organization, he deemed the time ripe to start off his revolt. In the autumn of that year, he set out for the hills of Galilee with a small band of followers. Their slogan was: 'This is jihad, victory or a martyr's death!' (*Hādhā djihād, naṣr aw istishhād*). On 20 November, the group was spotted by the police. In the ensuing fight al-Qassām and a number of his companions were killed, the rest were captured. Al-Qassām's funeral resulted in a mass demonstration against the British government.[154]

A few months after his death Palestine revolted. During the revolt, which lasted more than three years, most nationalist leaders were deported by the British, or were forced to flee from the country. At the same time many local guerilla bands were formed, consisting mainly of villagers. Although they lacked coordination and were torn by rivalries, they succeeded in paralyzing the civil government and, sometimes, in keeping large areas under control. Many of these bands were led by followers of al-Qassām[155] and clearly showed a religious inspiration by calling their struggle jihad. Thus we read in a proclamation of the General Command of the Arab Revolt:

> The fighters (*mudjāhidūn*) have sold themselves to Allah and they have set out in obeyance to Him, only in order to strive for His goal, for the jihad in His way and for success by [obtaining] His recompense and His satisfaction. They do not desire therewith [worldly] recompense nor power. They have remained true to the covenant they have concluded with Allah. . . . They try to get ahead of one another [in hurrying] to the battlefield of jihad and martyrdom, in order to support what is right, to establish justice and to defend their noble community (*ummah*) and their holy country. . . . We call upon any Moslem and Arab to set out for the jihad in the way of Allah and to help the fighters (*mudjāhidūn*) in defending the holy land.[156]

They also established a revolutionary tribunal that was to judge according to the prescriptions of the *sharīʿah*.[157] This religious inspiration can be explained by the fact that these bands were recruited from the rural population and consisted almost exclusively of Moslems,[158] so that there was no need to form a common front with Christians after the example of the nationalist political bodies. Moreover, the peasants tended to express their feelings of resistance in Islamic rather than nationalistic concepts. During the 1920 and 1929 disturbances, when they came to the towns in order to demonstrate, they used to shout their war-cry: 'The religion of Mohammed was erected by the sword!' (*Dīn Muḥammad qām bi-l-sayf*).[159]

That the nationalist leaders did not sound the call for jihad, does not imply that they were disinclined to use religious feelings for their political ends. The position of Jerusalem as a holy city in Islam was bound to bring up the issue of the holy places in the national struggle against zionism. The Moslems feared that the Jews were planning to take over the Haram al-Sharīf area, the ancient site of the Jewish temple. Immediately after its creation in 1922, the Supreme Moslem Council had set up a scheme for the restoration of the al-Aqṣā Mosque.

In order to raise funds and make propaganda at the same time, delegations were sent to various Arab and Islamic countries. The most important of these was the one that set out for Mecca during the *ḥadjdj*-season in July 1922 and the one that travelled to India in October 1923.[160] Though based on sincere concern, the theme of the holy places was very opportune. It was the continuation of a long tradition dating from the time of the Crusades, when propaganda literature was written extolling the virtues of Jerusalem in order to rouse pugnacity amongst the Moslems.[161] Thus it served a dual purpose: it was meant to add to the nationalist fervour of the Palestinians and, simultaneously, it was intended for external consumption, since the holy places were a concern of all Moslems, wherever they might live, and could justify appeals for moral and financial aid. On the other hand, the campaign would not antagonize the Palestinian Christians. On the contrary, it offered opportunities for cooperation, since the Christians entertained similar fears as to the safety of their own holy places. During the 1930s they launched a parallel campaign in the Christian world.[162]

Since Ottoman times the Jews had a customary right to perform prayer services near the Wailing Wall (*al-Burāq*). Several times during the 1920s they attempted to extend these rights and change the *status quo*. These attempts aroused great indignation amongst the Palestinian Moslems. After an incident on 24 October, 1928, the Supreme Moslem Council decided to take action. Mass meetings were held in the Dome of the Rock, telegrams were sent to Arab sovereigns and Islamic Organizations, asking for support and in November of that year an international congress of *ʿulamāʾ* convened, with delegations from Damascus, Beirut and Transjordan.[163] Besides the already existing Committee for the Defence of *al-Burāq* (*Ladjnat al-difāʿ ʿan al-Burāq al-sharīf*), another organization with a similar aim was established, viz. the Society for the Protection of al-Aqṣā Mosque (*Djamʿiyyat ḥarāsat al-Masdjid al-Aqṣā*) with local branches all over Palestine.[164] The tension between Arabs and Jews increased and there were constant and frequent provocations. The situation exploded in August, 1929, when, at the occasion of the festival of *Mawlid al-Nabī*, many peasants from the neighbouring regions had come to Jerusalem. The discontent of the Arabs with Jewish immigration and land purchases, in addition to the sufferings of the rural population due to economic recession and bad harvests caused by a locust plague and serious drought, found an outlet in large-scale violence against Jewish lives and properties. The political leaders, and especially the *Muftī*, had stepped up the campaign in the months before the outbreak, in order to put the British government under pressure to settle the Wailing Wall issue finally.[165] The violent popular reaction, however, which got out of their control, took them aback and they tried to wield a moderating influence.[166]

During and after the outbreak of August, 1929, it became apparent that the external campaign concerning the holy places had borne fruits and that the Arab and Islamic world took a keen interest in Palestine. In Damascus, Bagdad and Cairo meetings were held to express solidarity with the Palestinian Arabs and to remonstrate against the British and zionist policies. In India there was a strong movement in favour of the Palestinians among the Indian Moslems.[167] In view of this atmosphere of sympathy for the Palestinian cause, it was decided to organize an international Islamic conference in Jerusalem.[168] The conference assembled in December, 1931, and was attended by some 150 participants from all over the Islamic world, amongst whom were many Moslem political leaders and scholars of renown. The conference passed resolutions on the holiness of *al-Burāq* and on the importance of Palestine in the eyes of all Moslems and censured the British colonial and pro-zionist policy in Palestine. There was no overt mention of jihad, only the firm determination was proclaimed of all Moslems to defend *al-Burāq*. The Jerusalem Conference inaugurated a period of unremitting concern for Palestine in the Islamic world. This concern had a strong religious component. During the 1933 outbreak in Palestine the *ʿulamāʾ* of Iraq issued a *fatwā* on the boycotting of zionist products[169] and the *ʿulamāʾ* of Qum, Iran, started a campaign in support of the Palestinians.[170] There were also sympathetic reactions amongst the Indian Moslems.[171] This display of Islamic solidarity reached its high point during the 1936-1939 revolt. The first wave of protests from outside Palestine was occasioned by the publication of the British partition plan for Palestine. This plan was met with strong opposition throughout the Islamic world.[172] The leaders of the All India Moslem League decided to show their solidarity by sending a deputation to visit Islamic and European countries in order to make public the Indian Moslem point of view on Palestine and the Moslem members of the Indian Central Legislature adopted a resolution saying:

> We, the Muslim members of the Central Legislature, representing every shade of Muslim opinion in India, have been following events in Palestine most painfully. Our Arab brethren have our cordial sympathy for their great fight against heavy odds to safeguard their legitimate rights and save holy lands from aggression. . . . The present repressive and pro-Jewish policy must be stopped forthwith; otherwise there is great danger of Britain losing its friendly position of the Muslim world and forcing Indian Muslims to act according to the dictates of Islam.[173]

In fact, this was a barely concealed threat of proclaiming jihad. The campaign to support the Palestinians extended as far as the Dutch East Indies, Zanzibar and the Moslem part of Yugoslavia.[174] In this period the first overt jihad declarations were published. In Egypt, where the Society of Moslem Brethren actively supported the Palestinian cause, the Palestine Information Bureau published in 1937 a pamphlet stating that jihad for the sake of Palestine had become a duty to all Moslems.[175] Of similar content was an article published by a Beirut daily in April, 1938.[176] In August of the same year two famous Iraqi *ʿulamā'*, Muḥammad al-Ḥusayn Kāshif al -Ghiṭā' and Ibrāhīm al-Rāwī issued *fatwās* to the same effect.[177] A congress of Syrian *ʿulamā'* endorsed these *fatwās.*[178] The Egyptian *ʿulama'* wanted to do the same. However, the Rector of al-Azhar University, Muṣṭafā al-Marāghī, a close friend of the British, persuaded the *Hay'at Kibār al-ʿUlamā'* to adopt a rather moderate statement.[179] From 1938 many pamphlets and articles were published, which exalted the jihad of the Palestinians and incited the Moslems all over the world to support them:

> O Moslems! It is not allowed for you, according to Allah's religion, that you resign yourselves to the fact that the English and the Jews are taking possession of the holy land of Palestine, which Allah has distinguished amongst the surrounding towns and villages with the al-Aqṣā Mosque, whither Allah has caused our Lord Mohammed to travel. Nor [is it allowed for you] that you accept that they lay their hands on it [the al-Aqṣā Mosque] or on one inch of Palestine. For the Companions of the Messenger and, later, your faithful and fighting forbears have sacrificed their valuable lives and pure blood for it. Nor [is it allowed for you] that you remain silent on their designs of establishing a Jewish state in this blessed country, which is like the heart of the Islamic world. . . . The messenger of Allah has warned you against abandoning jihad, saying: *'As soon as people abandon jihad, Allah will chastise them all'.*[180]

On the whole, however, the ideology of Palestinian resistance against the British and the zionists was not essentially a religious one. As nearly everywhere in the Islamic world, nationalism, which could contain religious elements, but was basically secular, had become the leading ideology of anti-colonial struggle. On the level of nationalist politics, religion played a secondary role. Islam was invoked only when this could result in popular support for nationalist issues or as an appeal to religious solidarity from abroad. As we have explained, the doctrine of jihad was of no use for the nationalist leaders, as an appeal to it would imply armed struggle and mass mobilization, which ran counter to their tactics of negotiation and diplomacy and would endanger the cooperation with the Palestinian Christians. On the level of popular movements, however, like al-Qassām's organization or the peasant bands operating during the 1936-1939 revolt, religion played a considerably greater part. Al-Qassām's organization in many aspects resembled the earlier jihad-movements, envisaging the struggle in purely religious terms and calling it jihad. For the peasant bands the religious motive was strong too, though as far as they maintained relations with the nationalist leaders, not exclusive and all-embracing. The notion of jihad in relation with the struggle of the Palestinians came mainly from abroad, as a response to the campaign for the rescue of the holy places. This situation prevails down to the present day. After the establishment of the State of Israel in 1948 and the expulsion of the Palestinians, the Arab-Israeli conflict became one between national states. Until the emergence of the Palestinian resistance organizations in the middle of the 1960s, the Palestinians, left without a state of their own, did not play any part in it. As for the ideology of the Palestinian liberation movement, that has since become active, this was a completely secular one.[181]

Since 1948 four wars have been fought between Israel and its Arab neighbours (1948-49, 1956, 1967 and 1973). As for the concomitant war propaganda, this was mainly cast in nationalist terms: it appealed to the duty to defend one's fatherland and to Arab solidarity. Only when the *ʿulamāʾ* as faithful and loyal servants of the state took up their pens or mounted their pulpits in order to contribute their share in the war effort, was the duty of jihad mentioned. Thus, during and after every war, jihad-*fatwās* and exhortative pamphlets appeared, composed and published by societies of *ʿulamāʾ*, Islamic institutions like the Azhar University and fundamentalist Islamic organizations like the Moslem Brethren. The Arab governments, with the exception, however, of Saudi Arabia[182] did not themselves call for jihad, for fear that an appeal to purely Islamic values might prove to be a divisive factor in view of the large Christian minorities. Of course the governments concerned welcomed jihad-*fatwās* and religious propaganda of the *ʿulamāʾ* and Islamic institutions and it is likely that they encouraged them in this activity. As a result of the prevailing secular nationalist ideology, and the increasing separation between politics and religion, the doctrine of jihad was relegated from the political to the religious domain. The present-day function of jihad declarations has thus become similar to the blessing of arms or the sprinkling of holy water on tanks by the Christian clergy in case of war: an expression of religious approval and endorsement.[183]

4

The Doctrine of Jihad in Modern Islam

4.1 INTRODUCTION

In the previous Chapter we have become acquainted with writings on jihad that had a definite mobilizing character. They were written in order to mobilize Moslems for a specific occasion, a revolt or a war, and in order to expound the prescriptions of the *sharīʿah* with regard to problems the leaders of these struggles were confronted with. This, however, is not the only motive for writing on the topic of jihad. Many books and articles on jihad have been and are still published with the sole aim of spreading knowledge and information on the 'true' doctrine of jihad as seen by their authors, who generally reacted against unfavourable Western opinions on Islam. If we analyze modern writings on jihad with the help of these motives, i.e. the desire to mobilize people and the desire to instruct people, we find that they form some sort of continuum with, on the one extreme, writings with a purely mobilizing character, on the other, writings with a merely instructive character and in between the bulk of modern jihad literature, combining both motives in all shades of intensity.

The publication of writings with a purely mobilizing character is generally occasioned by a specific, well-defined political situation or occurrence. It is a *genre* as old as Islamic history itself. In fact, one is justified in considering the Koran as the first instance of this type, as it contains scores of verses with a clearly mobilizing character, such as: *'O ye who have believed, shall I point you to a trade which will save you from a punishment painful? Ye will believe in Allah and His messenger, and strive (perform jihad) with goods and person in the way of Allah; that is better for you if ye have knowledge. And he will forgive you your sins and will cause you to enter Gardens through which the rivers flow, and good dwelling-places in the Gardens of Eden; that is the mighty success.'* (K 61:10-12), and: *'O ye who have believed, what is the matter with you? When one says to you: "March out in the way of Allah", ye are weighed down to the ground; are ye so satisfied with this nearer life as to neglect the Hereafter? The enjoyment of this nearer life is in comparison with the Hereafter only a little thing. If you do not march out He will inflict upon you a painful punishment, and will substitute (for you) another people; ye will not injure Him at all; Allah over everything hath power'* (K 9:38-39). The second century H. saw the appearance of collections of Traditions, exclusively devoted to the theme of jihad. The first one was compiled by ʿAbd Allāh al-Mubārak, who died in 181 H.[1] Later on works were written that generally included mobilizing Koranic verses and traditions, chapters on the virtues of jihad and the rewards of the martyr in the Hereafter and short stories on the heroism of early Moslem personalities.[2] On the other hand, many *fatwās* were published, elucidating specific points of the law with regard to jihad.

If we look at the modern writings with a purely mobilizing character, we see that both types are still extant. We find treatises, published on the occasion of a war or revolt, extolling the virtues of jihad and the bliss of the martyrs in the Hereafter and quoting the relevant Koranic verses and Traditions. A typical example is a booklet, published by the Azhar University on the occasion of the June war of 1967 under the title *'Jihad in Islam'*[3] which consists of the following chapters: *Jihad in the Holy Koran*, an enumeration of Koranic verses with regard to jihad, to the reward of the martyrs and to the Jews, being 'the worst enemies of humanity', *Jihad in the texts of the Sunnah*, a collection of Traditions on about the same topics, and a last chapter with the title: *Marvellous Islamic images of sacrifice*, dealing with feats of Moslem heroism and contempt of death from Mohammed's time up to the Palestine war of 1948.

Fatwās concerning jihad have been published in great numbers in recent times. Generally they were to the effect that jihad had become an individual obligation (*farḍ ʿayn*), because the enemy had invaded Islamic territory. Illustrative of this type of *fatwās* is the one issued in April 1948 by the *muftī* of Egypt (*muftī l-diyār al-Miṣriyyah*) Ḥasanayn Muḥammad Makhlūf. He was asked to expound the position of Islam concerning personally volunteering for, or financially contributing to the struggle in Palestine. His response was:

> The answer is that jihad in person, or by means of financial contributions in order to rescue Palestine is legally obligatory upon those inhabitants that are able to do so, as well as upon the inhabitants of the Islamic states, since Jewish zionists attempt by force of arms to establish a Jewish state in one of the most honourable Arabic and Islamic countries, to wit Palestine, and this not only in order to take possession of Palestine, but also to dominate all Islamic states and to eliminate their Arabic character and their Islamic culture. . . . However, as today the methods of war have become complex, it is obligatory for anyone personally participating in jihad to submit to the rules that the states of the Arab League lay down for participation in jihad, in order that the expected victory be realized.[4]

It is obvious that the content of these *fatwās* is to a large extent political, as the application of the *sharīʿah* in a given situation, depends on the political evaluation of that situation and may give rise to different answers. In this *fatwā* the political element pops up in the last sentence, which is directed against the bands of Egyptian Moslem Brethren operating in Palestine without the approval of the Arab governments. One has to bear in mind that this *fatwā* was issued in April 1948, a month before the official military involvement of the Arab states in the Palestine war. Another illustration of the political character of these *fatwās* is the declaration issued by the Congress of the Academy of Islamic Research (*Madjmaʿ al-Buḥūth al-Islāmiyyah*) held in Cairo in November 1977. Whereas on previous occasions this congress, in which Islamic scholars from all over the Islamic world participate, had declared that, in view of the prevailing circumstances, jihad against Israel had become an individual duty of all Moslems with the aim of realizing the aims of the Palestinian people,[5] which can only mean the destruction of the zionist State of Israel and the establishment of a Palestinian State on the territory of mandatory Palestine, it now issued a statement to the effect that the aim of the jihad against Israel was the liberation of the territories occupied in 1967, the establishment of an independent Palestinian state therein and the return to Jerusalem. Thus the Congress conformed to the new policy of Egypt and most other Arab states with regard to Israel.[6] Besides these *fatwās* declaring that jihad in the given circumstances, has become an individual duty, many *fatwās* are issued, establishing that a certain struggle or revolt is to be considered as jihad so that the combatants are exempt from the obligation of fasting during the month of *Ramaḍān.*[7] Finally there are *fatwās* that deal with all kinds of legal aspects of war, e.g. the question whether those who collaborate with the (non-Moslem) enemy are to be considered apostates, or whether the conclusion of a peace-treaty is allowed in the given circumstances, or whether emigration from a country occupied by a non-Moslem power is obligatory.[8] Since, as we have seen, the content of *fatwās* on jihad is largely determined by political motives, they can be used as instruments of psychological warfare. In Chapter 3 I have described how both the British and the French managed to obtain *fatwās* to the effect that they were the legal rulers and that rebellion against them was not allowed.[9]

We now come to literature with a dual character, written with the aim of both instructing and mobilizing people. At first, the mobilizing aspect will be treated. In general one can say that in works with this dual character, the intended mobilization is not occasioned by a concrete and specific political occurrence, but that it more or less fits in a more general framework of struggle against colonialism, imperialism, zionism or communism. The subjugation of the Islamic countries to colonial powers, the impotence of the Arab world *vis-à-vis* the establishment of the state of Israel and the economic backwardness, for all these phenomena, there is, in the view of their authors, one fundamental thing to blame: the fact that the Moslems have abandoned the prescriptions of Islam, and thus have cut off themselves from their principal source of strength. The remedy is self-evident:

> If the Moslems want to get out of the situation they are in, what they must do is join forces, believe sincerely in Allah (He is exalted), act in accordance with Allah's Book and the teachings of His messenger (may Allah bless him and grant him salvation), take their matters firmly in hand as a preparation for fighting, mobilize themselves for struggle and offer themselves as a sacrifice for their religion and their land.[10]

Or from a more military view, as formulated by the Iraqi general Maḥmūd Shīt Khaṭṭāb:

> The human factor is still the decisive factor in war; it is still the most important force for any weapon or any equipment. However, man without creed is like foam, the foam of a torrent. The Arabs have a heavenly creed that has led them to victory, for their victories were no doubt victories produced by creed. When the Arabs became weak, their creed protected them against disintegration and collapse. . . . The return to Islam will entail the proclamation of Islamic jihad. In that case, there will be 75 million Moslem fighters on the battlefields facing Israel. They will be able to eliminate Israel, even without weapons. . . . The way to return to Islam is to revise the education of the young generation and to lay down new programs for educating them, based on the teaching of the true religion, and to act according to the teachings of Islam, to the letter and to the spirit.[11]

In this connexion, some authors have pointed out that the Israeli military successes were due to the religious inspiration of the Israelis, and especially the Israeli army.[12] Whereas this kind of mobilization is directed against an outside enemy, there is also another form that emphasizes the need to spread Islam, to establish a truly Islamic government and to struggle against tyranny and oppression. These calls for jihad came from fundamentalist movements like the *Djamāʿat-i Islāmī* in India and Pakistan and from the *Society of Moslem Brethren* in the Middle East and were in the first place directed against the local governments, that were not really Islamic governments:

> What I want to clarify in connexion with the topic we are discussing now, is that Islam is not only a set of theological dogmata and a collection of ceremonies and rites, as nowadays the word religion seems to be understood. In fact, it is an all-embracing order that wants to eliminate and to eradicate the other orders which are false and unjust, so as to replace them by a good order and a moderate program that is considered to be better for humanity than the other orders and to contain rescue from the illnesses of evil and tyranny, happiness and prosperity for the human race, both in this world

> and in the Hereafter. The call of Islam for this cause . . . does not concern only one nation with the exclusion of others, or one group with the exclusion of others, for Islam calls all people to its Word. . . . Whosoever believes in this call and accepts it in a proper way, becomes a member of the *'Islamic party'*. . . . As soon as this party has been established, it starts with jihad for the aim for which it has been founded. For by the nature of its existence, it will spare no efforts to eliminate and eradicate the regimes that are not founded on the bases of Islam and to replace them by a moderate cultural and social order.[13]

In works with a predominantly mobilizing character, the instructive aspect generally derives from their main function: the people that are to be rallied for the jihad should first be informed as to their rights and duties. When, however, the instructive aspect gets the upper hand, we can generally observe that the major aim of these writings is to defend Islam against the ideological attacks of the West. As the Western powers often justified their colonial expansion by the idea of a *mission civilisatrice*, it served their interests if Moslem society was depicted as backward and Islam as a religion of bloodthirsty, lecherous fanatics. Therefore, the unfavourable mediaeval image of Islam was revived. The writings on jihad with an instructive character, generally represent an ideological defence against the *'scimitar-syndrome'* in the West: the idea that Islam is a violent and fanatical creed, spread by savage warriors, carrying the Koran in one hand and a scimitar in the other. They are apologetical in that they try to refute false ideas on Islamic jihad and to demonstrate that the Islamic prescriptions of warfare are morally and practically superior to those of the Christian West. The accusations against which the authors feel obliged to defend Islam are the following:

> Firstly, that [Islam] is based on subjugation and conquest with the aim of imposing itself by power and strength on Allah's creatures of all races and religions;
> Secondly, that it denies Man freedom of opinion and creed;
> Thirdly, that Islam, in propagating its message, has declared war against all peoples and races of different religious communities and sects;

> Fourthly, that war is the fundamental relationship between Islam and all other nations and states and that peace can only exist for a fixed time in view of a temporary necessity;
> Fifthly, they claim that Islam does not heed pledges, does not keep obligations and does not respect treaties and pacts;
> Sixthly, some authors on international law went as far as to include the Moslems among the barbaric peoples to whom the honour of belonging to the international community must be denied.[14]

At first, as in the case of the Indian modernists of the latter half of the nineteenth century, the defence against the unfavourable image of Islam was only timidly voiced. Convinced of the superiority of the West and Western culture as they were, they tried to show that Islam was a 'respectable' religion that fostered the same values as Christendom and Western civilization in general. Later, many Moslem thinkers came to see these accusations as a functional part of the European colonial policy towards the Islamic world. Since Islam, in their view, was the ideological stronghold against Western penetration they regarded these Western accusations as attempts to weaken Islam so as to be able to subject the entire Islamic world. Thus their tone in refuting these Western allegations against Islam became bolder and more aggressive. They pointed at the political implications and violently denounced the evil designs and cunning methods of the Western powers. The Western accusations with regard to the doctrine of jihad were, in their view, to be placed in this political context:

> Many of them [= the Western orientalists] have written on certain aspects of it [= jihad], on the basis of what their fanaticism, their whims and their repulsion have dictated to them, with the aim of attacking Islam in its scientific and intellectual origin. For this is the very reason why orientalism came into being and why orientalists began launching their attacks against the Islamic East by assailing its nationalism, its language and its religion. Their main interest was jihad, as this is the principle that forms the foremost rank for protecting Islam. Therefore, they made it the object of a large-scale attack, in order to weaken the morale of the Moslems and to make them feel that *they* are the oppressors of other peoples. They still depict the Moslems as ferocious animals, lying

> in wait to hurl themselves upon the world in order to destroy all traces of civilization and culture. This will make people averse to accepting Islam in this form and will diminish the alleged danger of the Moslems for the Christians. However, it is well known that the opposite is true, for orientalism was resuscitated in order to pave the way for colonial domination by spreading scepticism about the fundamental values of the Arabs and Moslems and in order to turn the attention to Western civilization by means of articles and books that the authors try to disguise as scientific research, but that in fact are only meant to have a venomous influence and to serve evil purposes.[15]

A typical feature of these apologetical writings, and a feature that one can also observe in other branches of this literature, is the comparison between Western and Christian practice on the one hand and Islamic ideals on the other. It is not difficult to guess to whose advantage this comparison always turns out. Thus the excesses of warfare by Western powers are fully emphasized and opposed to the Islamic rules of war-conduct. In order to put an end to the problem of atrocities in warfare, a general application of the Islamic rules is proposed.[16]

A specific type of apologetic literature on jihad, which is entirely instructive in character and lacks any mobilizing aspects, are those writings that expound the theory of jihad as a form of international law. Their apologetical character lies in the emphasis on the basically peaceful character of the relationship between the Islamic and the other states and in the demonstration that Islam has been capable of constructing a detailed, just and merciful system of international law. Generally this system is depicted as being by far superior to positive international law, of Western origin, and being more capable of promoting world peace and security. This type of literature will be dealt with in par. 4.5.

4.2 MODERN AND CLASSICAL JIHAD LITERATURE COMPARED

In this section classical and modern literature on jihad will be compared as to style and as to the topics that are dealt with. In general, it is evident that differences between these two derive from differences in function. Thus we see that the works whose main function is mobilization, treatises as well as *fatwās*, hardly differ from each other in both periods. On the other hand there is a clear difference with regard to writings with an instructive character, which can be explained by the fact that the classical *fiqh*-texts on jihad had no aim other than expounding the sacred law on a specific subject. As the authority of the *sharīʿah* had not been challenged, there was no need to justify the rules with general moral or rational concepts. This situation, however, underwent a marked change in the latter half of the nineteenth century because of the accelerated European expansion. As the economic and social changes required the introduction of western codes, the supremacy of the *sharīʿah* was no longer self-evident. Consequently, the authors on legal subjects were forced back into the defensive and had to exert themselves in finding justifications for applying the *sharīʿah*. This accounts for a very clear alteration in style. Modern writings on jihad are less legalistic and do not indulge in the casuistic quibbles and legal niceties, that were the result of the classical lawyers' desire to give solutions for all thinkable cases. At the same time, these writings do not show any differentiation as to *madhhab*. The authors do not feel themselves bound to a specific School. In presenting the topic, they emphasize more the moral justifications and the underlying ethical values of the rules, than the detailed elaboration of those rules. This also explains a certain shift in the importance of certain topics. Whereas in modern jihad literature topics of a merely technical character do not get any attention, there are also many topics in modern literature, that are hardly or not dealt with in classical literature. The most important of these topics are:

The definition of jihad. As we shall see in par. 4.3, this definition generally includes all kinds of moral and spiritual jihad, that are hardly touched upon in classical *fiqh*-literature.

The principle of peaceful relations between the Islamic and the other states. The classical doctrine of jihad considered all wars against unbelievers as legal wars, sanctioned by the *sharīʿah*. In fact, the *sharīʿah*. required that the head of state organize once a year a military raid into enemy territory. Since the second half of the nineteenth century, however, modernist authors have asserted that the relationship between the Islamic and the other states had essentially a peaceful character. They argue that this principle is firmly rooted in the Koran and cite the following verses: '. . . *If then they withdrew from you and do not fight against you, but offer you peace, Allah hath not opened for you a way against them'* (K 4:90); '. . . *Do not say to one who gives you the peace-greeting, "Thou art not a believer", in desire of the chance gain of this world'* (K 4:94), and *'If they incline to make peace, incline thou to it, and set thy trust upon Allah'* (K 8:61).[17] The classical interpretation that the fundamental relation between the Islamic and the other states is war, is, according to modernist authors, due to the situation prevalent during the first centuries of Islam, as the Islamic state was then surrounded by bitter enemies. A logical complement of this modernist exegetical *volte-face* was the development of a set of rules for determining *when* war is allowed. This is closely related to the next topic.

The legal aims of jihad. Defining the legal aims of jihad is indispensable for answering the question when jihad is allowed. Therefore this theme receives a great deal of attention in modern literature, whereas, in classical literature, the question of the aim of jihad, is only perfunctorily treated by using very general and abstract formulae like: *'voiding the earth of unbelief'* or *'making Allah's word the highest'*. From this, one could infer that this question did not arouse much interest in the classical period. To this topic par. 4.4 will be devoted.

A survey of early Islamic military history. Surveys of the military *faits et gestes* of Mohammed and the first Moslems differ to some extent according to their function. The most common purpose of these surveys is to explain that Mohammed's intentions were basically peaceful, but that the obstinacy and enmity displayed by the unbelievers *vis-à-vis* the Islamic mission, made recourse to arms inevitable:

> These were the stages the Messenger went through, before and after the emigration. It is obvious that the polytheists of Mecca had been fighting the Prophet right from the start of his Mission, and that they were the first to commit aggression: time and again they chased the believers from their dwellings, they tyrannized the oppressed, subjecting them to all kinds of maltreatment and torture. It is also apparent that the Jews of Medina were not attacked by the Messenger until they had broken their pledge and had begun to offer resistance, just as the polytheists had done before. From all these events it appears clearly that the Messenger only fought those who fought him, and that his fighting had no other aims than repelling oppression, warding off rebellion and aggression and putting an end to persecution for the sake of religion.[18]

Another purpose of these surveys is to inspire the reader with combativeness and fervour, to be derived from the example of the Prophet. There are even special books that entirely serve this purpose.[19]

Women and jihad. Many books on jihad contain sections on the participation of women in fighting. The treatment of this topic certainly serves some apologetical aims, as thus the authors try to prove that women have played an important role in early Islamic society and that they belonged to its enthusiastic supporters:

> If the Westerners are proud of their high national feelings and of their alert national consciousness, and adduce as an example that their women always hasten to spend their property for the sake of the defence of their countries, then the women of the Moslems have preceded them in this virtue.[20]

At the same time it served the purpose of demonstrating that women occupied a position (nearly) equal to men in early Islam:

> Islamic history has established that Moslem women marched out just like men marched out, and participated in jihad side by side with them. . . . Of course, women did not carry weapons to fight with, since their nature differs from the nature of men and since their capacities in this field are limited. Therefore, they performed those tasks that were suitable to them, provisioning. These tasks

> are important and valuable for the fighters, for an army in combat needs an uninterrupted stream of food, water and weapons.[21]

These sections generally consist of an enumeration of Traditions demonstrating that women accompanied the armies and that they provided the fighters with drinks, cooked the meals, nursed the wounded and raised the morale of the combatants.[22]

The strategical and tactical lessons of the Koran. Many authors devote part of their books on jihad to the strategical and tactical prescriptions of the Koran. This subject shows great similarity to a modern genre of Koran exegesis, known as scientific exegesis (*tafsīr ʿilmī*)[23] as they both proceed from the basic assumption that the Koran mentions or hints at the essential elements of all modern sciences, arts and crafts.

> If one studies these verses [i.e. verses connected with the practical side of warfare] of Allah's Book, one will discover that they lay down general prescriptions for the Moslems, constituting a handbook for warfare ranking very high among similar institutions of modern civilization.[24]

In the first place, the Koran deals with the spiritual side, i.e. with the morale of the combatants. Many verses speak of the reward that awaits those who struggle in the path of Allah, e.g. K 4:74-76, K 9:19-22, 111. Other verses warn the believers against factors that may lead to cowardice and weakness: *'Say: "If your fathers and your brethren and your wives and your clan, and properties which ye have acquired, and trade which ye fear may go slack, and dwellings which please you, are dearer to you than Allah and His messenger and striving in His cause, then wait until Allah cometh with His affair; Allah guideth not the people who are reprobates"'* (K 9:24). Many verses inspire the believers with hope by reminding them that Allah is on their side and will aid them: *'(Recall) when thou wert saying to the believers: "Will it not suffice you that your Lord reinforces you with three thousand of the angels sent down? Ay! If ye endure and act piously, and they come upon you in this very rush of theirs, your Lord will reinforce you with five thousand of the angels, designated!" Allah only set that forth as good news for you, that your hearts thereby might be at peace; Help cometh only from Allah, the Sublime, the Wise.*" (K 3:124-126). As war is a costly enterprise, the believers must continuously be exhorted to partake in jihad with their wealth by financially contributing to the war-efforts. The Koran abounds in verses to this effect. As regards the practical aspects of warfare, K 8:60 is often quoted: *'Prepare (ye) for them whatsoever force and cavalry ye are capable of (gathering) to overawe thereby the enemy of Allah and your own . . .'*. This verse contains many useful lessons for the Moslems. It orders them to prepare their power according to their capabilities and possibilities. Thus, the Moslems must themselves produce military equipment such as guns, rifles, tanks, aeroplanes and battleships, so that they are not at the mercy of those who produce ammunition and war equipment.[25] It also orders them to deploy their armies at the frontiers of countries since there the enemies are likely to attack. Further it points out that the preparation of strength depends on the possibilities available, so that it differs according to time and place. The aim of this preparation is to deter the enemy and to maintain a situation which in modern military usage is called armed peaces.[26] Another verse quoted in this connexion is K 9:123: *'O ye who have believed, fight the unbelievers who are near to you, and let them feel a rough temper in you, and know that Allah is with those who show piety'*. In modern literature, this verse is usually interpreted as a tactical instruction concerning the order of attack: the Moslems must first attack the nearest enemy, then the next-nearest and so on, in order to clear the road of any hostile obstacle for the army. By means of this interpretation, modernist authors dissociate themselves from the classical, mainly Hanafite, opinion, that this is one of the verses that order the Moslems to fight all unbelievers.[27]

4.3 THE DEFINITION OF JIHAD

In general, literature on jihad is for the greater part devoted to jihad in the sense of struggle, of fighting. However, almost all of these writings lay stress on the fact that the word jihad has a much wider semantic content. They point out that it is derived from the verb *djāhada*, exerting oneself or striving, and thus has a friendlier connotation than the word *qitāl* (fighting). The latter notion necessarily entails killing and bloodshed, whereas jihad, meaning exerting oneself for some praiseworthy aim, does not.[28] Therefore, the translation of jihad by *'Holy War'* is considered to be incorrect and resented.[29] This wider meaning of jihad includes those notions that developed in classical Islam as a consequence of the *'internalizing'* (intérioration) of the jihad-doctrine.[30] Like the classical authors modern authors also mention *djihād al-nafs*, the struggle against oneself and *djihād al-shayṭān*, the struggle against the devil. Both notions imply the struggle against one's bad inclinations and against seduction and enticement by nearby pleasures. This form of jihad is usually called the *'Greater Jihad'*, on account of a saying of the Prophet. Once, when he came home from a raiding party, he said: *'We have now returned from the Smaller Jihad to the Greater Jihad'*. When asked what he meant by Greater Jihad, he answered: 'The jihad against oneself'. Although this Tradition is quite famous and frequently quoted, it is not included in one of the authoritative compilations.

Another notion of jihad is the struggle for the good of Moslem society and against corruption and decadence. In fact, it is coextensive with the concept of *al-amr bi-l-maᶜrūf wa-l-nahy ᶜan al-munkar* (commanding what is good and forbidding what is abominable). All Moslems must partake in this struggle and 'work with all their intellectual and material abilities for the realization of justice and equality between the people and for the spreading of security and human understanding, both among individuals and groups.'[31] Inasmuch as this notion of jihad implies the realization of the Islamic values in Moslem society, education is very crucial. Therefore, some authors speak of *djihād al-tarbiyah* (educational jihad).[32] In Tunisia, this notion of jihad was applied to the field of economy, when President Bourguiba called the struggle to overcome economic backwardness jihad:

> Tunisia, which is an Islamic country, suffers from a certain degree of decline and backwardness, that brings disgrace upon us in the eyes of the world. The only possibility to free ourselves from this

> shame is continuous and assiduous work and fruitful and useful labour. Escaping from this backwardness is jihad-obligation, ruled by the same prescriptions as jihad by means of the sword.[33]

This interpretation was brought forward as an argument in a discussion on the fasting of *Ramaḍān*. As during this month production stagnates, Bourguiba was looking for arguments to prove that fasting was not religiously obligatory for workers. Since the participants in jihad are excused from the duty to fast during *Ramaḍān*, he claimed that the struggle against economic underdevelopment could be put on a par with jihad with the sword.[34] This new interpretation was later accepted by the *ʿulamā'*.[34]

Related to the notion of *djihād al-tarbiyah* (educational jihad), which means the spreading of the Islamic values in Moslem society and may be compared with the idea of *home mission*, is the notion of *djihād al-daʿwah*, spreading Islam amongst the unbelievers by peaceful means, such as argumentation and demonstration,[36] and thus equivalent to *external mission*. This notion is sometimes termed *djihād al-lisān* or *djihād al-qalam* (jihad of the tongue or jihad of the pen). It is founded on K 16:125 (*'Summon to the way of thy Lord with wisdom and goodly admonition and argue against them with what is better'*). Some modern authors hold that this is nowadays the most important form of jihad. As during the first period of Islam means of communication were lacking, conquest was the only method for spreading the message of Islam. Nowadays, intensive communication is possible without having recourse to military expeditions. Therefore, fighting as a means of propagation of Islam, has become obsolete and must now be replaced by the concept of *djihād al-daʿwah*.[37] Some authors fear lest the emphasis on the peaceful side of the jihad-concept, may divert the Moslems from the necessary struggle. Therefore, they try to connect these peaceful forms of jihad with the idea of fighting. They interpret these forms of spiritual and moral jihad as a prerequisite for fighting in the way of Allah:

> Jihad begins with jihad against oneself by purifying one's soul from [bad] inclinations and passions and with its orientation towards Allah, [for one ought] not [to struggle] out of love for fame, or desire for pleasure or in hope of worldly matters.

> Whoever fights to show his courage and to acquire fame and money, cannot be regarded a *mudjāhid*, for a *mudjāhid* fights only to please Allah, to obtain what He has in store for him, to raise the truth and to make Allah's word the highest.[38]

The same motive, the fear that the Moslems would be distracted from fighting, played a role in the frontal attack by the fundamentalists against these notions of moral and spiritual jihad. They hold that there is no justification whatsoever for calling spiritual and moral jihad the *'Greater Jihad'*, as the Tradition: *'We have now returned from the Smaller Jihad to the Greater Jihad'* cannot be regarded as authentic. They believe that this idea has been spread on purpose to weaken Moslem combativeness.[39] Consequently, they stress the militant aspects of jihad, the notion of *al-djihād bi-l-nafs* (partaking in jihad by putting one's life at stake, i.e. fighting) or *al-djihād bi-l-sayf* (jihad with the sword). This is in fact the most important notion in nearly all writings on jihad and therefore receives most attention. Jihad in the sense of fighting, however, is restricted by the phrase *fī sabīl Allāh*, in the way of Allah. This implies that jihad is not just plain, ordinary war, but must be somehow connected with religion and the interest of the believers:

> The way of Allah is the road that leads to His gratification, by means of which His religion is protected and the situation of His worshippers thrives.[40]
>
> Fighting in the way of Allah is fighting in order to raise Allah's word, to safeguard His religion, to spread His mission and to defend His party, so that they will not be robbed of their rights and not prevented to bring their affair [= religion] to the open. Therefore, it comprises more than fighting for the sake of religion, because it includes defence of the religion and protection of its mission, but also the defence of territory when an aggressor covetously plans to take possession of our countries and to enjoy the riches of our land.[41]

The implications of these restrictions, i.e. the legal aims of jihad, will be dealt with in the next chapter. Jihad, however, is not only the act of fighting itself, but also everything that is conducive to victory, like contributing money to provide for military equipment (*al-djihād bi-l-māl*):

> Any activity that strengthens the military front and supports the jihad is also jihad in the way of Allah, like e.g. stepping up productivity, strengthening the internal front, financially contributing to war-efforts and looking after the fighters' families. The Prophet has said: *'Whoever supplies a warrior in the way of Allah with equipment, is also a warrior and whoever takes the place of a warrior in his family by means of* [*his*] *wealth, is also a warrior'*.[42]

In peacetime Moslems must fulfil their collective jihad-duty by military training and material preparation for warfare.[43]

4.4 THE LEGAL AIMS OF JIHAD

As it appears from the works on *fiqh*, there was no great concern about the justification of fighting against unbelievers in classical Islam. If mentioned at all, the subject was only briefly touched upon and summarily formulated as 'strengthening Islam', 'protecting the believers' of 'annihilating unbelief'. Apparently this topic was not of great importance as fighting against unbelievers was justified in itself. When modern authors accepted the principle of peaceful relations between the Islamic state and the rest of the world, a theory was required for deciding what wars against non-Moslems were legal and could be called jihad, and what wars were not. Thus the idea of jihad as *bellum justum* won through. Some modern authors,[44] however, hold that the idea of *bellum justum* did already exist in classical Islam. They quote in this connexion the famous Arab historian Ibn Khaldūn (d. 1406), who distinguishes between 'wars of jihad and justice' (*ḥurūb djihād wa-ʿadl*) and 'wars of sedition and persecution' (*ḥurūb baghy wa-fitnah*). The first kind he defines as punitive wars against rebels and wars out of zeal for Allah and His religion, 'what in the *sharīʿah* is called jihad'. The other form of warfare consists, according to Ibn Khaldūn, in wars conducted by tribes and barbaric nations that live on spoils and booty.[45] It is, however, doubtful whether Ibn Khaldūn's statement may be regarded as a legal distinction between just and unjust wars in the modern sense. Probably it amounts to no more than a distinction between wars fought by the

Islamic state on the one hand, and all other wars, like those between non-Islamic states, outside attacks on the Islamic states, internal rebellion against Islamic legal authority and intertribal warfare on the other. Nevertheless, it is not wholly unjustified to speak of jihad as *bellum justum* in classical Islam, for there was some embryonic development of *jus ad bellum* (the rules with regard to the beginning of wars, as opposed to *jus in bello*, the rules that must be observed during actual warfare). As we have seen in Chapter 2, a formal declaration of war was obligatory under certain circumstances, and truce imposed certain restrictions as to when warfare could be resumed. Moreover, there was a rule, although never explicitly formulated as it ran counter to the conception of the Islamic state as a whole, that an Islamic state could not wage war upon another Islamic state, unless it were established that the other state was to be regarded as a rebellious force against which punitive action was allowed. In practice, however, these prescriptions had only some importance inasfar as they necessitated Islamic rulers to have their military actions justified by *fatwās*, issued by the state-*muftī*.

The theory of jihad as *bellum justum* that developed in modern Islam, concentrates upon the causes of warfare waged by the Moslems. This cause must be 'in the way of Allah' (*fī sabīl Allāh*), which excludes fighting for territorial expansion, for booty, for vengeance and for other worldly aims.[46] Modern authors usually limitatively enumerate the causes for which war may be waged. These causes fall into two categories: those connected with the *propagation of Islam* and those connected with the idea of *defence*. Of the first kind are the following causes:

1. Strengthening monotheism and destroying polytheism and false gods. This is based on the nearly identical verses K 2:193 and K 8:39 (*'Fight them until there is no persecution and religion is (entirely) Allah's'*).

2. Protecting the Islamic mission against those who stand in its way. This is also called protecting freedom of religion.[47] This freedom of religion is to be realized by removing all obstacles that block free missionary activities. All men must be free to hear the call of Islam and to embrace Islam without any hindrance, oppression or

persecution on the part of the authorities or on the part of their fellow-men. This cause is also scripturally founded on K 2:193 and K 8:39 ('. . . *until there is no persecution* . . .'.

As for the causes connected with the idea of defence, these are:

1. Repelling aggression on Moslem lives and property in case of an actual or expected attack by enemy forces. This is founded on K 2:190 (*'Fight in the way of Allah those who fight you, but do not provoke hostility'*).

2. Preventing oppression and persecution of Moslems outside the Territory of Islam. This is closely linked up with the idea of protecting freedom of religion. It is based upon K 4:75 (*'What is wrong with you that ye fight not in the way of Allah and the oppressed, men, women, and children, who say: "Oh our Lord, take us out of this city of wrong-doing people* [i.e. Mecca], *and appoint for us from Thine own side a patron, and appoint for us from Thine own side a helper" '*).

3. Retaliating a breach of pledge by the enemy. This is supported by K 9:12 (*'But if they violate their oaths after they have made a covenant and attack your religion, fight the leaders of unbelief; no oath will hold in their case; mayhap they will refrain'*).

Without any exception, all authors emphatically state that fighting may never serve the aim of compelling people to conversion. Their main scriptural arguments are K 2:256 (*'There is no compulsion in religion; rectitude has become clearly distinguished from perversity, so whoever disbelieves in Tāghūt idols and believes in Allah has laid hold upon the firmest handgrip which never gives way; Allah is the one who hears and knows'*),[48] and K 10:99 (*'If thy Lord so willed, all those in the land would believe in a body; wilt thou then put constraint upon the people that they may be believers?'*). As additional arguments they adduce the Traditions that forbid to kill women, children and aged people, although they are unbelievers. Had jihad served the aim of forcing unbelievers to conversion, it would have been allowed to kill all unbelievers. Finally, it is pointed out that Islam is a logical religion based upon natural reason:

> Now, does such a Mission require force to make people believe in it? No, the use of force as a means of making people believe in this

> Mission, would be an insult to it, would be a discouragement to it and would put obstacles in its way. If a man realizes that he is being coerced, or forced into something, this will prevent him from respecting and esteeming it and reflecting upon it, let alone that he will be able to believe in it. Employing force as an instrument for conversion means wrapping this Mission in complexity, absurdity and obscurity and witholding it from the grasp of the human mind and heart.[49]

Generally, modern authors do not mention the prescriptions with regard to the unbelievers that are not qualified to become *dhimmīs* (i.e. the pagan Arabs or, according to others, all unbelievers except Jews and Christians), who only have the choice between Islam and the sword. Admittedly, this problem is of small practical importance nowadays, which may explain why it is passed over in silence. Those authors, however, who do deal with this subject, adduce that these pagan Arabs had committed aggression against the Moslems, so that fighting against them was justified for that reason.[50] Others, however, fully admit that these groups are to be excepted from the principle of freedom of religion and that they cannot be accorded the right to abide by their religion as polytheism and idolatry cannot be tolerated on Islamic territory:

> Islam has excluded the pagan Arabs from this principle and has allowed jihad in order to compel them to become Moslems, and that for very wise reasons, which are evident for those endowed with insight. The most important of these is that the souls of that magnificent nation must be purified from the evils of idolatry and that ignorance and barbarism must be eradicated from the Arab peninsula, which lies exactly between the realms of the East and those of the West.[51]

Surveying the field of modern literature on jihad, we see that modernist authors underline the defensive aspect of jihad, and hold that jihad outside Islamic territory is only permitted when the peaceful propagation of Islam is being hindered or when Moslems living amongst unbelievers are oppressed. Fundamentalist writers on the other hand do not depart to a great extent from the classical doctrine and emphasize the expansionist aspect.[52] As I have described in par. 3.2 the modernist, defensive tendency originated in India in the latter half of the nineteenth century. One of the first spokesmen of this current of thought was Sayyid Aḥmad Khān, who wrote in 1871, referring to the situation in India:

> First, what is *jihad*? It is war in defence of the faith *'fi sabílillàh'*. But it has its conditions, and, except under these, it is unlawful. It must be against those who are not only *Kafirs* [unbelievers, RP], but also 'obstruct the exercise of the faith' (K 47:1). The doctors of the law in all ages, not merely the Moulvies, Meccan or of Northern India, whom Mr. Hunter quotes, have laid down that to constitute the essential conditions for *jihad* on the part of the protected Musalmans as against a Christian power protecting them, there must be *positive* oppression or obstruction to the Moslems in the exercise of their faith; not merely want of countenance, negative withholding of support, or absence of profession of the faith; and further, this obstruction and oppression which justifies *jihad* must be, not in civil, but in religious matters; it must impair the foundation of some of the 'pillars of Islam', and not merely touch the existence of Kazees, the maintenance of tombs of saints (a practice declared by the stricter Moslems to be heretical), or the administration of the country through Moslem officials. These are merely negative abstentions from the faith (*kufr*), not that positive oppression (*zulm*) and obstruction to the exercise of the faith (*sadd*) which alone can justify *jihad*.[53]

Aḥmad Khān was not the only one to express these views. They were shared by many of his contemporaries.[54] By arguing in this fashion, Aḥmad Khān and the Indian modernists drastically restricted the scope of the jihad duty. Not only did they assert that jihad was essentially defensive, but they also limited this to defence against religious oppression impairing the pillars of Islam, i.e. the five ritual obligations of the Moslems (the profession of faith, prayer, ritual taxes, fasting and pilgrimage), thereby excluding from it all other kinds of political oppression. Thus they introduced a separation between the religious and political spheres, an obvious innovation with regard to a religion that claims to dominate all domains of human activity. This irenic interpretation of the jihad doctrine was prompted by the fact that the British regarded the Indian Moslems as the main instigators of the 1857 revolt. Hence they distrusted them and discriminated against them in favour of the Hindus with regard to government employment and army commissions. Since these were precisely the professions upon which the livelihood of the upper and middle class Moslems depended, the latter wanted to show that Islam was a respectable religion and that the doctrine of jihad was no obstacle for the loyal service of the British Empire. With their publications on jihad they tried to achieve two aims:

> My first object is that the Mohammedans ignorant of the texts bearing on Jihad and the conditions of Islam may become acquainted with them, and that they may not labour under the misapprehension that it is their religious duty to wage war against another people solely because that people is opposed to Islam. Thus they, by ascertaining the fixed conditions and texts, may be saved for ever from rebellion . . . . My second object is that non-Mohammedans and the Government under whose protection the Mohammedans live, may not suspect Mohammedans of thinking that it is lawful for us to fight against non-Mohammedans or that it is our duty to interfere with the lives and property of others, or that we are bound to convert others forcibly to Mohammedanism, or to spread Islam by means of the sword. The result of these two aims will, I hope, be that the bonds of concord will be drawn closer between the rulers and the ruled, and between British subjects generally and Mohammedans, so that peace and security may be established for ever in this country.[55]

By the end of the nineteenth century the idea that jihad is defensive warfare became current in the Middle East, and especially in Egypt, through the works of Muḥammad ʿAbduh and Muḥammad Rashīd Riḍā.[56] They, however, did not follow the narrow interpretation of the Indian modernists and emphatically asserted that the jihad duty also applied in case a foreign aggressor invaded Islamic territory for political and economic reasons. Hence they could appeal to the doctrine of jihad in order to resist colonial conquest. At the present, most authors on jihad follow this defensive tendency, although recently, there seems to take place a certain radicalization towards a more fundamentalist approach. Nevertheless, the text books for religious instruction used in Egypt all describe jihad as a defensive war.[57]

The point of departure of the modernists is that jihad is only to be waged as a reaction against outside aggression. Muḥammad Rashīd Riḍā formulated this as follows: 'Everything that is mentioned in the Koran with regard to the rules of fighting, is intended [to be understood] as defence against enemies that fight the Moslems because of their religion'.[58] They envisage various forms of aggression against which jihad is lawful, such as a direct attack of the territory of Islam or the suspicion thereof, and also the oppression of Moslems residing outside the frontiers of the Islamic state. Assistance to these and securing the missionary activities are both viewed as defence against an assault on the freedom of religion. The scriptural arguments they adduce are mainly derived from the Koran. The Koran abounds with verses that have a bearing on the relationship with the unbelievers. These verses range from prescriptions to preach Islam peacefully to unconditional commands to fight them. In classical Islam, as we have seen in par. 2.4, this contradiction was solved by means of abrogation. Departing from the gradual evolution in the relationship between Mohammed and the unbelievers, which was reflected in the Koran, it was assumed that the unconditional command to fight the unbelievers, to be found in those verses that were revealed in the latest stage of Mohammed's life, had abrogated all other prescriptions. The modernists, however, have rejected this method of interpretation. They have taken the verses that explicitly mention the causes for fighting and, in general belong to the last stage but one, the period in which Allah permitted the believers to offer resistance against the attacks of the unbelievers, as the verses determining the causes of warfare against non-Moslems. The most important of these are: K 2:190 ('*Fight in the way of Allah those who fight you, but do not provoke hostility; verily Allah loveth not those who provoke hostility*'); K 2:192 ('*But if they refrain (from fighting) then Allah is forgiving, compassionate*'); K 2:194 ('*The sacred month for the sacred month, things sacred being (subject to the law of) of retaliation; so if any make an attack upon you, make a like attack upon them; show piety towards Allah, and know that Allah is with those who show piety'*); K 4:75 (*'What is wrong with you that ye fight not in the way of Allah and the oppressed, men, women, and children, who say: "O our Lord, take us out of this city of wrong-doing people, and appoint for us from Thine own side a patron, and appoint for us from Thine own side a helper"'*); K 4:90-91 (*'If they then withdraw from you, and do not fight against you, but offer you peace, Allah hath not opened for you a way against them. If they do not withdraw from you, and offer you peace, and restrain their hands, take them and kill them wherever ye come upon them'*); K 9:13-14 (*'But if they violate their oaths after they have made a covenant and attack your religion, fight the leaders of unbelief; no oath will hold in their case; mayhap they will refrain. Will ye not fight against a people who have violated their oaths, and had it in mind to expel the messenger and who took the initiative with you the first time? Are ye afraid of them? It is more in order that ye should be afraid of Allah, if ye be believers'*); K 8:61 (*'If they incline to make peace, incline thou to it, and set thy trust on Allah; verily He is the Hearer the Knower'*), and K 60:8 (*'Allah doth not forbid you to act virtuously towards those who have not fought against you in the matter of religion, and have not expelled you from your dwellings, or to deal fair with them – Allah loveth those who deal fairly'*). Having quoted these and similar verses, one of the modernist authors exclaims:

> Read those verses . . . , then you will realize that they were revealed with regard to people recalcitrantly practising persecution, amongst whom the elements of depravation were so deeply rooted that they did not respect pledges anymore and that virtue became meaningless to them. There is no doubt that to fight these people, to purify the earth from them and to put an end to their persecution is a service to the commonweal and a benefaction to mankind as a whole.[59]

Taking the aforementioned verses as the decisive ones in the relationship with unbelievers, modernists were obliged to re-interpret the verses that were traditionally understood as giving an unconditional command to fight them. They accomplished this task by means of contextual exegesis. Thus, K 9:5 (*'Then, when the sacred months have slipped away, slay the polytheists wherever ye find them, seize them, beset them, lie in ambush for them everywhere'*), which is traditionally taken as the sword-verse, must, according to the modernists, be read in the context of the first part of *sūrah* 9 (*sūrat al-tawbah*), directed against the Meccans that had broken their treaty-obligations with the Moslems. This must be regarded as the immediate cause for the command to fight in K 9:5, although it is not expressly mentioned in this verse. In the same way K 9:29 (*'Fight against those who do not believe in Allah, nor in the Last Day and do not make forbidden what Allah and His messenger have made forbidden, and do not practise the religion of truth, of those who have been given the book, until they pay the jizya off-hand, being subdued'*) is re-interpreted. The modernists deny that this verse contains an unconditional command to fight all People of the Book (Jews and Christians) until they pay poll-tax (*djizyah*), but infer from the context that only those Jews and Christians were meant that had violated their pledges and assailed the propagation of the Islamic mission. An additional argument for this interpretation is to be found in the phrase *'being subdued'*, which implies, according to modernist authors, that previously, they were recalcitrant and that there had been reasons for the Moslems to fight them. This verse also shows, that unbelief is not the reason for fighting the People of the Book, for, if this were the case, fighting ought to be continued until conversion and not to cease when they agree to pay poll-tax. As for K 9:123 (*'O ye who have believed, fight the unbelievers who are near to you, and let them feel a rough temper in you and know that Allah is with those who show piety'*), we have seen in par. 4.2 that this verse is to be taken as a tactical instruction, not as a general command to fight the unbelievers. Finally the modernists had to cope with the Tradition according to which Abū Bakr has said: *'I have been ordered to fight the people until they profess that there is no god but Allah and that Mohammed is the messenger of Allah, perform the ṣalāh and pay the zakāh. If they do so, their lives and property are inviolable to me, unless* [*when*] *the* [*law of*] *Islam permits them* [*to be taken*]*'*. This was done by interpreting the word *'people'* in the restricted sense of *'polytheist Arabs'*, who had committed aggression against the Moslems.

The fundamentalists[60] also hold that jihad aims at defending Islam. They repudiate, however, the view that this is the sole aim and emphasize, on the contrary, the function of jihad in propagating Islam. The most important objects of jihad are, in their view, to bring about: an end to the domination of man over man and of man-made laws, the recognition of Allah's sovereignty alone, and the acceptance of the *sharīʿah* as the only law. Jihad, in trying to realize these objectives, is a permanent revolutionary struggle for the sake of the whole of mankind:

> For Islam is not concerned with the interest of one nation to the exclusion of others and does not intend to advance one people to the exclusion of others. It is not at all interested in what state rules and dominates the earth, but only in the happiness and welfare of humanity. Islam has a concept and a practical program, especially chosen for the happiness and progress of human society. Therefore, Islam resists any government that is based on a different concept and program, in order to liquidate it completely. . . . Its aim is to make this concept victorious, to introduce this program universally, to set up governments that are firmly rooted in this concept and this program, irrespective of who carries the banner of truth and justice, or whose flag of aggression and corruption is thereby toppled. Islam wants the whole earth and does not content itself with only a part thereof. It wants and requires the entire inhabited world. It does not want this in order that one nation dominates the earth and monopolizes its sources of wealth, after having taken them away from one or more other nations. No, Islam wants and requires the earth in order that the human race altogether can enjoy the concept and practical program of human happiness, by means of which Allah has honoured Islam and put it above the other religions and laws. In order to realize this lofty desire, Islam wants to employ all forces and means that can be employed for bringing about a universal all-embracing revolution. It will spare no efforts for the achievement of this supreme objective. This far-reaching struggle that continuously exhausts all forces and this employment of all possible means are called jihad.[61]

This concept and this program aim at establishing an Islamic order of society, where the *sharīʿah* is the leading principle:

> Islam proclaims the liberation of man on earth from the subjection to something that is not Allah. Therefore, Islam has to march out in order to put an end to the actual situation that conflicts with this universal proclamation, by means of both elucidation and action. It has to deliver blows at the political forces that make men the slaves of something that is not Allah, i.e. that do not rule them according to the *sharīʿah* and the authority of Allah, those forces that prevent them from hearing the elucidation and from freely embracing the Creed, without being hindered by any authority. [It has to destroy those forces] in order to establish a social, economic and political order that allows this liberation movement to proceed effectively, after having put an end to the dominating power, regardless of whether this is purely political, or obscured by racialism or by the ideology of class-supremacy within one race. However, Islam does not seek to force people to embrace the Creed. . . . In the first place it aims at putting an end to these regimes and governments that are based on the principle that human beings rule human beings and on the subjection of men to other men. Thereupon it actually sets the individual free to choose the creed according to his own free will, after having liberated him from political pressure and after having given him elucidation that illuminates his soul and intellect.[62]

These quotations from the works of the fundamentalists are illustrative of their style and way of presentation. In fact, this is the sole feature that distinguishes fundamentalist from classical texts on jihad, since both views on the relationship with unbelievers are essentially identical. The fundamentalists have wrapped up these old ideas in a modern packing, by using phrases like 'permanent revolution', 'liberation of man', 'practical program', e.t.q., that are all borrowed from modern political usage. This style shows striking resemblances with that of the tracts of the various Jesus-movements in Western Europe and the U.S.A., that by using similar catch-phrases with a politically progressive connotation, try to disguise their conservative message.

In contrast with the modernists, the fundamentalists adhere to the classical doctrine of *marḥaliyyah*, the gradual evolution in the relationship between Mohammed and the unbelievers, culminating in the unconditional command to fight them.[63] Illustrative of the controversy between both groups, are their interpretations of K 2:193 and 8:39 (*'Fight them until there is no persecution and religion is (entirely) Allah's'*). The modernists emphasize the first part of this verse and point out that, in this case, fighting is lawful as a defence against persecution,[64] whereas the fundamentalists stress the second part and read this verse as a command to fight against the unbelievers with the aim of establishing a universal Islamic order, ruled by Allah's law.[65] Because of their defensive stand, the modernists are under serious attack by the fundamentalists, who accuse them of *'defeatism'* for having yielded to the ideological assaults of orientalists. For that is the reason why they have transformed the classical doctrine of jihad into a doctrine of defensive war, by interpreting the relevant Koranic verses separately and not in their historical order and by trying to demonstrate that all wars the Prophet has fought, were defensive wars:

> We shall now have a look at the impact of the malicious attacks by the orientalists on Moslem scholars, and at how the latter responded to it and defended jihad. In this connexion I am interested in the response of those scholars that have spiritually and intellectually capitulated to the attacks of the orientalists, under the pressure that at present is exerted upon the Moslems, the scholars that tried to rid their religion of these insinuations, without, however, realizing the serious consequences of what they were writing. They began to cast about for excuses for jihad, to interpret clear Koranic verses and to falsify historical facts in order to be able to say to those orientalists: 'We have nothing to do with the jihad and the sword. Jihad has been made obligatory because of certain incidental and temporary circumstances. Now, it is not obligatory anymore, since the cause has disappeared. We hold that jihad has no other aim than defence of our lives and of the country we live in'.[66]

The fundamentalists are of the opinion that one cannot apply the categories *'offensive'* or *'defensive'* to jihad, because, in their view, jihad is universal revolutionary struggle. Looking for moral justifications for jihad, as the modernists do, is senseless, since Koranic prescriptions do not require any justification. If one really wants to apply the categories *'offensive'* and *'defensive'* to jihad, one will see that there are offensive as well as defensive aspects. The offensive aspect is that all states and governments will be resisted as long as they are based on principles contradictory to Islam, especially if they are founded on the principle of the sovereignty of Man. The defensive aspects are, firstly, the self-evident fact that the present territory of Islam must be protected as a basis for expansion and, secondly, the fact that the Islamic movement protects Man against all factors that hinder his freedom and emancipation, regardless of whether these factors consist in religious convictions and ideas, social structures, or political regimes. So, if one wants to call Islam peaceful, one has to bear in mind that:

> When Islam strives for peace, it does not want a cheap peace, a peace that does not mean more than that one is safe in that particular territory where people embrace the Islamic faith. No, it wants a peace wherein all religion belongs to Allah, which means that all people worship Allah alone and that they do not take each other as objects of worship to the exclusion of Allah.[67]

These last words bring another difference between the modernists and the fundamentalists to light. The latter lay stress upon the Koranic words: *'How shall the polytheists have a covenant with Allah and with His messenger'* (K 9:7), and hold that a peace treaty with polytheists is not allowed.[68]

They only accept peace when it is the result of the final victory of Islam. The modernists on the other hand, accept the principle of peaceful coexistence between the Islamic state and the rest of the world. On the authority of K 8:61 (*'If they incline to make peace, incline thou to it and set thy trust upon Allah; verily He is the Hearer, the Knower'*)[69] they consider it obligatory for the Moslems to respond positively if the enemy asks for a peace treaty, even, according to some, if they harbour suspicions that this request has been made perfidiously and treacherously, or that the enemy wishes to benefit from the cessation of fighting in order to prepare a new war.[70]

The divergence between the modernist and the fundamentalist view on the doctrine of jihad goes back to an essential difference in political outlook. The modernists accept to a great extent the situation they live in. Consciously or unconsciously they have adopted the Western liberal values that became current in the Islamic world as a result of economic and political penetration. Their attempts to reform Islam aimed at incorporating these values in their religion. They seem to have acquiesced in the division of the Islamic world in national states and Islamic unity is for them some vague ideal that can be invoked for the sake of certain political issues connected with religion. The Indian modernists of the latter half of the nineteenth century even condoned colonial rule and limited the scope of the jihad obligation to such an extent that resistance against colonialism was excluded. Later modernists did not go that far. They were opposed to colonial domination but accepted the fact that the struggle against foreign rule was waged within the framework of a secular nationalist ideology and that religion played but a secondary role. Hence they often referred to jihad as being a struggle 'for the sake of the fatherland and the defence of religion' (*fī sabīl al-waṭan wa-l-difāʿ ʿan al-dīn*).[71] Although this notion of jihad is in complete conformance with the classical doctrine that makes jihad an individual duty whenever an outside enemy attacks the territory of Islam, the novelty lies in the wording and the use of the word fatherland (*waṭan*).[72] For many modernists the concept of jihad has now become coextensive with that of a national war conducted by an Islamic state against a non-Islamic state, and hence they apply it to the wars between the Arab states and Israel. This identification went so far that during the October war of 1973, the Rector of the Azhar-University, ʿAbd al-Ḥalīm Maḥmūd, stripped the concept of jihad of its exclusively Islamic character by declaring that:

> Jihad is an obligation for all, without distinction between Moslems and Christians. It is the first duty of all who live under the sky of Egypt, the fatherland of all. . . . Being killed (*istishhād*) for the sake of the fatherland gives access to Paradise. This is confirmed by all divine laws (*sharāʾiʿ samāwiyyah*) that have been revealed to the People of the Book.[73]

The fundamentalists, on the other hand, do not acquiesce in the present situation. Their ideal is the establishment of a truly Islamic state founded upon the prescriptions of the *sharīʿah.* Jihad is for them the means of achieving this ideal. They wage their struggle against all who stand in the way of realizing this ideal and hence against those regimes in the Islamic world that do not apply the *sharīʿah,* against the Western powers and against communism and zionism. In fact they carry on the struggle of the early jihad movements, which were also motivated by the ideal of invigorating the Islamic world by returning to the fundamental principles of Islam. Only their language has been modernized and brought up to date. They do not admit of a separation between religion and politics. Religion is to dominate all their activities and they reject therefore secular ideologies such as nationalism.

In fact the modernist and the fundamentalist tendency represent two different reactions to Western penetration. The modernists have reacted in a defensive manner, by adopting Western values and reforming their religion in the light of these newly imported ideas. They have transformed Islam into a religion that is well suited for the Westernized elite. The fundamentalists, on the other hand, have reacted in a self-assertive manner, by rejecting everything Western and emphasizing the real Islamic values. Both reactions are clearly reflected in their views on the doctrine of jihad.

4.5 A NEW INTERPRETATION OF THE JIHAD DOCTRINE: ISLAMIC INTERNATIONAL LAW

As has been shown in the preceding paragraph, modernist authors have argued that the doctrine of jihad offers a theory of *bellum justum.* Some of them have elaborated this point and have interpreted this doctrine as *Islamic international law* or as *Islamic law of nations.*[74] This conception, however, was not really a new one. We can find it already in the works of some nineteenth-century European authors.[75] For a scholar like Pütter, who wrote in the first half of the nineteenth century, it was only logical to hold the view that there existed a separate Islamic international law, as a really general international law did not exist in his time. The law that dominated the domain of international relations between European states, was called Christian international law and was confined to the Christian states. This situation came to an end in 1856, when the Ottoman Empire was admitted to the advantages of the 'Public Law and Concert of Europe'. As a consequence, international law gradually lost its exclusively Christian character. Until quite recently, however, it was not a really universal law, as its application was restricted to civilized nations only. Thus, nearly all Asian and African nations remained outside the pale of international law. In view of this exclusive character of Western international law, the notion of Islamic international law could easily come into being. There is, however, a fundamental difference between both concepts. Christian as well as modern international law are founded on the fact that they are regarded as binding by all states concerned. On that basis they give prescriptions for international intercourse, which, in the case of Christian international law, is confined to the Christian nations. Islamic law, on the other hand, is not interested in the relations between the Islamic states as, ideally, there is but one. Its object is to provide Moslems with a code of behaviour in their relations with non-Moslems. Thus, its prescriptions are only binding for Moslems, be it individuals or the head of the state (*Imām*). It is not concerned with the question whether non-Moslems do also consider its rules as binding. Because of the Islamic claim to universality, it does not recognize non-Moslems and non-Moslem states as legal subjects equal to Moslems and the Islamic state. Thus, the Islamic rules are completely internal and unilateral. An enlightening illustration of this can be found in the rules concerning prisoners of war. On the one hand they prescribe how Moslems must treat enemy prisoners. On the other hand they decree how Moslems must act when they happen to fall into enemy hands. Whether the enemy regards these rules as equally binding or not, is of no concern to Islamic international law. With the exception of treaty obligations, non-Moslems, in as far as they are not protected by *amān* or *dhimmah*, cannot, in general, claim any right under Islamic international law.[76] In view of the divergence between Islamic doctrine and what is nowadays understood by international law[77] contemporary European authors deny the character of international law to the Islamic doctrine of jihad[78] or call it at the most 'resembling international law' (*völkerrechtsähnlich*).[79]

In the following I shall deal with two topics. The first is how modern Moslem authors view the relation between Islamic and positive international law and the viability of the Islamic system. Secondly I shall give a succinct exposé of how these authors now describe the practical rules of Islamic international law.

Although most of these authors profess Islamic international law to be a universal system, they actually adhere to the classical doctrine, as they define it as an internal law for Moslems in their relations with non-Moslems, irrespective of whether these last accept its obligatory character or not. Thus we find the following definitions of Islamic international law:

> L'ensemble des règles dont l'usage est imposé exclusivement aux musulmans pour régler leurs rapports de guerre et de paix avec les non-musulmans, individus ou états, dans le pays de l'Islam ou en dehors de ce pays;[80]
>
> That part of the law and custom of the land and treaty obligations which a Muslim de facto or de jure State observes with its dealings with other de facto and de jure States. . . . It depends wholly and solely upon the will of the Muslim State;[81]
>
> The sum total of rules and practices which Islam ordains or tolerates in international relations.[82]

Although other authors do not give express definitions, it is evident from their writings that they subscribe to this classical doctrine. Only two authors explicitly envisage the applicability of Islamic international law between separate Islamic states. Although this runs counter to the classical theory that recognizes but one single Islamic state, they argue that the Koran has admitted of the division of the Islamic world into separate political entities, where it says in K 49:9 (*'If two parties of the believers fight, set things right between them, and if one of the parties oppress the other, fight the one which is oppressive until it returns to the affair of Allah; then if it returns, set things right between them justly, and act fairly; verily Allah loveth those who act fairly'*).[83]

Most authors do not expressly discuss the problem raised by the conflicting claims to universality of both Islamic and modern international law. They pass it over in silence or, at best, touch upon it in a vague and contradictory manner. The following quotations from one and the same book – in which the italics are mine – offer an illustrative example of their ambiguous attitude:

> Obviously, it is not necessary that there should be only one set of rules, or one system of international law, at a time, for the conduct of all the States of the world. And several systems of international law *could* and in fact *did* exist in different parts of the globe.[84]
>
> We can see now that the relevant portions of the Qur'an and Sunnah *form permanent positive law* of the Muslims in their international dealings.[85]
>
> Modern international law, *in use practically all over the world*, is in fact the law originated in Western Europe.[86]
>
> The international conventions on law of air are now *part of Muslim law*, in so far as they have been adhered to by independent Muslim states.[87]

The authors evade the problem by presenting their writings as historical or comparative studies, by means of which they want to demonstrate that the standard of Islamic international law, in view of its adaptability to modern conditions and of its humane rules, is equal or even superior to that of positive international law.[88] Some authors, however, see possibilities for future application of Islamic law in the domain of international relations:

> It must be recalled that Article 30 of the International Court of Justice mentions the writings of the highly qualified publicists of other nations as the subsidiary source of law.[89] So far only the treatises of European jurists have been referred to as evidence of law. It is hoped that with increasing cooperation among the Muslim States and their insistence on the adoption of Islamic laws and judicial system will call for occasional reference to or reliance on the works of Islamic jurisprudence [*sic*]. A recognition of the merits of Islamic law becomes all the more imperative, now that

> the Western Powers no longer enjoy paramountcy in most Muslim countries, who, now freed from alien domination, are rediscovering their cultural heritage.[90]

Another author justifies his new interpretation of the classical doctrine with the contention that there is an increasing trend in the Moslem world towards the revival of Islam and the implementation of its concepts. As the rigid classical doctrine, in his view, is likely to cause a breach between the Islamic and non-Islamic states, 'it is about time to introduce an adequate interpretation to be of service to the cause of world peace and security. Apart from many details of considerable interest, Islamic legal theory presents an advance on modern thought as regards the fundamental problems of international law'.[91] Finally it has been proposed to use the principles of Islamic international law as a regional form of international law to be applied in the projected Arab Court of Justice.[92]

An important characteristic of the writings on Islamic international law is that in nearly all of them the point is stressed that Islamic international law, at least in its principles, is superior to positive international law.[93] The argument that one meets most frequently is that Islamic international law can boast of a venerable age of thirteen centuries, whereas the present system of international law was created only four hundred years ago. The illustrious and human principles of Islamic international law were formulated and applied at a time when, in the rest of the world, international relations were still dominated by barbaric anarchy and the savage law of the jungle. Muḥammad al-Shaybānī, the first Moslem author to compose a major work devoted exclusively to *siyar*, the Islamic law dealing with relations with non-Moslems, is often called the Hugo Grotius of Islam. In addition to this, there exists a thesis that has become popular and found many supporters amongst Moslem authors, to the effect that European international law has been strongly influenced by the *sharīʿah* via intercultural contacts during the Crusades and in Spain. E. Nys[94] and Baron Michel de Taube[95] were the first to assume a certain influence of Islamic law on Western international law. Moslem authors have run away with this thesis and usually present it in a much exaggerated form.[96] This idea, it be noted in passing, finds its parallel in the contention that European civil law is to a great extent indebted to the *sharīʿah*.[97]

Further evidence for the superiority of Islamic international law is, according to Moslem writers, to be found in the remarkable fact that Islamic international law has, since its inception, thirteen centuries ago, stood for principles that were only recently recognized in modern international law. The foremost of these is the principle of equality and reciprocality which, in modern international law, was formally accepted only with the creation of the United Nations. Previously, there existed a distinction between Christian and heathen nations, a distinction that was gradually replaced by one between civilized and uncivilized or savage nations. To these last full international personality was denied. Moslem authors enlarge upon this inequality and oppose it to the principle of equality and reciprocality as guaranteed in Koranic verses like: *'The people were one community; then Allah raised up the prophets as bringers of good tidings and warners, and with them He sent down the Book with the truth to judge amongst the people regarding that in which they had differed'* (K 2:213); *'Allah doth not forbid you to act virtuously towards those who have not fought against you in the matter of religion, and have not expelled you from your dwellings, or to deal fairly with them – Allah loveth those who deal fairly'* (K 60:8); *'The sacred month for the sacred month, things sacred being [subject to the law of] retaliation; so if any make an attack upon you, make a like attack upon them; show piety towards Allah and know that Allah is with those who show piety'* (K 2:194).[98] Actually, these sweeping assertions about Islam recognizing the equality of all mankind and the reciprocality in inter-state relations, amount to no more than gratuitous and non-committal slogans. When they come down to the details of the relations between Moslems and non-Moslems, they hardly depart from the classical doctrine and maintain the legal distinction between Moslems and non-Moslems and between the Islamic and the other states. Only one author attempts to give a more or less concrete and elaborate form to the notion of a community of equal states in Islamic international law. This community, however, does not embrace all states, as its membership is subject to certain restrictions. The author founds his theory on K 3:64 (*'O People of the Book, come to a word* [*which is*] *fair between us and you,* [*to wit*] *that we serve no one but Allah, that we associate nothing with Him, and that we do not take one the other as Lords apart from Allah'*). By *'a word* [*which is*] *fair'* (Ar.: *kalimat sawā'*) the author understands 'a word on the basis of equality, an agreement'. His interpretation then goes on:

> The Arabic text, thus, connotes that the agreement to which the Scriptuaries [i.e. the People of the Book, RP] are called is based on the principle of legal equality since the only condition is to admit the oneness of God, not to become Muslims. From the Islamic point of view the acknowledgement of the oneness of God is the preliminary prerequisite for establishing peaceful relations among the Muslims and the non-Muslims. In other words, the Islamic state could not tolerate being bound with another state by common interests unless the latter's civilization is based on the idea of unity of Deity. A state under Muslim international law is not entitled to claim the right of legal equality unless it attains a certain degree of civilization, that is to say when its civilization is moulded with the idea of the unity of God.[99]

The author compares this restriction to the conditions of membership of the United Nations, as mentioned in Article 4 of the Charter of the U.N.: 'Membership of the United Nations is open to all other peace-loving states which accept the obligations contained in the present charter and, in the judgement of the organization, are able and willing to carry out these obligations'.[100] The author doubts whether communist countries, 'with their dialectical materialism' could be admitted to the pale of international law.[101]

An argument of equal importance for establishing the superiority of Islamic international law is, according to modern authors, its peaceful character. From its beginning, thirteen centuries ago, it has recognized peace as the fundamental relationship between the Islamic and the other states. Moreover, it has developed clearcut definitions of the notions of *bellum justum* and of aggression, something which, if we may believe these authors, positive international law has, until now, not achieved. For more details and for the scriptural arguments for this opinion I refer to the paragraphs 4.2 and 4.4.

Treatises on Islamic international law can roughly be divided into two categories. Some authors take modern works on international law as a starting point and compare the various topics with the Islamic prescriptions. If they cannot find corresponding prescriptions, which occurs frequently, they develop them themselves by interpreting the Koran and the *Sunnah*. Thus, they pay much attention to theoretical topics like sources of Islamic international law, the nature of its rules, international legal personality, sovereignty, treaties and the like.[102] Other authors do not go deeply into the theories and notions of positive international law. They depart from the classical doctrine of the *sharīʿah*, which they reinterpret and rearrange so as to cast it in the mould of a more or less Western inspired system.[103] In the following I shall first deal with two points of a more theoretical character as expounded by authors of the first category, viz. the notion of international legal personality and the problem of the obligatory character of international law. Then I shall proceed with a succinct survey of the more concrete rules of Islamic international law.

International personality is still a hotly debated issue in international law. For a long time, modern international law has recognized as legal subjects only sovereign states. Exceptionally, as in the case of crimes against humanity, international legal norms are directly addressed to individuals, but in general, this takes place via municipal legislation codifying international legal rules. Only recently are voices heard advocating the extension of international personality to individuals and to colonized peoples, but prevailing opinion hesitates and is reluctant in conferring it to subjects other than states. This is connected with the doctrine that there exist two separate and distinct realms of law: that of international law and that of municipal law. Modern authors on Islamic international law assert that international personality does not offer any problem at all in Islamic law, precisely because it does not admit of a division between international and municipal law. The *sharīʿah* addresses its rules to individuals as well as collectivities. Although classical doctrine did not develop any theory on the corporate personality of collectivities, modern authors claim that the foundations of such a theory can be found in the following Koranic verses: *'O ye people, we have created you of male and female and made you races and tribes, that you may show mutual recognition; verily the most noble of you in Allah's eyes is the most pious; verily Allah is knowing, well-informed'* (K 49:13); *'And let there be [formed] of you a community inviting to good, urging what is reputable and restraining from what is disreputable; such are the prosperous'* (K 3:104); *'When We intend to destroy a town, We command its affluent people; thereupon*[104] *they act viciously therein, so that the sentence against them is justified; then We destroy it utterly'* (K 17:16).[105] One author elaborates on the theory of corporate personality in Islamic international law and contends that the *sharīʿah* offers better criteria for deciding whether international personality should be conferred to a given territorial community than positive international law does, viz.: territory, population and a sovereign government. Islam, according to this author, establishes the following criteria: (1) socio-cultural unity (which in classical Islam was called unity of religion); (2) representative political leadership (as, in classical Islam, the caliph should be public choice); and (3) unity of legal system (which in classical Islam was called unity of the *sharīʿah*). In his view, these three criteria can remedy the present situation in positive international law, whereby international personality is denied to colonized peoples and certain international organizations.[106]

In contemporary theory of international law, there is no unanimity as to the source of its obligatory character. This theoretical problem has, until now, not been solved in a satisfactory manner. Some hold that its source is to be found in the subjective will of the individual states. However, accepting this implies that states can shirk the obligations imposed by international law by merely withdrawing their consent. As law characteristically emanates from an authority of a higher order than that of its legal subjects, some have looked upon the collective will (*Vereinbarung*) of all states, as the source of the obligatory character of international law, as this must be of a higher authority than the will of the individual state. However, the weakness of this theory lies in the fact that it presupposes a unity of separate wills. As conflict of interests between states is rather the rule than the exception, it is hard to postulate the existence of this unified will. Other theories have turned away from these subjective principles. One of these derives the obligatory character of international law from the fact that every community presupposes the observance of certain rules to ensure mutual solidarity, for, if it fails to do so, this community would cease to exist. Thus, the basis of international law is to be found in the social fact (*fait social*) that the existence of a community depends on the observance of certain restrictions by its members. These restrictions develop into binding legal norms when the members of the community become conscious of them. This theory, however, can account for the existence of law, but it cannot explain what precisely is the basis of its binding character. Finally, there is a school of thought that holds that the validity of any legal rule must be derived from another rule that governs its creation. This presupposes the existence of one supreme fundamental norm from which the validity of all inferior rules are derived. However, the existence of such a rule is axiomatic and cannot be verified, which certainly weakens its explanatory force. *Vis-à-vis* these controversies and conflicting theories, Islam offers, according to modern Moslem authors, a clear and simple solution: the obligatory character of Islamic international law derives from divine revelation. Since the rules of the *sharīʿah* are Allah's commands, they are sanctioned by religion. Thus, legal rules in Islam have a moral dimension, which according to Moslem authors, is lacking in Western laws, and, especially, in positive international law. The enforcement of Islamic prescriptions is therefore enhanced by this religious or moral sanction. In the Koran, one repeatedly finds exhortations to fulfil pledges, like: *'Fulfil the covenant of Allah when ye have taken it, and do not violate oaths after their confirmation and your having set Allah as guarantor over you; assuredly Allah knoweth what ye do'* (K 16:91); '. . . *And fulfil the covenant; verily, a covenant is a thing for which one is responsible'* (K 17:36); *'Except those polytheists with whom ye have made a covenant and who then have not failed you in anything, or backed anyone up against you; fulfil their covenant up to (the end of) its period; Allah loveth those who show piety'* (K 9:4). This means that the principle of *pacta sunt servanda* is a religiously sanctioned norm in Islam. On the strength of K 9:4, this norm applies also in the domain of international relations. This, precisely, constitutes the superiority of Islamic to positive international law.[107] This same argument is also brought up by advocates of reintroduction of the *sharīʿah* in the field of civil and penal law.[108]

I shall now give a survey of the more concrete rules of Islamic international law as expounded by Moslem authors on the subject. Many of these topics have also been dealt with by other authors in their reinterpretation of the classical doctrine of jihad. In this exposé, I shall globally adhere to the systematic arrangement of the authors on Islamic international law. Generally, they group the subject-matter under two headings: international relations in peace-time and international relations in war-time. The topics that fall under the first heading are: the principle of peaceful relations between the Islamic and the other states, diplomacy and treaties. Because of its doctrinal pedigree, which goes back to truce and armistice, some authors discuss this last topic under the second heading. This heading, international relations in war-time, includes the following topics: lawful and unlawful wars, ultimatum and declaration of war, treatment of enemy persons and property, prisoners of war, safeconduct and quarter, and the conclusion of war.

As the principle of peaceful relations has been discussed in par. 4.2 I shall not go into it here. That diplomacy is dealt with as a peacetime institution is significant as it shows the desire of modern authors to emphasize the peaceful character of the doctrine of jihad. For the only classical rule with regard to envoys is that they are automatically granted safeconduct (*amān*), as we have seen in par. 2.13. Now, this only makes sense in case of hostile relations. Modern authors, however, put this automatically granted safeconduct on a par with the modern institution of diplomatic immunity. As the status of diplomats is hardly touched upon in the classical *fiqh*-books, most modern authors amplify this topic with historical instances of diplomacy between the Islamic and other states.[109]

As a consequence of the classical Islamic doctrine, that does not admit of permanent peaceful relations between the Islamic and the other states, the classical works on *fiqh* discuss only three kinds of treaties: collective *amān* or quarter, temporary armistice or truce and the permanent treaty of *dhimmah* whereby a population is brought under the sway of the Islamic state. In the last case, the non-Moslem population is allowed to abide by their own religion, but has to pay a special tax, *djizyah*. Modern authors, however, who hold that the relations between the Islamic and the other states are essentially peaceful, assert that all kinds of treaties are allowed in Islamic international law. In peace time, the Islamic state may conclude permanent commercial treaties, pacts of friendship and the like. They found their opinion on the general Koranic commands to fulfil pledges and on Mohammed's example, as tradition has it that he has concluded a treaty with the Jews of Medina.[110] In order to develop a general theory on permanent treaties, modern authors had to do away with the restrictions that the *sharīʿah* imposes on armistices and truces, for most schools hold that armistices can only be concluded for a limited period. The Hanafites did allow treaties with unlimited duration, but they stipulated that the *Imām* has the right to rescind treaties whenever this is in the interest of the Moslems.[111] According to modern authors, this last implicit condition, viz. that a treaty will remain valid as long as it is in the interests of the Moslems, closely resembles the doctrine of the *clausula rebus sic stantibus* in positive international law. Therefore, Hanafite opinion would be acceptable, were it not that it is contrary to the general Koranic injunctions to fulfil pledges and with K 8:58 (*'If thou fearest treachery at all from any people, cast back to them (thy covenant) equally'*), which requires that there be objective indications of treachery.[112] These same general Koranic injunctions and Mohammed's example in concluding a pact with the Jews of Medina, serve as arguments against the classical doctrine that only admits of temporary treaties.[113] Few authors mention the general conditions for the validity of treaties. They do not depart very far from the classical doctrine and enumerate the following requirements: Treaties must be concluded by the *Imām* or his proxy. In the latter case the treaty is subject to ratification by the *Imām* in order to ascertain that the proxy has not exceeded the limits of his mandate. The stipulations of treaties may not be contrary to the fundamental laws of Islam. This is founded on the Tradition: *'Every stipulation that is not to be found in the book, is void'.*[114] Treaties concluded under duress are null and void as they must be based upon mutual consent. Finally, the stipulations of treaties must be specific, so that the rights and obligations of the parties are well defined and do not admit of different interpretations. The Koran warns against treaties with obscure stipulations in K 16:94 (*'Do not regard your oaths as merely intrigue amongst you, so that a foot slip after it has been set firm, and ye taste evil for having turned* [*people*] *aside from the way of Allah and for you there be in store a punishment mighty'*).[115]

Under the heading international relations in wartime, we find, after a general discussion on lawful and unlawful wars, that we have dealt with before, the rules concerning declaration of war or ultimatum. This is the modern version of the summons to Islam (*daʿwah*), which according to the classical doctrine, must in some cases precede fighting. [116] Contrary to the classical rules, modern authors assert that previous notification of an attack accompanied by a summons to Islam or to the acceptance of *djizyah* is obligatory in all cases. Its aim is not only to warn the civil population in enemy territory of the coming hostilities, but also to inform the enemy that Islam fights for a religious cause and not for conquest or worldly gain. Proudly, the authors conclude that the Islamic injunctions concerning declaration of war are thirteen centuries older than modern international codification in this domain as embodied in the *Hague Convention on the Opening of Hostilities* of 1907. These rules, however, our authors hasten to add, are hardly observed in the West, as surprise attacks have rather become the rule than the exception. They ascribe this phenomenon to the fundamental weakness of positive international law, which lacks a religious or moral sanction, contrary to Islamic law.[117]

The law of warfare is the pet subject of modernist authors. Usually they give a selective anthology of the most humane regulations to be found in the classical works on *fiqh*[118] and compare them with modern international conventions on warfare. Characteristic is the subsequent quotation that follows an enumeration of the acts forbidden by modern conventions:

> As we have already said, Islam forbids all this and even more. It forbids to kill and to fight the wounded, it forbids to fight those who have shed their weapons, it forbids to kill monks and religious dignitaries and to destroy their cells and churches. Islam forbids sabotage, whereas modern international law allows the destruction of highways, bridges and anything that can be of use to the enemy.[119]

In general, they adopt the terminology of the modern regulations on warfare. Thus, the prohibition of killing women, infants and decrepit old men, is put on a par with the modern prohibition to attack the civilian population. Only occasionally is attention paid to the modern technological development of warfare. One author goes into the question whether Islam allows the use of the atomic bomb. On the strength of K 8:60 (*'Prepare* [*ye*] *for them whatsoever force and cavalry ye are capable of* [*gathering*] *to overawe thereby the enemy of Allah and your own . . .'*) he concludes that its production is permitted. Its use, however, is restricted to retaliation or defence in case of a nuclear attack by the enemy, because of K 2:194 (*'So if any make an attack upon you, make a like attack upon them . . .'*).[120] One other author touches upon modern methods of warfare. But as he is carried away by his enthusiasm over alleged early Moslem inventions of poisonous gas and the use of gliders in battles, he hardly goes into the legal implications, except that he holds that modern conventions on warfare, in as far as they have been adhered to by Moslem states, form part of Islamic international law.[121] Finally, some authors mention that Islam prohibits attacks upon ambulances, medical orderlies and stretcher bearers.[122]

According to classical doctrine, the *Imām* has the choice between four policies with regard to prisoners of war; he may kill them, enslave them, exchange them against a ransom or he may liberate them without any condition.[123] Modern authors, however, argue on the strength of K 47:4 (*'So when you meet those who have disbelieved* [*let there be*] *slaughter until when ye have made havoc of them, bind* [*them*] *fast* [i.e. take prisoners]*; then either freely or by ransom* [i.e. liberate them out of kindness or in return for ransom]*; until war lays down its burdens'*), that the *Imām*'s choice is restricted to liberating them with or without ransom. Killing of prisoners of war is forbidden according to these authors, who also adduce the opinion of some early lawyers in support of their theory. Individual prisoners, however, may be killed if there is some specific reason for it. Thus they explain the historical instances of killing of prisoners during Mohammed's lifetime. As to enslavement, they hold that in early days this was permitted, since the enemy acted likewise with Moslem prisoners of war. They found this opinion on K 16:126 (*'If ye take vengeance, take it only in the measure that vengeance was taken from you'*). Many authors remark that, just as the Geneva convention of 1929 prescribes, Islam considers prisoners of war as prisoners of the state and not as prisoners of the individuals or military units that have captured them. Prisoners of war must be treated well, fed and clothed. This prescription derives from K 76:8 (*'They give food for His love to the poor, the orphan and the prisoner'*).[124]

As the treatment of *amān* by modern authors remains within the traditional framework and does not offer striking examples of modernist interpretation, I shall not go into it, but proceed with the rules concerning the conclusion of war. The following possibilities are envisaged for wars to end: (1) mere cessation of hostilities; (2) victory of the Moslem army; (3) surrender of the enemy, i.e. conversion to Islam; and (4) treaty of peace or armistice.[125] Most authors, however, only discuss the last possibility, the termination of war by means of a treaty of peace or armistice. The crucial question in this connexion is whether the Moslems may conclude a permanent treaty of peace with unbelievers, since the classical doctrine only admits armistices with a limited duration or with a unilaterally revocable character.[126] As we have seen, most authors are of the opinion that in peace time all kinds of permanent treaties are allowed. Although they also profess that Moslems may conclude permanent peace treaties with their enemies in order to put an end to the war between them, they differ when it comes to details. For some assert that the only permanent treaty of peace that Islam allows is the pact of *dhimmah*. As this implies that the non-Moslems must recognize the suzerainty of the Islamic state and pay a special tax, the *djizyah*, one cannot really call it a treaty of peace. It rather has the character of surrender. Besides the pact of *dhimmah*, they only admit of temporary armistices. Thus they remain within the scope of the classical doctrine.[127] Other authors, however, hold that permanent treaties of peace other than the pact of *dhimmah* are possible, provided that the propagation of Islam is secured and is not subject to any hindrance on the part of the other state.[128]

It is evident that the writings I have discussed in this chapter have a highly apologetic character. The classical doctrine of jihad has been stripped of its militancy and is represented as an adequate legal system for maintaining peace in the domain of international relations. Emphasis is laid upon the ethical values underlying this system. Islamic international law, according to our Moslem Panglosses, is the best of all possible systems. It surpasses positive international law in peacefulness, tolerance, respect for human dignity, denunciation of colonialism and exploitation, fidelity to pledges and humanity. To enhance these exalted principles, they contrast them with the wicked practices of contemporary international intercourse, rife with dishonesty, atrocities and outrages against humanity. Moreover, many authors extol the legal genius of Islam, as it has been able to develop a theory of international law, long before modern international law came into being. This theory, they argue, is adaptable to satisfy present-day conditions and offers solutions to problems that modern international law has until yet not been able to cope with. Its superiority is a consequence of its religious character that bestows a moral sanction on it. As a result, its enforcement is achieved in a better way than in positive international law. The writings on Islamic international law are typically part of the mainstream of apologetic writings that defend Islam against an unfavourable image that used to be prevalent in the West. Apart from jihad, this defence is concerned with the position of women, slavery, penal law, human rights and the like. In all these fields, it is claimed that the Islamic rules can easily stand comparison with Western institutions.

5

Conclusions

In Chapter 3 we have analyzed the political aspect of jihad in modern history or, more specifically, to what extent the doctrine of jihad played a role in anti-colonial resistance in the Islamic world. During the early stages of colonial expansion, resistance was organized in religious movements that appealed to the doctrine of jihad in order to mobilize the population and to justify the struggle against the Western – Christian – rulers. I have described four movements of this type, viz. the *Ṭarīqa-i Muḥammadī* in India, ʿAbd al-Qādir's movement in Algeria, the Mahdist movement in Sudan and the Sanūsiyyah in its struggle against the Italians in Libya. In the societies where these movements arose, there was no clear distinction between the realm of politics and that of religion. Like in many pre-capitalist societies religion dominated the entire ideological superstructure. No wonder that movements of protest and resistance assumed an outwardly religious character. Islamic history offers a great many instances of this phenomenon, which, it may be added here, can also be observed in European history, as the example of the Anabaptist movement in Germany and the Low Countries may show.

The Islamic movements that developed in opposition to European colonial expansion show many common traits. Their leaders explained colonial expansion by pointing to the weakness of their own societies, which had given the European powers a chance to intrude into the Islamic world. The ultimate cause of this weakness was, in their view, religious laxity and decay and the abandonment of the pristine principles of Islam. Hence they could propose a clear and simple remedy: purification of Islam by returning to its original principles and purging it of un-Islamic innovations and corruption. They stressed the monotheistic character of Islam and rejected all kinds of polytheism (*shirk*) and unbelief (*kufr*). In fact, these movements fought on two fronts. On the one hand they strove for the purification of their own societies and attacked established institutions and practices that were, in the view of their leaders, incompatible with true Islam. On the other hand they waged an armed struggle against colonial rule which they totally rejected. Both aims converged in their endeavours to establish a purely Islamic state, where the *sharīʿah* was to be the supreme law. The four movements that I have described, succeeded in forming state-like nuclei with, however, flowing boundaries, due to the continuous warfare against the colonial powers. Within these states the *sharīʿah* was applied in its full vigour. Special stress was laid on the application of the Islamic taxes, which obviously reveals a widespread discontent with the existing systems of taxation. As a consequence of the existence of these state-like nuclei, the doctrine of *hidjrah* could be invoked after the example of the prophet Mohammed. This could serve as a subsidiary means of mobilization, as according to this doctrine those Moslems who were living outside the boundaries of the newly founded Islamic states and were subjected to non-Moslem rule, were obliged to emigrate to Islamic territory, thus reinforcing the Islamic camp. The organization of these movements resembled to a great degree that of the religious orders, the *ṭuruq*, in that they were based on a strict hierarchy and on a strong personal bond between the followers and their leader, formalized by an oath of allegiance, the *bayʿah*. That this was the case in Algeria and Libya is obvious, as the Qādiriyyah *ṭarīqah* in Algeria and the Sanūsiyyah *ṭarīqah* in Libya were the organizational pivots of anti-colonial resistance. In India and the Sudan, the *Ṭarīqa-i Muḥammadī* and the Mahdist movements respectively, pretended to supersede all existing *ṭuruq*. This, however, did not prevent them of borrowing their organizational model.

In reading the texts composed by the leaders of these movements or their propagandists one is struck by the appropriateness of the Koranic texts quoted by them to their circumstances. In fact, one can easily compare these circumstances with those of the nascent Islamic state under the leadership of the prophet Mohammed. The practical problems that Mohammed had to cope with were to a great extent similar to those which faced these puritanical movements fighting against colonial penetration: difficulty of recruitment due to the lukewarm reactions of their followers, tribal rivalries, financial difficulties and collaboration with the enemy. Hence, the leaders of these movements could readily resort to the Koranic verses dealing with these problems, rather than to the works on *fiqh* that hardly treated most of these topics. This can be explained by the fact that the Koran, and, for that matter, early Tradition came into existence in a period when the Moslems were constantly involved in warfare, whereas the *fiqh* was only laid down when the wars of conquest had ceased.

During the periods of early colonial expansion, only Islam could supply a unifying ideology that would motivate Moslems to join hands in an anti-colonialist struggle. However, as these Islamic movements strove for the establishment of a more or less centralized state, ruled by the *sharīʿah*, and thus threatened vested interests, they were from their inception faced with the problem of opposition on the part of groups that wanted to defend their privileges. The old ruling classes that had lost their lucrative positions, tribes that had been deprived of their fiscal privileges, rivalling *ṭuruq* that had lost their monopoly of dispensing justice and collecting the *zakāh* tax, these were the groups that were bent upon bringing about the failure of the new states. In order to achieve this, they often collaborated with the colonial enemy, despite the fulminations against them based on their transgression of religious precepts. Although this opposition has certainly contributed to the ultimate defeat of these movements, the main reason must be sought in the military and technical superiority of the colonial adversaries. The very existence of these militant movements, however, may have hastened European expansion in the areas where they operated. Had it not been for these nuclei of armed resistance at the frontiers of territories occupied by European powers, the latter would probably have delayed or even stopped their conquest. In the face of the constant threat from without, which also affected the attitude of the Moslems under their rule, they felt compelled to extirpate these inimical movements and to enlarge their territory.

A belated instance of a typical jihad-movement was the organization of *Shaykh* ʿIzz al-Dīn al-Qassām in Palestine. Ideologically this organization bore great resemblance to the earlier jihad-movements.

Its main inspiration was religious. Rejecting all foreign non-Moslem domination, it saw armed struggle as the only way of liberating Palestine from the British and the zionists. Although it was only active for a short while, it has exerted great influence during the 1936-1939 revolt in Palestine. In a way al-Qassām's movement was anachronistic, operating in a society where politics were dominated by a westernized elite that formulated its political goals in secular, nationalist terms and recognized foreign domination to the extent that it was prepared to negotiate with the British and sometimes even to cooperate with them. However, al-Qassām's movement certainly reflected the spirit of the mainly rural masses that suffered from the economic transformation of the country and had ceased to expect anything of the nationalist politicians.

The ʿUrābī revolt was different from the typical jihad-movements. It had originated as a movement of Arabic-speaking officers and, at a somewhat later stage, Arab landowners and civil servants, against the dominating position of the Turco-Circassian ruling class, that blocked their promotion and access to state power. The National Party that voiced their demands was never radical and advocated a reformist policy. It can only be regarded as opposed to European intervention inasmuch as it denounced the abuses of Anglo-French financial control and the privileged position of foreigners. Only when the movement became powerful and the British, out of fear for their financial and strategical interests, invaded the country, did this movement assume an anti-colonial character and offer armed resistance against the foreign occupiers. Since secular nationalism, which would have been more suitable to express its demands, did not or hardly exist at that time, it had recourse to the doctrine of jihad in order to mobilize the population. The movement itself and the political demands it had formulated, were not, as the jihad-movements were, dominated by religion. Religion played a role inasfar as it provided a sentiment of cohesion against the foreign enemy and this religious aspect was reinforced by the fact that religious dignitaries served as channels of propaganda. A further difference lies in the fact that, whereas the jihad-movements strove at establishing new states, to be ruled by the *sharīʿah*, ʿUrābī waged his struggle within the framework of the already existing Egyptian state. Although there were doubts as to the legality of ʿUrābī's authority, his struggle must nevertheless be viewed as the defence of a state against foreign intruders. As such it was a war between national states, whereby ʿUrābī could employ the normal state organs such as the army and the administrative apparatus. Just as the ʿUrābī movement was different from the earlier anti-colonial movements in the Islamic world, the use of the doctrine of jihad during the few months of Egyptian resistance against the British had deviated from its earlier models. Whereas the doctrine of jihad in the earlier jihad-movements was integrated in a puritanistic and revivalist Islamic ideology, it was now more or less isolated, since the ʿUrābī revolt did not take place in an exclusively religious ideological framework, and had a merely mobilisatory and propagandistic purpose.

This propagandistic aspect was even stronger and more manifest in the Ottoman jihad-declaration of 1914. The *fatwās* and the concomitant declarations were war-propaganda pure and simple, aimed at creating support for the Ottoman cause amongst the Moslem peoples under Russian, French and British colonial rule. It was intended for external, more than for internal consumption, and appealed to Pan-Islamic feelings. This appeal, however, failed. Nowhere did Moslems under colonial rule rise in large-scale revolts. This was mainly due to colonial oppression, but another reason lies in the fact that Pan-Islamism was no organized political movement. Although Pan-Islamic feelings were widespread, the strength of these feelings was grossly overrated in the West. The cry for Islamic unity had been raised by some Moslem intellectuals who began to discern the world-wide character of European imperialism. Unification of all Moslems was, in their view, the only way to block further colonial expansion. This ideological tendency coincided with the Ottoman ambitions towards a greater influence in the Islamic world by playing on the title of Caliph, one of the titles of the Ottoman sultan, with the implication that the Ottoman sultan was the spiritual leader of all Moslems, just as the Pope is the spiritual head of all Catholics. This policy was consciously pursued, especially *vis-à-vis* the Western powers and met to some extent with success. Thus we see that in the

Ottoman Empire the domain of politics had become separated from that of religion, in the sense that the latter was consciously used in pursuance of secular political aims. Despite the religious institutions connected with the state, and despite the religious authority of the Sultan, the Ottoman state had undergone a certain process of secularization, partly as a result of direct political pressure by the Western powers and partly as a consequence of the social and economic transformation of the country owing to Western economic penetration. As far as the doctrine of jihad is concerned, we can observe that its use had become part of the stock of propagandistic methods to be invoked by the state whenever it thought its use expedient.

This widening gulf between politics and religion that made the call for jihad dependent upon its political expediency and not upon the objective conditions laid down by the *sharīʿah*, became more manifest during the struggles of the Moslem peoples against foreign domination in the course of this century. Having realized that full-scale armed revolt had no chance to succeed in the face of the military superiority of the colonial powers, and being convinced that a greater amount of freedom could only be obtained by Western political methods such as negotiation and persuasion, occasionally backed up by mass demonstrations, their political leaders were not inclined to declare jihad. This is very clear with regard to Egypt and the Fertile Crescent, where there operated still other factors preventing the use of the jihad doctrine. Anti-colonial politics there were dominated by nationalism, either Arab nationalism or Egyptian nationalism. Both were based on ethnic and cultural and not on religious solidarity, and Christian Arabs played a significant role in the various national parties. Moreover, Arab nationalism, which was dominant in the Fertile Crescent, had developed in opposition to the centralizing tendencies within the Ottoman Empire, the bulwark of Islamic orthodoxy. Hence, it had a distinctly secular character. However, even where these factors did not exist and anti-colonial politics were based on Moslem communalism, as was the case on the Indian subcontinent, the doctrine of jihad has not been invoked.[1] Thus we see that the doctrine of jihad did not play any important part in nationalist politics in the Islamic world in this century. There was, however, one political issue, in connection with which the call for jihad has several times been raised: the zionist colonization of Palestine. Although the Palestinian nationalist leaders, just as their colleagues in the neighbouring countries, had not called for jihad, yet they had played on religious feelings by means of their campaign for the rescue of the holy places in order to gain support all over the Islamic world. When the situation in Palestine became critical for the Arabs during the 1936-1939 revolt, Moslem leaders and religious dignitaries all over the Islamic world responded by issuing jihad-declarations. Their actual effect, however, was rather small. Some fund-raising campaigns were conducted, but no volunteers ever came to Palestine from the non-Arab Islamic world. These declarations must therefore be understood as Platonic statements of solidarity.

Besides the mainstream of nationalist politics, dominated by a westernized bourgeoisie, there arose, during the 1920s and 1930s some groups that bore great resemblance to the earlier jihad movements and operated within the same tradition of Islamic puritanism and revivalism. The best-known and most influential of these groups were the *Djamāʿat-i Islāmī* in Pakistan and the Society of Moslem Brethren (*Djamʿiyyat al-Ikhwān al-Muslimīn* in Egypt and Syria. These movements rejected the separation between politics and religion and strove for an Islamic state, ruled by the *sharīʿah*. They did not consider themselves political parties since that would imply that they accepted the basic principles of the secularized national state. Jihad, in the sense of armed struggle, was considered by them as the way to achieve their aim, as we can learn from a slogan of the Eyptian Brethren: 'Allah is our goal. The Prophet is our leader. The Koran is our constitution. Struggle (*djihād*) is our way (*sabīl*). Death in the service of Allah is the loftiest of our wishes. Allah is great, Allah is great'.[2] They were not only concerned with the struggle against colonialism, but also with that against those regimes that prevented the full-scale application of the *sharīʿah* and did not take the Koran as their constitution. As for the Egyptian Brethren, they actively participated in armed struggles. During 1947-1948 many Brethren came to the rescue of the Palestinians in their fight against the zionists and in 1952 bands consisting of Brethren attacked the British army in the Suez Canal Zone. After the Egyptian revolution of 1952 they did not shun the use of violence against the political leaders of the country, which ultimately led to their dissolution by the government and the execution of a number of their leaders. The strength of these movements and their large popular following show that the secularization of politics is limited to a small westernized elite and has not fully permeated all Moslem classes. This conclusion is corroborated by the events during the Palestinian revolt of 1936-1939 when the peasant bands that operated independently from the national leadership expressed their feelings in religious terms and used the concept of jihad.

At present the political role of jihad seems to lie exclusively in the field of propaganda with regard to the Arab-Israeli conflict. However, with the exception of Saudi Arabia, secularization of politics has progressed to the extent that the governments do not issue jihad-declarations anymore. The Ottoman State in the beginning of this century was secularized to a certain degree, but the Sultan-Caliph still claimed religious authority and on the strength of that jihad-declarations were issued at the outbreak of the First World War. Modern governments in the Islamic world do not claim this authority anymore. Although they call themselves 'Islamic' in their constitutions and stipulate that the *sharīʿah* is one of the sources of the law, this has significance in the domain of justice only, hardly any in that of politics. Therefore, they leave it to the *ʿulamāʾ* to appeal to the doctrine of jihad in case of war against a non-Moslem state, in practice Israel.[3] The function of this is to secure maximal internal support for the national war efforts and, to a lesser degree, to gain political support from other Islamic countries. In countries with a large Christian minority, Christian leaders also issue declarations in order to lend religious sanction to the war. Jihad-declarations have now become downright statements of support for war explicitly based upon national considerations. Jihad is now, if we are to believe ʿAbd al-Ḥalīm Maḥmūd, at the time Shaykh al-Azhar, a national duty, incumbent upon Moslems as well as Christians.[4]

Summing up, we can discern the following evolution in the

political significance of the idea of jihad in modern history. During the first stages of colonial expansion in the Islamic world, the doctrine of jihad provided a suitable ideology for movements of resistance, since these formulated their goals entirely in religious terms and rejected therefore all foreign, non-Moslem rule. They tried to mobilize the Moslem masses in order to offer resistance against foreign invaders. Owing to the unequal balance of powers, these movements ultimately failed to achieve their aim, the establishment of a truly Islamic state. The social and economic transformation brought about by Western penetration, and the increasing cultural impact of the West resulted in a process of secularization of politics: politics came to be separated from religion and nationalism was to become the ideology of resistance against foreign domination. In view of the prevailing military superiority of the colonial powers, the westernized elite that dominated nationalist politics, adopted western political methods and only occasionally resorted to violence. These factors were incompatible with the use of the doctrine of jihad. As a reaction against the growing Western influence and in opposition to the nationalist groups whose activities often balanced on the verge of collaboration with the colonial powers, a fundamentalist tendency rose during the 1920s and 1930s, embodied in organizations like the Society of Moslem Brethren and the *Djamāʿat i Islāmī*. These groups operated within the tradition of the earlier, religiously inspired anti-colonial movements. They did not recognize a separation between religion and politics and jihad was an essential part of their ideology. Despite their large popular support, they were suppressed by the national governments after independence. As a result of decolonization and the formation of sovereign national states that were to a great extent secularized, the doctrine of jihad lost its significance in politics. Only with regard to the Arab-Israeli conflict jihad continues to play a certain role. Saudi Arabia excepted, jihad declarations are now being issued not by the state, but by religious authorities that have increasingly come to identify jihad with national war. Thus the doctrine of jihad has entirely been relegated to the realm of subsidiary religious propaganda for national politics.

We now come to the second part of our original questions: how did the doctrine of jihad develop during the modern period, or, more specifically, what was the impact of colonial expansion upon the doctrine of jihad? The change in ideas with regard to jihad has been the subject-matter of Chapter IV of this study. The need to come to a new interpretation of the doctrine of jihad was felt after the defeat of the jihad-movements and the subsequent awareness of Moslem thinkers of the fact that the colonial powers were firmly established in large parts of the Islamic world. They realized the futility of large-scale armed resistance in the face of the military superiority of the colonial rulers. Some of them justified their position of quiescence by referring to the classical rule that the Moslems are not bound to wage jihad if they do not stand any chance of gaining the victory and *fatwās* to this effect were solicited and obtained by colonial governments.[5] By invoking this rule, they left the jihad obligation basically intact, but regarded it as being temporarily suspended. The Moslem modernists, however, followed a different path by elaborating a new interpretation that restricted the obligation to wage jihad.

This new interpretation was first formulated in India. After the bloody suppression of the 1857 revolt the Moslem upper and middle classes were singled out as scapegoats by the British. They suffered from discrimination with regard to government employment and the military profession. Realizing that British rule was firmly rooted in India, that close cooperation with the British was the only means of putting an end to this discrimination, and that continuation of British rule would protect them from Hindu domination, they wanted to win the favour of the British by showing that Moslems could be loyal subjects of the British Crown. This involved a new interpretation of the jihad-doctrine so as to demonstrate that Moslems were not obliged by their religion to offer armed resistance against colonial rule. Sayyid Aḥmad Khān, their most outstanding intellectual representative, supplied this new interpretation by restricting the scope of the jihad-obligation to wars for religious reasons, i.e. armed struggle in order to defend Moslems against religious oppression, and excluding from it wars for temporal reasons like e.g. wars for territorial conquest or armed resistance against civil oppression. Since the British did not aim at the extirpation of Islam and did not hinder the Moslems from performing their religious duties, jihad against them was, in his view, unlawful. By distinguishing between religious and secular aims, Aḥmad Khān prepared the way for a separation between religion and politics and thus for the secularization of politics.

Although the Indian discussion on jihad during the 1870s and 1880s was directly occasioned by the political situation of the Indian Moslems and the British attitudes towards them, it must also be placed within the context of Islamic modernism. This current of thought, which was to gain acceptance all over the Islamic world, originated in India. The Indian Moslems were the first to articulate modernist ideas in a coherent and systematic way. Just as the leaders of the jihad-movements, they were well aware of the weakness of the Islamic world. But unlike them, they were acquainted with the West and Western culture. Conscious of the overwhelming technical, economic and military superiority of the West, they thought that the source of this superiority was to be found in the character of Western culture and ideas and in Western methods of education. The remedy for the backwardness of Islamic society was, in their view, the adoption of Western values and ideals and the introduction of Western educational models. Rejecting the rigidity of the blind imitation of the early religious authorities (*taqlīd*), they claimed a right to reinterpret the sources of Islam (*idjtihād*). Thus they set out to expound Islam in such a way as to show that its basic principles were not opposed to the nineteenth-century values like Progress, Science, Liberty, Tolerance, etc., sometimes going at great length to prove that Islam had fostered these values even before they gained currency in the West. In doing so, they had a double purpose in mind. On the one hand they wanted to remove religious obstacles for the introduction of Western culture and sciences. On the other hand they were thus defending Islam against Western ideological attacks. This latter aim gave many of their writings a distinct apologetical flavour. Since the doctrine of jihad was a major target of the occidental ideological attacks, this topic occupied an important position in the apologetical literature. Concludingly we can say that the writings on jihad by the Indian modernists were determined by three closely connected tendencies: the desire for a *rapprochement* between the Indian Moslems and the British, the wish to reform Islam in order to remove religious impediments for the introduction and adoption of Western culture and, finally, the need to defend Islam against ideological attacks from the West.

The modernist writings on jihad that were published in other parts of the Islamic world, and particularly in Egypt, had much in common with Indian modernist literature. They lacked, however, the ardent sympathy for the West and Western culture. The Egyptian reformer Muḥammad ʿAbduh never enthusiastically supported the British rule in Egypt, as Aḥmad Khan had done in India. Yet he was not really opposed to the British, especially after his return from exile, since he had an open eye for the advantages of the British presence in Egypt as a means of bringing progress to the country. Later thinkers such as his pupil, Rashīd Riḍā, became increasingly more critical of the West. Thus the strongest stimulus for the Indian Moslems to write on jihad, the desire to win the favour of the British and to cooperate with them, was absent in Egyptian modernism. This explains the difference between the ideas on jihad in Indian and Egyptian modernism. These ideas agreed as far as the defensive character of jihad was concerned. The Indian notion of jihad, however, was more restrictive, as the Indian modernists confined it to wars of defence against religious oppression. The Egyptian modernists held that jihad was a struggle against all kinds of oppression, both religious and political. This implied that the struggle against colonial domination could be classified as jihad, precisely that what the Indian modernists had wanted to exclude. Under the influence of Djamāl al-Dīn al-Afghānī, many Egyptian modernists called for jihad against colonialism, and later, against zionism and communism, without abandoning the thesis that jihad is essentially defensive. These calls, however, were of little more than academic interest. The struggle against colonial domination was, as we have seen, waged under the banner of nationalism and the calls for jihad were no more than the expression of support for this struggle on the part of the religious authorities.

The apologetical approach of the modernists does not only show itself in the notion that jihad is defensive warfare. An important place in modernist writings is taken by the exposition of the laws of warfare, with the aim of showing that these laws are based upon lofty principles such as tolerance and humanity and that they guarantee the protection of religious liberty and peaceful coexistence between the various nations and religious groups. In this, according to the modernist authors, the Islamic prescriptions compare favourably with present-day positive international law of Western origin. These points are eleborated in those books that present the doctrine of jihad as Islamic international public law. The aim of these books is merely apologetical and not mobilisatory. They have a theoretical and academic character since their authors are well aware of the fact that Islamic international law is nowhere being applied. Some of them, however, expressly advocate its implementation, arguing that, because of its lofty standards, it will contribute to world peace and the welfare of mankind. Other authors propose that Islamic international law be applied in the sphere of international relations between Islamic states. This movement, which strives for the reintroduction of the *sharīʿah* in the domain of international relations, is part of a more general tendency that favours the application of the *sharīʿah* in civil and penal law. It has started as a corollary of nationalism. Resentment against Western domination, both politically and culturally, led to a search for indigenous cultural values, deriving from the Islamic cultural tradition. In the domain of law, the predominance of Western codes and Western juridical principles was resented and the reintroduction of Islamic law and its underlying principles in their stead was proposed. For a long time, this movement booked little progress, except that by way of lip service in some constitutions and civil codes the *sharīʿah* is mentioned as one of the sources in case of silence of the law. Recently, however, one can observe a break-through in this field: a number of Islamic states have reintroduced the Koranic punishments for certain offences like theft and drinking alcohol. In the domain of international relations, however, it is hardly to be expected that the *sharīʿah* will ever be applied.

Although the modernist interpretation that underscores the defensive character of jihad is now widely accepted and is being taught in schools as a generaly received theory, it is not the only interpretation that one meets in present-day writings on the subject. Apart from the few authors that expound the doctrine of jihad in the traditional way by copying the phrases from the classical works on *fiqh*, there exists a distinct fundamentalist school of thought that combines traditional content with a highly modernized vocabulary. This tendency has found its political expression in movements like the *Djamāʿat-i Islāmī* in Pakistan and the Society of Moslem Brethren in the Middle East. Their ideology is entirely dominated by religion and they do not recognize a separation between politics and religion. Hence they reject nationalism and recognize only religious solidarity. Continuing the tradition of the earlier jihad movements, their aim is to establish Islamic rule all over the earth. Thus they want 'to liberate mankind', i.e. to create circumstances wherein one can freely choose to be converted to Islam or not. They strongly condemn the existing governments in the Islamic world, since, in their view, these are not really Islamic, being based on the authority of man and not on the authority of Allah. Jihad is the means of achieving their aims and they consider it as a 'permanent revolutionary struggle' for the propagation of Islam. Thus they emphasize the expansionist character of jihad. Just as the modernist tendency, this self-assertive current must be regarded as a reaction against Western political and cultural influence. But whereas the modernists reacted by conforming to Western values and accepting Western political concepts, in order to show that Islam is a 'respectable' religion, fundamentalists have expressly rejected these and try to seek their inspiration in Islam only, emphasizing the real Islamic values and opposing them to occidental culture. They vehemently denounce the modernists' view of jihad which they regard as defeatism in the face of Western attacks, and hold that one cannot apply categories like 'offensive' and 'defensive' to the concept of jihad. Jihad as a struggle for the propagation of Islam is good in itself and need not be justified by moral values that are alien to Islam.

By way of conclusion we can say that the modern views on jihad are the expression of certain attitudes towards colonial rule and Western culture. The Indian Moslems' view in the latter half of the nineteenth century that jihad is only to be waged in defence against religious oppression is clearly connected with the cooperative stand of the Indian middle and upper classes towards British colonial rule, which was dictated by their desire to secure their share in the administration and in the military professions, and with their conviction that the key to progress was to be found in Western culture. Their view on jihad, apart from being meant to bring home to the British that Moslems could loyally serve British colonial rule, shows that they had implicitly adopted values like the desirability of peaceful coexistence and of a separation between politics and religion. Later modernists – mainly concentrated in Egypt, but also to be found in other parts of the Islamic world – espoused the view that jihad is essentially a defensive struggle, regardless of whether this is against political or religious oppression. This view reflects the attitude of the Westernized elite that was critical of colonial domination and generally supported nationalist movements. At the same time, however, they appreciated Western culture and were convinced that Islamic society could benefit from it. The views on jihad being held by the fundamentalists, the heirs of the earlier jihad-movements, are in content identical to the classical doctrine and represent the attitude of the lower, mainly rural classes. They suffered most from the radical economic and social changes brought about by Western penetration. Having little direct contact with Western culture, they resorted to their own cultural tradition and especially Islam for the expression of their political feelings.

List of consulted works on *fiqh*

1. WORKS ON IKHTILĀF

(1) Muḥammad ibn Djarīr al-Ṭabarī (d. 310/923), *Kitāb ikhtilāf al-fuqahā'* (v. GAL I 149, S I 218: GAS I 328). Ed. by J. Schacht. Leyden: Brill, 1933, xvi + 274 pp.

(2) Abū l-Walīd Muḥammad ibn Aḥmad ibn Muḥammad ibn Rushḍ (Averroes) (d. 595/1198), *Bidāyat al-mudjtahid wa-nihāyat al-muqtaṣid*, 2 vols. (v. GAL S I 836). 3rd ed., Cairo: Muṣṭafā l-Bābī al-Ḥalabī, 1379/1960.

2. HANAFITE WORKS

(3) Muḥammad ibn Aḥmad al-Sarakhsī (d. 483/1090), *Sharḥ kitāb al-Siyar al-Kabīr li-Muḥammad al-Shaybānī* (d. 189/804), 5 vols. (v. GAL S I 291, 638; GAS I 430 ff.). Ed. by Ṣalāḥ al-Dīn al-Munadjdjid. Cairo: Maʿhad al-Makhṭūṭāt bi-l-Djāmiʿah al-ʿArabiyyah, 1971.

(4) Abū l-Ḥasan ʿAlī ibn Abī Bakr al-Marghīnānī (d. 593/1197), *al-Hidāyah sharḥ bidāyat al-mubtadi'*, 4 vols. (v. GAL S I 644). Cairo: Muṣṭafā l-Bābī al-Ḥalabī, 1384/1965.

(5) ʿAbd al-Raḥmān ibn Muḥammad Shaykhzādeh (d. 1078/1667), *Madjmaʿ al-anhur sharḥ multaqā l-abḥur* (by Ibrāhīm al-Ḥalabī, d. 956/1549), 2 vols. (v. GAL S II 643). Istanbul: Dār al-ʿAmirah li-l-Ṭibāʿah, 1301 H.

(6) Muḥammad Amīn ibn ʿĀbidīn (d. 1252/1836), *Radd al-muḥtār ʿalā l-durr al-mukhtār* (by Muḥammad ibn ʿAlī al-Ḥaṣkafī, d. 1088/1677), *sharḥ tanwīr al-abṣār* (by Muḥammad ibn ʿAbd Allāh al-Timirtāshī, d. 1004/1595), 5 vols. (v. GAL S II 428, 773). Būlāq: Dār al-Ṭibāʿah al-Amīriyyah, 1299 H.

3. MALIKITE WORKS

(7) Saḥnūn ibn Saʿīd al-Tanūkhī (d. 240/854), *al-Mudawwanah al-kubrā*, 16 vols. (v. GAL S I 229/300; GAS I 469 ff.). Cairo: Maṭbaʿat al-Saʿādah, 1323 H.

(8) Ṣāliḥ ʿAbd al-Samīʿ al-Azharī (d. ?), *al-Thamr al-dānī fī taqrīb al-maʿānī sharḥ Risālat ibn Abī Zayd al-Qayrawānī* (d. *c.* 386/996). (v. GAL I 177, S I 301; GAS I 478; Azharī and his commentary, however, are not mentioned). Cairo: Muṣṭafā l-Bābī al-Ḥalabī, 1363/1944, 531 pp.

(9) Abū l-Qāsim Muḥammad ibn Aḥmad ibn Djuzayy (d. 741/1340), *al-Qawānīn al-fiqhiyyah* (v. GAL S II 377). New and rev. ed. N.p., n.d., 350 pp.

(10) Abū ʿAbd Allāh Muḥammad ibn Muḥammad al-Ḥaṭṭāb (d. 953/1546), *Mawāhib al-djalīl li-sharḥ mukhtaṣar Khalīl* (d. 767/1365), 6 vols. (v. GAL 11 84). Tripoli (Libya): Maktabat al-Nadjāḥ, n.d.

(11) Abū ʿAbd Allāh Muḥammad ibn Yūsuf al-Mawwāq (d. 896/1492), *al-Tādj wa-l-iklīl li-mukhtaṣar Khalīl*, 6 vols. (v. GAL II 84). Tripoli: Maktabat al-Nadjāḥ, n.d. (printed in the margin of Ḥaṭṭāb's *Mawāhib al-djalīl.*).

(12) Muḥammad ibn ʿArafah al-Dasūqī (d. 1230/1815), *Ḥāshiyah ʿalā l-sharḥ al-kabīr* (a commentary on Khalīl's *Mukhtaṣar* by al-Dardīr, d. 1201/1786), 4 vols. (v. GAL II 84, 485). Cairo: Dār Iḥyā' al-Kutub al-ʿArabiyyah, n.d.

4. SHAFIʿITE WORKS

(13) Muḥammad ibn Idrīs al-Shāfiʿī (d. 204/820; GAS I 486), *Kitāb al-Umm*, 7 vols. (GAL I 190, S I 304). Būlāq: al-Maṭbaʿah al-Kubrā al-Amīriyyah, 1321-1325 H.

(14) Abū l-Ḥasan ʿAlī ibn Muḥammad al-Māwardī (d. 450/1058), *al-Aḥkām al-sulṭāniyyah* (v. GAL I 386, S I 668). 2nd impr. Cairo: Muṣṭafā l-Bābī al-Ḥalabī, 1386/1966, 264 pp.

(15) Abū Zakariyā' Yaḥyā ibn Sharaf al-Nawawī (d. 676/1278), *Minhādj al-ṭālibīn* (v. GAL I 395). Ed. by L. W. C. van den Berg, *Le guide des zélés croyants, Manuel de jurisprudence selon le rite de Chāfiʿi.* Texte ar. . . . *avec tr. et ann.* 3 vols. Batavia: Impr. du Gouvernement, 1882-1884.

(16) Badr al-Dīn Abū ʿAbd Allāh Muḥammad ibn Burhān al-Dīn Abī Isḥāq Ibrāhīm ibn Djamāʿah (d. 733/1333), *Taḥrīr al-aḥkām fī tadbīr millat al-Islām* (v. GAL II 74). Ed. by H. Kofler. *Islamica*, Vol. VI, pp. 349-411, Vol. VII, pp. 1-34.

(17) Ibrāhīm al-Bādjūrī (d. 1276/1860), *Ḥāshiyah ʿalā Fatḥ al-Qarīb* (by Ibn Qāsim al-Ghazzī, d. 918/1512), *sharḥ al-Taqrīb fī l-fiqh* (by Abū Shudjāʿ, d. 500/1106), 2 vols. (v. GAL I 392, II 487). Cairo: ʿĪsā l-Bābī al-Ḥalabī. 1340/1922.

5. HANBALITE WORKS

(18) Abū Muḥammad ʿAbd Allāh ibn Aḥmad ibn Muḥammad ibn Qudāmah (d. 620/1223), *al-Mughnī sharḥ ʿalā Mukhtaṣar al-Khiraqī* (d. 333/944), 10 vols. (all publ.). (v. GAL I 398; GAS I 513). Ed. by Ṭāhā Muḥammad al-Zaynī, a.o. Cairo: Maktabat al-Qāhirah, 1388-89/1968-69.

(19) Abū l-ʿAbbās Aḥmad ibn ʿAbd al-Ḥalīm ibn Taymiyya (d. 728/1328), *al-Siyāsah al-sharʿiyyah fī iṣlāḥ al-rāʿī wa-l-raʿiyyah* (v. GAL II 127, S II 124-5). Ed. by Muḥammad Ibrāhīm al-Bannā and Muḥammad Aḥmad ʿĀshūr. Cairo: Dār al-Shaʿb, 1971, 191 pp.

6. ZAHIRITE WORKS

(20) Abū Muḥammad ʿAlī ibn Aḥmad ibn Saʿīd ibn Ḥazm (d. 456/1064), *al-Muḥallā*, 11 vols. (v. GAL S I 695). Beirut: al-Maktab al-tidjārī li-l-ṭibāʿah wa-l-nashr wa-l-tawzīʿ, n.d., al-Mawsūʿah al-Islāmiyyah.

7. TWELVER SHIʿITE WORKS

(21) Djaʿfar ibn al-Ḥasan al-Ḥillī al-Muḥaqqiq al-Awwal (d. 676/1277), *Sharāʾiʿ al-Islām fī masāʾil al-ḥalāl wa-l-ḥarām*, 4 vols. (v. GAL I 406, S I 711). Ed. by Abū Ḥusayn Muḥammad ʿAlī. al-Nadjaf: Maṭbaʿat al-Ādāb, 1389/1969.

8. ISMAʿILITE WORKS

(22) al-Nuʿmān ibn Muḥammad al-Tamīmī (known as al-Qāḍī l-Nuʿmān) (d. 363/974), *Daʿāʾim al-Islām fī l-ḥalāl wa-l-ḥarām wa-l-qaḍāyā wwl-aḥkām ʿan ahl Bayt Rasūl Allāh*, 2 vols. (v. GAL S I 325; GAS I 572, 576). Ed. by A. A. A. Fyzee. Cairo: Dār al-Maʿārif, 1370-79/1951-60.

Notes

NOTES TO CHAPTER 1: 'INTRODUCTION'

1. Cf. Willem Elsschot, *Lijmen*. In: *Verzameld Werk* (6th ed., Amsterdam; 1963), pp. 285-286, 302-303.
2. Cf. Muḥammad Ṣāliḥ Dja'far al-Ẓālimī, *Min al-fiqh al-siyāsī fī l-Islām* (Beirut: Dār Maktabat al-Ḥayāh, 1971), p. 44. The classical Shī'ite texts carefully distinguish between jihad, which has an expansive character and is conditional upon the presence of the Imam, and defensive wars, that are under certain conditions obligatory, regardless of whether the Imam is present or not. Despite this distinction, however, some Persian *'ulamā'* have called for jihad on the occasion of the wars between Russia and Iran in the nineteenth century, with the aim of enhancing their religious character and thereby increasing popular support. Cf. A. K. S. Lambton, 'A 19th century view on jihad', *SI* 32 (1970), pp. 181-192; Etan Kohlberg, 'The development of the Imāmī Shī'ī doctrine of jihād', *ZDMG* 126 (1976), pp. 64-86.
3. In this study I shall distinguish between 'modernism' and 'fundamentalism'. By modernism I understand those Islamic currents of thought that attempt to adapt Islam to 'modern life', i.e., the values and practices of Western, capitalist society. Fundamentalists are those that expressly reject Western influence and want to model society after the example of the early Islamic community. The terminology is not entirely satisfactory, since the modernists have also recourse to early Islam in order to find support for their new interpretations. However, I wanted to avoid the word conservative, since a distinction between modernists and conservatives could imply a value judgement, which I wanted to exclude.
4. H. Th. Obbink, *De heilige oorlog volgens den Koran* (Leiden: E. J. Brill, 1901), 123 pp.
5. Louis Mercier, *'Aly ben 'Abderrahman ben Hodeil el Andalusy. L'Ornement des âmes et la devise des habitants d'el Andalus. Traité de guerre sainte Islamique* (Paris: Geuthner, 1939), pp. 75-96.
6. Adriaan Reland, *Verhandeling van de godsdienst der Mahometaanen alsmede van het krygs-recht by haar ten tyde van oorlog tegens de Christenen gebruykelyk* (Utrecht: 1718; originally published in Latin).
7. Here I shall list only the most recent and important works:
(1) Alfred Morabia, *La Notion de gihad dans l'Islām médiéval. Des origines à al-Gazālī* (Thèse Univ. Paris IV, 1974; Lille: Service de réproduction des thèses

Université de Lille III, 1975), 638 pp. A comprehensive study dealing with the doctrinal aspects of jihad as well as with their historical setting.
(2) Wahbah al-Zuḥaylī, *Āthār al-ḥarb fī l-fiqh al-Islāmī. Dirāsah muqārinah* (Beirut: Dār al-Fikr, 1965), 890 pp. The richest and best documented account of the classical doctrine according to the various schools. In a number of cases, however, the author rides apologetical hobbyhorses, but since these elaborations are clearly distinguishable from his survey of the classical texts, they do not diminish the value of the book.
(3) Majid Khadduri, *War and Peace in the Law of Islam* (Baltimore, etc.: The Johns Hopkins Press, 1955), 321 pp. A good survey of the classical doctrine, though it lacks the depth of al-Zuḥaylī's work in that it has used considerably fewer primary sources on *fiqh*.
(4) Muhammad Hamidullah, *The Muslim conduct of State. Being a Treatise on Siyar, that is the Islamic Notion of Public International Law, Consisting of the Laws of Peace, War and Neutrality, Together with Precedents from Orthodox Practice and Preceded by a Historical and General Introduction* (3rd ed., Lahore: Sh. Muhammad Ashraf, 1953), 389 pp. Besides suffering from an apologetical approach, this work attempts to schematize the subject-matter according to concepts derived from modern public international law. Nevertheless it is one of the best of its kind owing to the author's erudition and extensive recourse to classical sources. It cannot, however, be regarded as representing the classical doctrine.
The same can be said of (5) Ahmed Rechid, 'L'Islam et le droit des gens'. In: *Académie de Droit International. Recueil des Cours – La Haye 1937* (Paris: Sirey, 1938), Vol. II, pp. 375-504.
(6) Albrecht Noth, *Heiliger Krieg und heiliger Kampf in Islam und Christentum. Beiträge zur Vorgeschichte und Geschichte der Kreuzzüge* (Bonn: Ludwig Röhrscheid Verlag, 1966; Bonner Historische Forschungen, 28), 160 pp. This study is mainly concerned with the historical setting of jihad immediately before and during the Crusades. The author attempts to compare the doctrine of jihad with parallel notions in Christianity.

8. Cf. A manifesto published by the Communist Party of Palestine in May, 1921: '. . . the struggle (*djihad*) against these capitalists, both Arabs and Jews . . .'. Full text in: Ghassān Kanafānī, 'Thawrat 1936-1939 fī Filasṭīn. Khalfiyyāt wa-tafāṣīl wa-taḥlīl', *Shu'ūn Filasṭīniyyah* 6 (Jan. 1972), p. 50.
9. Cf. Ṭāhā Ḥusayn, *Ḥadīth al-Arbiʿā'* (Cairo: Dār al-Maʿārif, n.d.), Vol. II, p. 3.
10. Cf. Ibrāhīm Khalīl Aḥmad, *Al-istishrāq wa-l-tabshīr wa-ṣilatuhumā bi-l-imbiriyāliyyah al-ʿālamiyyah* (Cairo: Maktabat al-Waʿy al-ʿArabī, 1973), p. 58.
11. On this point, cf. Noth (1966), pp. 47-61, 87-92.
12. Cf. *Fatāwā khaṭirah fī wudjūb al-djihād al-dīnī al-muqaddas li-inqādh Filasṭīn wa-ṣiyānat al-Masdjid al-Aqṣā wa-sā'ir al-muqaddasāt* (Cairo: al-Maṭbaʿah al-Salafiyyah, n.d.), 32 pp.; Muḥammad Ismāʿīl Ibrāhīm, *Al-djihād*

rukn al-Islām al-sādis (Cairo: Dār al-Fikr al-ʿArabī, 1964), pp. 56, 139; Muḥammad Faradj, *Al-madrasah al-ʿaskariyyah al-Islāmiyyah* (Cairo: Dār al-Fikr al-ʿArabī, n.d.), p. 26.

13. A typical example where this image is elaborated and brought into relation with the prescriptions of jihad is John Laffin's *The Arab Mind* (London, 1975).
14. Mercier (1939), p. 18.
15. ʿAbbās Maḥmūd al-ʿAqqād, *Mā yuqāl ʿan al Islām* (Cairo: Maṭbaʿat al-ʿUrūbah, n.d.), p. 168.
16. Maxime Rodinson, *Islam and Capitalism* (Engl. tr. by Brian Pearce. London: Allen Lane, 1974), 296 pp.

NOTES TO CHAPTER 2: 'THE DOCTRINE OF JIHAD IN CLASSICAL ISLAM'

1. Joseph Schacht, *An Introduction to Islamic Law* (London, etc.: Oxford University Press, 1964), pp. 205-206.
2. As for the primary sources of *fiqh* that I have consulted, see the Appendix, pp. 167-170. Further I have relied on the following secondary sources: Ömer Nasuhı Bilmen, *Hukuki Islamiyye ve Istılahatı Fıkhiyye Kamusu*, 6 vols. (Istanbul: Istanbul Üniversitesi Hukuk Fakültesi, 1949-1952); Muhammad Hamidullah, *Muslim Conduct of State* (3rd ed., Lahore: Sh. Muhammad Ashraf, 1953), 389 pp.; Majid Khadduri, *War and Peace in the Law of Islam* (Baltimore: The Johns Hopkins Press, 1955), 321 pp.; Alfred Morabia, *La Notion de ǧihad dans l'Islām médiéval. Des origines à al-Gazālī* (Thèse Univ. Paris IV, 1974; Lille: Service de réproduction des thèses, Université de Lille III, 1975), 638 pp.; Albrecht Noth, *Heiliger Krieg und heiliger Kampf in Islam und Christentum. Beiträge zur Vorgeschichte und Geschichte der Kreuzzüge* (Bonn: Röhrscheid Verlag, 1966; Bonner Historische Forschungen, 28), 160 pp.; Wahbah al-Zuḥaylī, *Āthār al-ḥarb fī l-fiqh al-Islāmī. Dirāsah muqārinah* (Beirut: Dār al-Fikr al-ʿArabī, 1965), 890 pp.
3. al-Tahānawī, *Kitāb kashshāf iṣṭilāḥāt al-funūn* (Teheran, 1967), Vol. I, p. 197; Shaykhzādeh, Vol. I, p. 587; Ibn ʿAbidīn, Vol. III, p. 301; Azharī, p. 306; Ḥaṭṭāb, Vol. III, p. 347; Bādjūrī, Vol. II, p. 268.
4. Tahānawī (1967), *loc. cit.*; Bādjūrī, Vol. II, p. 268; Djār Allāh Maḥmūd ibn ʿUmar al-Zamakhsharī, *Al-kashshāf ʿan ḥaqā'iq al-tanzīl wa-ʿuyūn al-aqāwīl* (Cairo: Muṣṭafā l-Bābī al Ḥalabī, 1966), ad. K 9:122.
5. Mawwāq, Vol. III, p. 346; Abū l-Faḍl Djamāl al-Dīn Muḥammad ibn Makram Ibn Manẓūr, *Lisān al-ʿArab* (Beirut: Dār Ṣādir/Dār Bayrūt, 1955/1373), Vol. III, p. 135; for another distinction between the various meanings of jihad, cf. Abū Muḥammad ʿAlī ibn Aḥmad ibn Saʿīd Ibn Ḥazm, *Kitāb al-fiṣal fī l-milal wa-ahwā' al-niḥal* (Cairo: 1318-20/1899-1902), Vol. IV, p. 135; Abū Ḥāmid Muḥammad al-Ghazālī, *Iḥyā' ʿulūm al-dīn* (Cairo: Dār Iḥyā' al-Kutub al-

ʿArabiyyah/ʿĪsā l-Bābī al-Ḥalabī, n.d.), Vol. II, pp. 307-308. For a good survey of the various spiritual and moral connotations of the word jihad, cf. Morabia (1975), pp. 480-487, 512-555.

6. Throughout this study I have made use of R. Bell's translation of the Koran (Edinburgh, 1939) for rendering Koranic verses in English.
7. Sarakhsī, Vol. I, p. 188; Marghīnānī, Vol. II, p. 135; Shaykhzādeh, Vol. I, p. 387; Ibn ʿĀbidīn, Vol. III, p. 301; Azharī, p. 306; Mawwāq, Vol. III, p. 346; Ḥaṭṭāb, Vol. III, p. 347; Ibn Taymiyyah, p. 144; Bilmen, Vol. III, p. 356; Khadduri (1955), pp. 55-57, 59-60; Hans Kruse, *Islamische Völkerrechtslehre. Der Staatsvertrag bei den Hanafiten des 5./6. Jahrhunderts d.H. (11./12. Jahrh. n. Chr.).* (Göttingen; 1953), pp. 45-50; Noth (1966), pp. 22-25; E. Tyan, *Djihād.* In: *EI*[2], Vol. II, pp. 538-540.
8. Ibn Rushd, Vol. I, p. 381; Ibn Taymiyyah, p. 146; Mawwāq, Vol. III, p. 357; Dasūqī, Vol. II, p. 183; Ibn Djuzayy, p. 110; Shāfiʿī, Vol. IV, pp. 90, 155-156; Ḥillī, Vol. I, p. 310; Hamidullah (1953), p. 189; Khadduri (1955), p. 80.
9. Sarakhsī, Vol. I, pp. 6-7; Ibn ʿĀbidīn, Vol. III, p. 301; Azharī, pp. 312-313; Ibn Qudāmah, Vol. IX, p. 203; Ḥillī, Vol. I, p. 309; Ibn Ḥazm, Vol. VI, p. 353; Bilmen, Vol. III, pp. 372, 397-398; Khadduri (1955), pp. 81-82; Noth (1966), pp. 66-87.
10. Sarakhsī, Vol. V, pp. 1856-1857, 2165; Shaykhzādeh, Vol. I, p. 609; Ibn ʿĀbidīn, Vol. III, pp. 349-350; Shāfiʿī, Vol. IV, pp. 103-104, 192; Māwardī, p. 138; Tahānawī (1967), Vol. I, p. 466; A. Abel, *Dār al-ḥarb.* In: *EI*[2], Vol. II, p. 126; A. Abel, *Dār al-Islām.* In: *EI*[2], Vol. II, p. 127; Bilmen, Vol. III, pp. 394-396; H. İnalcık, *Dār al-ʿahd.* In: *EI*[2], Vol. II, p. 116; Khadduri (1955), pp. 155-157, 170-171; Kruse (1953), pp. 58-63; F. Løkkegaard, *Islamic Taxation in the Classic Period* (Copenhagen: Branner og Korch, 1950), pp. 81-83; D. B. Macdonald and A, Abel, *Dār al-ṣulḥ.* in: *EI*[2], Vol. II, p. 131; Morabia (1975), pp. 312-317; Zuḥaylī (1965), pp. 166-194.
11. *On the legal qualification*: Ibn Rushd, Vol, I, pp. 380-381; Sarakhsī, Vol. I, pp. 187-189; Marghīnānī, Vol. II, p. 135; Shaykhzādeh, Vol. I, pp. 587-588; Ibn ʿĀbidīn, Vol. III, pp. 302-303; Azharī, p. 303; Ibn Djuzayy, pp. 109-110; Ḥaṭṭāb, Vol. III, pp. 346-347; Mawwāq, Vol. III, pp. 346-348; Dasūqī, Vol. II, pp. 173-175; Shāfiʿī, Vol. IV, pp. 84-85, 90-91; Nawawī, Vol. III, pp. 255-259; Bādjūrī, Vol. II, p. 268; Ibn Qudāmah, Vol. IX, pp. 196-197, 213-214; Ibn Taymiyyah, pp. 149-150; Ḥillī, Vol. I, pp. 307, 309; Qāḍī Nuʿmān, Vol. I, pp. 399-401, 438-439; Bilmen, Vol. III, p. 379; Khadduri (1955), pp. 60-62; Morabia (1975), pp. 337-340; Noth (1965), pp. 33-35; Zuḥaylī (1965).

    On the exemptions: Ibn Rushd, Vol. I, p. 381; Sarakhsī, Vol. I, pp. 184-185, 191-204, Vol. IV, pp. 1448-1454; Marghīnānī, Vol. II, pp. 135, 137; Shaykhzādeh, Vol. I, pp. 588, 590; Ibn ʿĀbidīn, Vol. III, pp. 304-306, 309; Saḥnūn, Vol. III, p. 5; Azharī, pp. 308, 313; Ibn Djuzayy, p. 110; Ḥaṭṭāb, Vol. III, pp. 347-348; Mawwāq, Vol. III, pp. 347-350; Dasūqī, Vol. II, pp. 174-176,

178; Shāfiʿī, Vol. IV, pp. 85-87; Nawawī, Vol. III, pp. 257-258; Bādjūrī, Vol. I, pp. 270-271; Ibn Qudāmah, Vol. IX, pp. 197-210, 214-215, 300; Ibn Ḥazm, Vol. VII, p. 299; Ḥillī, Vol. I, pp. 307-308; Qāḍī Nuʿmān, Vol. I, p. 402; Bilmen, Vol. III, pp. 383-384; Khadduri (1955), pp. 83-87.

12. Ḥillī, Vol. I, 307; Kohlberg (1976), pp. 79-80.
13. Sarakhsī, Vol. I, p. 188; Ibn ʿĀbidīn, Vol. III, p. 302; Shāfiʿī, Vol. IV, pp. 83-85; Ibn Taymiyyah, pp. 139-140. Although all authors agree upon the unconditioned command to fight the unbelievers, there is some controversy as to the precise relationship between the various relevant verses and as to the extent of abrogation. Cf. Abū Bakr Muḥammad ibn ʿAbd Allāh Ibn al-ʿArabī, *Aḥkām al-Qur'ān* (Ed. by ʿAlī Muḥammad al-Badjāwī. 4 vols. 2nd ed., Cairo: ʿĪsā l-Bābī al-Ḥalabī, 1387/1967), Vol. I, pp. 102-104, 147, 232-234, Vol. II, pp. 864-865, Vol. III, p. 302; Abū Bakr Aḥmad ibn ʿAlī al-Rāzī al-Djaṣṣāṣ, *Aḥkām al-Qur'ān* (Ed. by Muḥammad al-Ṣādiq al-Qamḥāwī. 5 vols. 2nd ed., Cairo: Dār al-Muṣḥaf, n.d.), Vol. I, pp. 319-328.
14. Cf. A. J. Wensinck, a.o. (eds.) *Concordance et indices de la tradition Musulmane* (7 vols. Leiden: E. J. Brill, 1936-69), Vol. I, p. 99.
15. Sarakhsī, Vol. I, p. 187; Ibn al-ʿArabī, Vol. I, p. 103.
16. Cf. Wensinck (1936-69), Vol. IV, p. 487.
17. Ibn Qudāmah, Vol. IX, p. 195.
18. Cf. Wensinck (1936-69), Vol. IV, p. 180.
19. Cf. Wensinck (1936-69), Vol. I, p. 389.
20. This Tradition is not to be found in any of the authentic collections.
21. Cf. Wensinck (1936-69), Vol. I, p. 388.
22. Cf. Wensinck (1936-69), Vol. VI, p. 35.
23. Ṭabarī, pp. 2-3; Ibn Rushd, Vol. I, pp. 386-387; Sarakhsī, Vol. I, pp. 75 77, Vol. V, pp. 2231-2232; Marghīnānī, Vol. II, p. 136; Shaykhzādeh, Vol. I, p. 589; Ibn ʿĀbidīn, Vol. III, pp. 307-308; Saḥnūn, Vol. III, pp. 2-3; Azharī, p. 307; Ibn Djuzayy, p. 110; Ḥaṭṭāb, Vol. III, p. 350; Mawwāq, Vol. III, pp. 350-351; Dasūqī, Vol. II, pp. 176, 201; Shāfiʿī, Vol. IV, p. 157; Māwardī, pp. 37-38; Ibn Qudāmah, Vol. IX, pp. 210-211; Ḥillī, Vol. I, p. 311; Qāḍī Nuʿmān, pp. 422-423; Bilmen, Vol. III, pp. 387-388; Hamidullah (1953), pp. 190-193; Khadduri (1955), pp. 94-101; Morabia (1975), pp. 356-360; Zuḥaylī (1965), pp. 147-158.
24. Cf. Wensinck (1936-69), Vol. II, p. 131.
25. Ṭabarī, pp. 3-9; Ibn Rushd, Vol. I, pp. 385-386; Sarakhsī, Vol. I, p. 110, Vol. IV, pp. 1467-1475; Marghīnānī, Vol. II, pp. 136-137; Shaykhzādeh, Vol. I, pp. 590-591; Ibn ʿĀbidīn, Vol. III, pp. 308-309; Saḥnūn, Vol. III, pp. 7-8, 24-25; Ibn Djuzayy, p. 111; Ḥaṭṭāb, Vol. III, pp. 352-353; Mawwāq, Vol. III, pp. 351-352; Dasūqī, Vol. II, pp. 177-179; Shāfiʿī, Vol. IV, pp. 160-161, 199, Vol. VII, p. 318; Māwardī, pp. 52-53; Nawawī, Vol. III, pp. 261-262; Ibn Djamāʿah, pp. 412-414; Ibn Qudāmah, Vol. IX, pp. 287-289; Ḥillī, Vol. I,

pp. 311-312; Qāḍī Nuʿmān, Vol. I, p. 440; Bilmen, Vol. III, pp. 390-391; Hamidullah (1953), pp. 204-208, 225-231; Khadduri (1955), pp. 102-107; Zuḥaylī (1965), pp. 506-507.

26. Cf. Wensinck (1936-69), Vol. II, p. 175.
27. Ṭabarī, pp. 9-12; Ibn Rushd, Vol. I, pp. 383-385; Sarakhsī, Vol. I, pp. 41-43, Vol. IV, pp. 1415-1417, 1429-1443; Marghīnānī, Vol. I, pp. 137-138; Shaykhzādeh, Vol. I, pp. 590-591; Ibn ʿĀbidīn, Vol. III, pp. 309-311; Saḥnūn, Vol. III, pp. 6-7; Azharī, p. 308; Ibn Djuzayy, p. 110; Ḥaṭṭāb, Vol. III, pp. 350-352; Mawwāq, Vol. III, pp. 350-352; Dasūqī, Vol. II, pp. 176-177; Shāfiʿī, Vol. IV, pp. 156-157, 197-198; Māwardī, p. 41; Nawawī, Vol. III, p. 261; Ibn Djamaʿah, p. 412; Ibn Qudāmah, Vol. IX, pp. 310-313; Ibn Taymiyyah, pp. 144-145; Ibn Ḥazm, Vol. VII, p. 296-299; Ḥillī, Vol. I, p. 312; Qāḍī Nuʿmān, Vol. I, pp. 439-440; Bilmen, Vol. III, pp. 393-394; Hamidullah (1953), pp. 204-208; Khadduri (1955), pp. 102-107; Morabia (1975), pp. 367-368, 376-377; Zuḥaylī (1965), pp. 106-109, 495-506.
28. Cf. Wensinck (1936-69), Vol. V, p. 290.
29. Cf. Wensinck (1936-69), Vol. V, p. 285.
30. Cf. Wensinck (1936-69), Vol. III, p. 227.
31. Ibn Rushd, Vol. II, p. 286; Sarakhsī, Vol. I, pp. 43-54, Vol. IV, pp. 1467-1475; Marghīnānī, Vol. II, p. 142; Shaykhzādeh, Vol. I, pp. 594-595; Ibn ʿĀbidīn, Vol. III, pp. 308, 317-318; Saḥnūn, Vol. III, pp. 8, 40; Ibn Djuzayy, p. 111; Ḥaṭṭāb, Vol. III, pp. 355-356; Mawwāq, Vol. III, pp. 355-356; Dasūqī, Vol. II, pp. 180-181; Shāfiʿī, Vol. IV, p. 199, Vol. VII, p. 324; Māwardī, pp. 42, 52; Nawawī, Vol. III, pp. 263-264; Ibn Qudāmah, Vol. IX, pp. 289-292; Ibn Ḥazm, Vol. VII, pp. 294-296; Ḥillī, Vol. I, p. 312; Qāḍī Nuʿmān, Vol. I, p. 434; Bilmen, Vol. III, pp. 391, 394; Morabia (1975), pp. 364-367.
32. Cf. Wensinck (1936-69), Vol. V, p. 462.
33. Cf. Wensinck (1936-69), Vol. VI, p. 387
34. Ibn Rushd, Vol. I, p. 387; Sarakhsī, Vol. I, pp. 123-125; Azharī, p. 307; Ibn Djuzayy, p. 111; Ḥaṭṭāb, Vol. III, p. 353; Mawwāq, Vol. III, p. 353; Dasūqī, Vol. II, pp. 178-179; Shāfiʿī, Vol. IV, p. 92; Māwardī, pp. 44-45; Nawawī, Vol. III, pp. 262-263; Ibn Djamāʿah, pp. 410-411; Ibn Qudāmah, Vol. IX, pp. 317-320; Ibn Ḥazm, Vol. VII, pp. 292-293; Ḥillī, Vol. I, p. 311; Qāḍī Nuʿman, Vol. I, p. 434; Khadduri (1955), pp. 135-136; Morabia (1975), pp. 354-355; Zuḥaylī (1965), pp. 751-752.
35. Sarakhsī, Vol. IV, pp. 1422-1423, 1515; Ibn ʿĀbidīn, Vol. III, p. 325; Ḥaṭṭāb, Vol. III, p. 350; Dasūqī, Vol. II, p. 178; Shāfʿī, Vol. IV, pp. 89, 177; Ibn Qudāmah, Vol. IX, pp. 256-257; Bilmen, Vol. III, p. 392; Morabia (1975), pp. 347-348.
36. Cf. Wensinck (1936-69), Vol. IV, p. 443.
37. Sarakhsī, Vol. IV, pp. 1567-1574, 1408-1409; Marghīnānī, Vol. II, p. 139; Ibn ʿĀbidīn, Vol. III, pp. 312-313; Ibn Ḥazm, Vol. VII, p. 349; Bilmen, Vol. III,

pp. 396-397; Hamidullah (1953), pp. 262-266; Khadduri (1955), pp. 167, 225-228; Zuḥaylī (1965), pp. 512-523.

38. Ibn Rushd, Vol. I, pp. 382, 385; Sarakhsī, Vol. III, pp. 1024-1035, 1148, Vol. IV, pp. 1587-1592, 1516-1522; Marghīnānī, Vol. II, pp. 137, 141-142; Shaykhzādeh, Vol. I, pp. 590, 594; Ibn ʿĀbidīn, Vol. III, pp. 316-317; Saḥnūn, Vol. III, p. 7; Ibn Djuzayy, p. 112; Ḥaṭṭāb, Vol. III, pp. 350, 353-354; Mawwāq, Vol. III, pp. 353-354; Dasūqī, Vol. II, pp. 179, 184; Shāfiʿī, Vol, IV, pp. 162, 198-199; 156; Māwardī, pp. 50, 53; Nawawī, Vol. III, pp. 264-267; Ibn Djamāʿah, pp. 3-4; Ibn Qudāmah, Vol. IX, pp. 286-287, 220-225; Ibn Taymiyyah, p. 146; Ḥillī, Vol. I, pp. 317-318; Qāḍī Nuʿmān, Vol. I, pp. 440-441; Bilmen, Vol. III, pp. 427-432; Erwin Gräf, 'Religiöse und rechtliche Vorstellungen über Kriegsgefangenen im Islam und Christentum', *WI*, n.s. 8 (1962-63), pp. 89-139; Hamidullah (1953), pp. 213-224; Khadduri (1955), pp. 126-132; Morabia (1975), pp. 368-377; Zuḥayli (1965), pp. 404-471.
39. Cf. Wensinck (1936-69), Vol. IV, p. 488, Vol. VI, p. 169.
40. Cf. Wensinck (1936-69), Vol. IV, p. 164.
41. This Tradition is not to be found in any of the authoritative collections.
42. For the discussion on the permissibility of killing prisoners, Ibn Rushd, Vol. I, p. 282; Sarakhsī, Vol. III, p. 1024; Ibn Qudāmah, Vol. IV, p. 221.
43. Djaṣṣāṣ, Vol. IV, p. 258; Ibn al-ʿArabī, Vol. II, pp. 867-869.
44. Ṭabarī, pp. 25-43; Ibn Rushd, Vol. I, pp. 382-383; Sarakhsī, Vol. I, pp. 252-368, Vol. II, pp. 410-582, Vol. IV, p. 1280, Vol. V, pp. 1788, 1853-1870; Marghīnānī, Vol. II, pp. 139-140, 152-156; Shaykhzādeh, Vol. I, pp. 592-593, 607; Ibn ʿĀbidīn, Vol III, pp. 313-314, 341-342, 349; Azharī, p. 308; Ibn Djuzayy, p. 117; Ḥaṭṭāb, Vol. III, pp. 359-361, Mawwāq, Vol. III, pp. 359-361; Dasūqī, Vol. II, pp. 185-187; Shāfiʿī, Vol. IV, pp. 111, 201, Vol. VII, p. 319; Māwardī, p. 52; Nawawī, Vol. III, p. 271; Ibn Djamāʿah, pp. 22-23; Ibn Qudāmah, Vol. IX, pp. 241-247, 295, 317, 322; Ḥillī, Vol. I, pp. 313-315; Qāḍī Nuʿmān, Vol. I, pp. 440, 442-443; Bilmen, Vol. III, pp. 404-411; Hamidullah (1953), pp. 123-124, 148-150, 209-212, 259-262; Julius Hatschek, *Der Musta'min. Ein Beitrag zum internationalen Privat- und Völkerrecht des islamischen Gesetzes* (Berlin: Walter de Gruyter, 1920), 108 pp. (but see also the reviews by W. Heffening, *Der Islam* 13 (1923), pp. 144-149 and by R. Hartmann, *OLZ* 26 (1923), pp. 345-346); Willi Heffening, *Das islamische Fremdenrecht bis zu den islamisch-fränkischen Staatsverträgen* (Hannover: Heinz Lafaire, 1925), 219 pp.; Khadduri (1955), pp. 163-169, 243; Kruse (1953), pp. 77-82; Morabia (1975), pp. 331-336; Joseph Schacht, *Amān*. In: *EI*[2], Vol. I, pp. 429-430; J. Wansbrough, 'The Safe-conduct in Muslim chancery practice', *BSOAS* 34 (1971), pp. 20-35; Zuḥaylī (1965), pp. 220-319, 330-335.
45. Cf. Wensinck (1936-69), Vol. I, p. 398.
46. Cf. Wensinck (1936-69), Vol. I, p. 398.

47. This Tradition is not to be found in any of the authoritative collections.
48. Cf. Wensinck (1936-69), Vol. II, p. 184.
49. Cf. Wensinck (1936-69), Vol. II, p. 260.
50. Ṭabarī, pp. 14-20; Ibn Rushd, Vol. I, pp. 387-388; Sarakhsī, Vol. I, p. 304, Vol. V. pp. 1689-1788, 1856-1857; Marghīnānī, Vol. II, pp. 138-139; Shaykhzādeh, Vol. I, pp. 591-592; Ibn ʿĀbidīn, Vol. III, pp. 312-313, 430; Ibn Djuzayy, p. 118; Ḥaṭṭāb, Vol. III, pp. 386-387; Mawwāq, Vol. III, pp. 386-387; Dasūqī, Vol. II, p. 205; Shāfiʿī, Vol. IV, pp. 107-113; Māwardī, pp. 51-52; Nawawī, Vol. III, pp. 288-290; Ibn Djamāʿah, p. 20; Ibn Qudāmah, Vol. IX, pp. 296-302; Ibn Ḥazm, Vol. VII, p. 307; Ḥillī, Vol. I, pp. 332-334; Qāḍī Nuʿmān, Vol. I, p. 443; Bilmen, Vol. III, pp. 413-420; Hamidullah (1953), pp. 226-228, 270-282; Khadduri (1955), pp. 202-213, 215-222; Majid Khadduri, *Hudnah*. In: *EI*², Vol. III, pp. 546-547; Kruse (1953), pp. 86-151; Morabia (1975), pp. 319-324; Zuḥaylī (1965), pp. 345-403, 663-690.
51. Ibn Rushd, Vol. I, pp. 389-390; Sarakhsī, Vol. IV, p. 1036; Marghīnānī, Vol. II, p. 160; Shaykhzādeh, Vol. I, pp. 614-615; Ibn ʿĀbidīn, Vol, III, p. 370; Azharī, p. 370; Ibn Djuzayy, p. 118; Ḥaṭṭāb, Vol. III, pp. 350, 380-381; Mawwāq, Vol. III, p. 380; Dasūqī, Vol. I, p. 201; Shāfiʿī, Vol. IV, pp. 91, 94, 155-156; Māwardī, pp. 143-144; Ibn Qudāmah, Vol. IX, pp. 212-214, 328-333; Ibn Taymiyyah, p. 136; Ibn Ḥazm, Vol. VII, p. 345; Ḥillī, Vol. I, p. 327; Qāḍī Nuʿmān, Vol I, p. 444; C. Cahen, *Djizya*. In: *EI*², Vol. II, pp. 359-362; C. Cahen, *Dhimma*. In: *EI*², Vol. II, pp. 227-231; Khadduri (1955), p. 189; Zuḥaylī (1965), pp. 638-648, 691-714.
52. Cf. Wensinck, Vol. II, p. 552.

NOTES TO CHAPTER 3: 'JIHAD AND RESISTANCE AGAINST COLONIALISM'

1. P. M. Holt, Ann K. S. Lambton and Bernard Lewis (eds.), *The Cambridge History of Islam* (Cambridge: The University Press, 1970), Vol. 2, pp. 159, 179; F. M. Pareja, A. Bausani and L. Hertling, *Islamologia* (Rome, 1951), pp. 245, 255, 257, 345; P. J. Veth, 'De Heilige Oorlog in den Indischen Archipel', *Tijdschrift voor Nederlandsch Indië* (1870), pp. 168-176.
2. Holt, a.o. (1970), Vol. 1, pp. 445, 511.
3. Holt, a.o. (1970), Vol. 2, p. 394.
4. For these movements, see: Pareja, a.o. (1951), p. 286; Holt, a.o. (1970), pp. 367-368, 376; J. H. Willis, 'Jihād fī sabīl Allāh; Its doctrinal basis in Islam and some aspects of its evolution in 19th century West Africa', *Journal of African History* 8 (1967), pp. 395-417; M. C. Smith, 'The Jihad of Shehu dan Fodio, Some problems'. In: I. M. Lewis (ed.). *Islam in Tropical Africa* (London, etc.: Oxford University Press, 1966), pp. 408-420; Peter Waterman, 'The

Jihad in Haussaland', *Kroniek van Afrika* 5 (1975), 2, pp. 141-153.

5. Cf. Wensinck (1936-69), Vol. I, p. 164.
6. Cf. Wensinck (1936-69), Vol. VII, p. 67.
7. al-Djaṣṣāṣ, Vol. IV, p. 262; Ibn al-ʿArabī, Vol. II, p. 876; Abū l-Walīd Muḥammad ibn Rushd, *Kitāb al-Muqaddamāt* (Cairo: Maṭbaʿat al-Saʿādah, 1325/1907), Vol. II, p. 285; Shāfiʿī, Vol. IV, p. 84; ʿAbd al-Ḥamīd al-Shirwānī, *Ḥāshiya ʿalā Tuḥfat al-Muḥtādj sharḥ al-Minhādj li-Zakariyā' Yaḥyā l-Nawawī* (Mecca: al-Maṭbaʿah al-Mīriyyah, 1304-5), Vol. VIII, pp. 62-63; Ibn Qudāmah, Vol. IX, pp. 293-295; on the *fatwās* with regard to the obligation to emigrate after the *Reconquista*, cf. Mercier (1939), pp. 60-62.
8. Charles-Robert Ageron, *Les Algériens Musulmans et la France (1871-1919)* (Paris: Presses Universitaires de France, 1968), Vol. II, pp. 1079-1093.
9. F. S. Briggs, 'The Indian Hijrat of 1920', *MW* 20 (1930), pp. 164-168; A. C. Niemeijer, *The Khilafat Movement in India, 1919-1924* (The Hague: Martinus Nijhoff, 1972), pp. 102-106.
10. *Mūl s-sāʿa*, Lord of the Hour, is the North African vernacular designation of the *Mahdī*.
11. Ch. Richard, *Les mystères du peuple arabe* (Paris: 1860), p. 107; quoted in Ahmed Nadir, 'Les ordres religieux et la conquête française (1830-1851)', *Rev. Alg. des Sc. Jur., Écon. et Pol.* 9 (1972), p. 856.
12. C. Snouck Hurgronje, *De Atjehers* (Batavia/Leiden: Landsdrukkerij/E. J. Brill, 1894), Vol. 2, pp. 388-389.
13. Ageron (1968), Vol. I, p. 59, Vol. II, p. 921 and 1028; Peter von Sivers, 'The realm of Justice. Apocalyptic revolts in Algeria (1849-1879)', *Humaniora Islamica* (The Hague), 1 (1973), pp. 47-60.
14. R. C. Majumdar, *The Sepoy Mutiny and the Revolt of 1857* (2nd ed., Calcutta: Mukhopadhyay, 1963), p. 60.
15. W. W. Hunter, *The Indian Musulmans. Are They Bound in Conscience to Rebel Against the Queen?* (2nd ed., Lahore: Premier Book House, 1974), pp. 35-36, 47-50.
16. A. Schölch, *Ägypten den Ägyptern. Die politische und gesellschaftliche Krise der Jahre 1878-1882 in Ägypten* (Zürich: Artemis Verlag, n.d.), p. 46.
17. Percival Spear, *India: A Modern History* (Ann Arbor: The University of Michigan Press, 1971), pp. 262-263; Hunter (1974), pp. 134-140, 158-162.
18. Angus Maddison, *Class Structure and Economic Growth in India and Pakistan Since the Moghuls* (London: Allen & Unwin, 1971), pp. 53-55.
19. The omission of the article in *dār Islām* and *dār ḥarb* follows the rule of the Arabic grammar: *Dār Islām* is only a part of *the dār al-Islām* and *dār ḥarb* only a part of *the dār al-ḥarb*.
20. Zuḥaylī (1965), pp. 182-192.
21. Hunter (1974), pp. 114-116; P. M. Holt, a.o. (1970), Vol. 1, p. 73; Tahanāwī (1967), Vol. I, p. 466.

22. Shāh ʿAbd al-ʿAzīz, *Fatāwā-yi ʿAzīzī* (2 vols. Deoband: n.d.), Vol. 1, pp. 30-31; Engl. transl. also to be found in: M. Mujeeb, *The Indian Muslims* (London: Allen and Unwin, 1967), pp. 390-391; Muhammad Abdul Bari, 'The politics of Sayyid Ahmad Barelwi', *IC* 31 (1957), p. 162; Ziya-ul-Hasan Faruqi, *The Deoband School and the Demand for Pakistan* (London: Asia Publishing House, 1963), pp. 2-3; for similar *fatwās* and opinions, cf. Hunter (1974), pp. 120-121; Mujeeb (1967), p. 391; Muin-ud-Din Ahmad Khan, *History of the Fara'idi Movement in Bengal, 1808-1906* (Karachi: Pakistan Historical Society, 1965), pp. 78-80; Muhammad Nurul Karim, 'Part played by Haji Shariʿatullah and his son in the socio-political history of East Bengal', *Proceedings of the Pakistan History Conference* (5th session), 1955, p. 177.
23. On this movement, see: Aziz Ahmad, 'Le mouvement des Mujahidin dans l'Inde au XIXᵉ siècle', *Orient* 15 (1960), pp. 106-116; Qeyamuddin Ahmad, *The Wahabi Movement in India* (Calcutta: Mukhopadhyay, 1966), 391 pp.; Muhammad Abdul Bari (1957), pp. 156-164; Freeland Abbott, 'The jihad of Sayyid Ahmad Shahid', *MW* 52 (1962), pp. 216-222; Hunter (1974), *passim*; Ishtiaq Husain Qureshi, *The Muslim Community of the Indo-Pakistan Subcontinent, 610-1947. A Brief Historical Analysis* (The Hague: Mouton, 1962), pp. 194-207; E. Rehatsek, 'The history of the Wahhabys in Arabia and India', *Journal of the Bombay Branch of the Royal Asiatic Society* 14 (1878-80), pp. 274-401; Muin-ud-Din Ahmad Khan (1965), pp. xxxvi-lxxxi.
24. Shāh Ismāʿil, *Ṣirāṭ-i mustaqīm* (n.p., n.d.), pp. 105-106. Engl. transl. of this par. also to be found in: Hunter (1974), pp. 50-51, and: Ahmad Khan Bahadur, *Review on Dr. Hunter's Indian Musalmans* (Benares: Medical Hall Press, 1872), pp. 30-31.
25. Hunter (1974), pp. 35-36, 47-50.
26. Q. Ahmad (1966), pp. 358-363, where many of these pamphlets are listed; Rehatsek (1878-80), pp. 379-401.
27. For this movement, see: Khan (1965); M. Nurul Karim (1955), pp. 175-182; Qureshi (1962), pp 209-220; Abdul Bari, 'The Fara'idi Movement', *Proceedings of the Pakistan History Conference* (5th session), pp. 197-207.
28. This is contrary to the established Hanafite opinion, which the Farā'iḍis usually followed. Cf. Ibn ʿAbidīn, Vol. I, pp. 589 and 594. This divergence must probably be ascribed to *Wahhābī* influence. Cf. on this point Khan (1965), pp. 67-80.
29. Abdul Bari (1955), p. 205.
30. Faruqi (1963), pp. 16-20; R. C. Majumdar, *The Sepoy Mutiny and the Revolt of 1857* (2nd ed., Calcutta: Mukhopadhyay, 1963), pp. 59, 113, 318-319, 400-401.
31. Engl. transl. in Lini S. May, *The Evolution of Indo-Muslim Thought after 1857* (Lahore: Sh. Muhammad Ashraf, 1970), pp. 440-448.
32 Wilfred Cantwell Smith, *Modern Islam in India. A Social Analysis* (2nd ed., London: Gollancz, 1946), p. 162.

33. Hunter (1974), pp. 140-147; Qureshi (1962), pp. 213-225, 232-233; Smith (1946), p. 163.
34. May (1970), pp. 24-28; P. Hardy, *The Muslims of British India* (Cambridge: Cambridge University Press, 1972), pp. 108-115.
35. Engl. transl. in Hunter (1974), p. 186, and Ahmad Khan (1872), p. iii.
36. Maulavi Karamat Ali, *Abstract of the Proceedings of the Muhammadan Literary Society of Calcutta on Wednesday, 23rd November 1870. Being a Lecture by Maulavi Karamat Ali of Jawnpur on a Question of Muhammadan Law, Involving the Duty of the Muhammadans in British India towards the Ruling Power* (Calcutta: 1871); partly quoted in Hunter (1974), p. 187.
37. Ahmad Khan (1872), pp. iv-xxii.
38. Hunter (1974), p. 186, cf. also pp. 62-63.
39. Ibid., p. 187.
40. Ahmad Khan (1872), p. xviii.
41. Ibid., p. xvi.
42. Ibid., p. xix.
43. Engl. transl. of these *fatwās* in Hunter (1974), pp. 185-186; Ahmad Khan (1872), pp. i-ii.
44. C. Snouck Hurgronje (1894), Vol. 2, pp. 387-388.
45. Faruqi (1963), pp. 24, 40.
46. For an exposé of the different orders in Algeria and the factors that brought the *Qādiriyyah* to the foreground, see: Ahmed Nadir, 'Les ordres religieuses et la conquête française (1830-1851)', *Rev. Alg. des Sc. Jur., Écon. et Pol.* 9 (1972), pp. 826-834.
47. For the text of this *bayʿah*, see: Muḥammad b. ʿAbd al-Qādir al-Djazā'irī, *Tuḥfat al-za'ir fī ta'rīkh al-Djazā'ir wa-l-Amīr ʿAbd al-Qādir* (2 vols. Ed. by Mamdūḥ Ḥaqqī. 2nd ed., Beirut: Dār al-Yaqaẓah al-ʿArabiyya, 1384-1964), Vol. 1, p. 159.
48. For the details of his army organization, see: Djazā'irī (1964), Vol. 1, pp. 191-209.
49. Y. Lacoste, A. Nouschi and A. Prenant, *L'Algérie passé et présent. Le cadre et les étapes de la constitution de l'Algérie actuelle* (Paris: Éds Sociales, 1960), pp. 274-275.
50. For the texts of these letters, see: Charles Henry Churchill, *La vie d'Abd-el-Kader* (Transl. into Fr. by Michel Hobart. 2nd ed., Algiers: Société Nationale d'Édition et de Diffusion, 1974), pp. 189-196, 201-204; Ar. summaries in al-Djazā'irī (1964), pp. 349-353 and 359-360.
51. Nadir (1972), pp. 858-864.
52. For his religious views, see: Pessah Shinar, ''Abd al-Qadir and ʿAbd al-Krim. Religious influences on their thought and action', *Asian and African Studies* 1 (1965), pp. 139-174.
53. Al-Djazā'irī (1964), Vol. 1, pp. 316-317.
54. Fr. transl.: E. Michaux-Bellaire, 'Traduction de la Fetoua du Faqih Sidi ʿAly Et

Tsouli contenant le "Souāl" du Hādj Abdelqāder ben Mahi ed Dīn et la response', *Archives Marocaines* 11 (1907), pp. 116-128, 395-454; 15 (1909), pp. 158-184; Ar. summary in al-Djazā'irī (1964), Vol. 1, pp. 318-330.

55. This was politically an important point as the Moroccan Sultan had urged ʿAbd al-Qādir to denounce his treaty with the French. Having explained that the conclusion of an armistice with the enemy is only allowed in cases of necessity, in order to save Moslem lives and to protect their country, al-Tasūlī wrote: 'For necessity has its own rule and perhaps he who is present [at the scene of war] sees things that those who are not, may not see', thereby implying that for the Moroccans the necessity of concluding a peace treaty was not evident. al-Djazā'irī (1964), Vol. 1, p. 325.
56. Abū ʿAbd Allāh Muḥammad ʿIllaysh, *Fatḥ al-ʿalī al-mālik fī l-fatwā ʿalā madhhab al-Imām Mālik* (2 vols. Cairo: Maṭbaʿat al-taqaddum al-ʿilmiyyah, 1319), Vol. 1, p. 313.
57. Muḥammad ʿIllaysh was a professor at the Azhar University in Cairo. In 1854 he became Mālikite *muftī* of Egypt. In 1882, despite his great age, he actively took part in the ʿUrābī revolt.
58. ʿIllaysh (1319), Vol. 1, pp. 313-328. ʿAbd al-Qādir's son and biographer, Muḥammad ibn ʿAbd al-Qādir al-Djazā'irī, mentions that he has not seen the Egyptian *fatwā*. Cf. al-Djazā'irī (1964), Vol. 1, p. 329. The text of ʿIllaysh's *fatwā*, however, leaves no doubt as to the fact that it refers to the situation in Algeria at ʿAbd al-Qādir's time, although it does not expressly mention it.
59. Text in al-Djazā'irī (1964), Vol. 1, pp. 411-423.
60. Ibid., Vol. 1, p. 416.
61. Ibid., Vol. 1, pp. 384-385.
62. Ibid., Vol. 1, pp. 384-389.
63. Ibid., Vol. 1, pp. 472-473; ʿIllaysh (1319), Vol. 1, pp. 328-329.
64. ʿIllaysh (1319), Vol. 1, p. 330.
65. Von Sivers (1973).
66. M. Émerit, 'L'État d'esprit des Musulmans d'Algérie de 1847 à 1870', *Revue d'Histoire Moderne et Contemporaine* 8 (1961), pp. 103-120.
67. Ageron (1968), Vol. 2, pp. 1079-1092; Id. 'L'Émigration des Musulmans algériens et l'exode de Tlemcen', *Annales. Économies, Sociétés, Civilisations* 22 (1967), pp. 1047-1068.
68. Fr. transl. of the question and the *fatwās* in Octave Depont and Xavier Coppolani, *Les Confréries religieuses musulmanes* (Alger: Alphonse Jourdan, 1897), pp. 33-37; the authors do not mention whether the Malikite *muftī* had issued a *fatwā* or not. If there existed a Malikite *fatwā*, the French authorities may have suppressed it, as the position of the Mālikite *madhhab* with regard to emigration was more radical than the other *madhhabs*.
69. Ageron (1968), Vol. 2, pp. 1085-1092.

70. Richard Hill, *Egypt in the Sudan, 1820-1881* (London, etc.: Oxford University Press, 1959), pp. 13-18.
71. J. Spencer Trimingham, *Islam in the Sudan* (London, etc.: Oxford University Press, 1949), pp. 126-141, 195-202.
72. P. M. Holt, *The Mahdist State in the Sudan, 1881-1898. A Study of its Origins and Overthrow* (2nd ed., London, etc.: Oxford University Press, 1970), p. 18.
73. ʿAbd Allāh ʿAlī Ibrāhīm, *Al-ṣirāʿ bayn al-Mahdī wa-l-ʿulamāʾ* (Khartoum: Shuʿbat Abḥāth al-Sūdān, Kulliyyat al-Adāb, Djāmiʿat al-Khartūm, 1968), pp. 1-11.
74. Holt (1970), pp. 30 and 50, n. 2.
75. Naʿūm Shuqayr, *Tārīkh al-Sūdān al-qadīm wa-l ḥadīth wa-djughrāfiyyatuh* (3 vols. Cairo: Maṭbaʿat al-Maʿārif, 1903), Vol. 2, p. 139; Engl. transl. also in Holt (1970), p. 117.
76. Shuqayr (1903), Vol. 3, p. 365. This opinion had also been current in Moslem Spain. Cf. R. Brunschvig, 'Averroes Juriste'. In: *Études d'orientalisme, dédiées à la mémoire de Lévi-Provençal* (2 vols. Paris: Maisonneuve, 1962), Vol. I, pp. 35-68.
77. Shuqayr (1903), Vol. 3, pp. 122-124. As Abū Salīm's compilation of the *Mahdī*'s writings (Muḥammad Ibrāhīm Aḥmad Abū Salīm. *Manshūrāt al-Imām al-Mahdī*. 4 vols. Khartoum, 1963-64), was not accessible to me, I had to depend on Shuqayr (1903) for the text of the *Mahdī*'s letters and proclamations. According to Holt the texts as given by Shuqayr are reliable. Cf. Holt (1970), p. 274.
78. Shuqayr (1903), pp. 347-348.
79. This was not a new device. During the wars between the Ottoman Empire and Persia, the Ottoman *Shaykhs al-Islām* used to issue *fatwās* declaring the Persians to be unbelievers, in order to justify jihad against them. Cf. W. Björkman, *Kāfir*. In: *EI*[2], Vol. IV, p. 408.
80 Abū l-Barakāt Sayyidī Aḥmad al-Dardīr (d. 1201/1786) writes in his commentary on Khalīl's *Mukhtaṣar*: '[This definition of robber, *muḥārib*, also includes] the tyrannical rulers (*umarāʾ*) of Egypt and their likes, since they rob the properties of the Moslems, hinder them in finding their daily bread and raid their towns, whereas it is impossible for these Moslems to obtain help from the *ʿulamāʾ* or others.' Dasūqī, Vol. 4, p. 348 (*in margine*).
81. Shuqayr (1903), Vol. 3, p. 134.
82. The word *djizyah* is used here deliberately in order to emphasize the contention that the Turks treat the Sudanese as subjected non-Moslems.
83. Ibrāhīm (1968), pp. 42-43.
84. Holt (1970), pp. 112-114.
85. Text of the letter in Shuqayr (1903), Vol. 3, pp. 466-467.
86. The *ḥadīth al-qudsī* is a class of traditions that relate the words of Allah.
87. Shuqayr (1903), Vol. 3, pp. 349-350.

88. Ibid., p. 350. What he probably did not know, was that large groups in Egypt were awaiting his coming in order to deliver them from the taxes, the debts and the Europeans. Cf. Jacques Berque, *L'Égypte. Impérialisme et Révolution* (Paris: Gallimard, 1967), p. 122.
89. Shuqayr (1903), Vol. 3, p. 374.
90. Text in: Muḥammad al-ʿAbbāsī al-Mahdī, *Al-Fatāwā l-Mahdiyyah fī l-waqāʾiʿ al-Miṣriyyah* (7 vols. Cairo: Al-Maṭbaʿah al-Azhariyyah, 1301), Vol. 2, pp. 28-32.
91. For an analysis of the ideological struggle between the *Mahdī* and the *ʿulamāʾ*, see: Ibrāhīm (1968).
92. Text in Shuqayr (1903), Vol. 3, pp. 383-391.
93. Text in Shuqayr (1903), Vol. 3, pp. 375-383.
94. This was obviously a sneer at the *Mahdī*'s fiscal policy, as he wanted to reintroduce the taxes prescribed by the *sharīʿah.*
95. Holt (1970), pp. 109-110.
96. Shuqayr (1903), Vol. 3, p, 374.
97. Muḥammad Rashīd Riḍā, *Tārīkh al-Ustādh al-Imām, al-Shaykh Muḥammad ʿAbduh* (3 vols. Cairo: Maṭbaʿat al-Manār, 1351/1931), Vol. 1, pp. 370, 380.
98. Trimingham (1949), pp. 158-159.
99. Alexander Schölch, *Ägypten den Ägyptern! Die politische und gesellschaftliche Krise der Jahre 1878-1882 in Ägypten* (Zürich, etc., Atlantis Verlag, n.d. [1972]), p. 54.
100. The word *ḥizb* at the time did not denote any kind of organized political party in the modern sense, but rather a group of people with more or less the same political interests and views. Cf. Schölch (1972), pp. 118-119.
101. For the text of the program of the National Party, see: ʿAbd al-Raḥmān al-Rāfiʿī, *Al-thawrah al-ʿUrābiyyah wa-l-iḥtilāl al-Inglīzī* (Cairo: Maṭbaʿat al-Nahḍah, 1355/1937), pp. 145-148.
102. In 1882 there were 1,355 foreigners among the 9,200 state officials. They occupied the highest posts. Cf. Rifʿat Saʿīd, *Al-asās al-idjtimāʿī li-l-thawrah al-ʿUrābiyyah* (Cairo: Dār al-Kātib al-ʿArabī li-l-Ṭibāʿah wa-l-Nashr, 1387/1967), p. 101.
103. Schölch (1972), p. 146.
104. Schölch considers it likely that the British had a hand in these riots, but cannot bring forward conclusive evidence. Schölch (1972), p. 219.
105. Ibid., pp. 345-346.
106. Rāfiʿī (1937), pp. 426, 430.
107. Text in: Salīm Khalīl al-Naqqāsh, *Miṣr li-l-Miṣriyyīn* (9 vols. Alexandria: Maṭbaʿat Djarīdat al-Maḥrūsah, 1302/1884), Vol. 5, p. 201.
108. Schölch (1972), p. 244.
109. Ibid., p. 245.

110. From a sermon by *Shaykh* Ḥamīdah al-Damanhūrī. Text in Naqqāsh (1884), Vol. 5, p. 195.
111. From a sermon by Muḥammad Abū l-Waṣl. Text in Naqqāsh (1884), Vol. 5., p. 194.
112. From a sermon by *Shaykh* ʿAlī Mulayḥī. Text in Naqqāsh (1884), Vol. 5, p. 150.
113. Muṣṭafā ʿIzz, *Kitāb ṭarīq al-rashād fī l-ḥathth ʿalā l-djihād* (Cairo: Maṭbaʿat Djarīdat al-Hidāyah, 1317), 16 pp. The author was the Shāfiʿite *mufti* of Egypt. His pamphlet was posthumously published by his son in 1899/1900. Internal evidence shows that the text must have been written during the last month of the war, as it mentions the occupation of Suez by the British, but not ʿUrābī's surrender: 'They have also attacked us from other directions than Alexandria and Suez, but time and again we have been victorious over them. However, although the final victory is beyond doubt, there are still apprehensions that, if it takes much longer, those who are weak of heart and faith will be overcome with dismay and anxiety. The remedy for this inveterate malady is to obey the orders of Allah, to avoid what He has forbidden and to do penance.' (p. 4).
114. Ibid., pp. 2-3.
115. Naqqāsh (1884), Vol. 5, p. 188.
116. Ibid., Vol. 5, pp. 186-189.
117. E. E. Evans-Pritchard, *The Sanusi of Cyrenaica* (London, etc.: Oxford University Press, 1949), p. 99.
118. Ar. text and Germ. transl. in: Erich Graefe, 'Der Aufruf des Scheichs der Senūsīja zum Heiligen Kriege', *Der Islam* 3 (1912), pp. 141-150.
119. Ibid., pp. 144-145.
120. Evans-Pritchard (1949), p. 116; Ageron (1968), Vol. 2, p. 912; Niemeijer (1972), p. 56.
121. Graefe (1912), p. 142; Muḥammad Rashīd Riḍā, 'Al-djihād fī l-Islām', *Al-Manār* 15 (1912), p. 34.
122. The Ottoman government thus exploited the erroneous idea that the Sultan-Caliph was the spiritual leader of all Moslems, as the Pope was for all Catholics. This had become standard practice since the Treaty of Küçük Kaynarca (1774), when, for the first time, the Ottoman Empire was compelled to cede territory inhabited by Moslems to a Christian power. The treaty with Austria, concluded in 1908, over Bosnia contained similar terms. On this question, see: T. W. Arnold, *The Caliphate* (2nd ed., London: Routledge and Kegan Paul, 1965), pp. 177-179; C. A. Nallino, 'Appunti sulla natura del "Califfato" in genere e sul presunto "Califfato ottomana".' In: *Raccolta di scritti* (Rome, 1941), Vol. 3, pp. 249-254.
123. Evans-Pritchard (1949), p. 110.
124. Ibid., p. 115.

125. Al-Sayyid Muḥammad al-Mahdī Aḥmad ibn al-Sayyid Muḥammad al-Sharīf ibn al-Sayyid Muḥammad ibn ʿAlī al-Sanūsī al-Khaṭṭābī al-Ḥasanī al-Idrīsī, *Bughyat al-musāʿid fī aḥkām al-mudjāhid fī l-ḥathth ʿalā l-djihād* (Cairo: Maṭbaʿat Djarīdat al-Shaʿb, 1332/1913-4), 58 pp. There is an obvious textual relationship between this treatise and the aforementioned proclamation. With the exception of the introduction and the end, the latter is composed of fragments that can literally be found in the *Bughyah*. Hence, it is plausible to assume that the *Bughyah* has been written earlier. It seems, however, that the final text was not drafted until the Turks had left, since the proclamation refers – be it in passing – to the Caliph (Graefe, 1912, p. 144), whereas the parallel text in the *Bughyah* has conspicuously dropped this reference (*Bughyah*, p. 6).
126. *Bughyah*, p. 3.
127. Ibid., p. 7.
128. Ibid., pp. 35-36.
129. Ibid., pp. 18-22.
130. Ibid., p. 37.
131. Ibid., pp. 40-43.
132. Turkish text in: *Der Islam* 5 (1914), pp. 391-392; Germ. transl.: Ibid., pp. 392-393; *WI* 3 (1915), pp. 2-3; Engl. transl.: *IQ* 19 (1975), pp. 157-158.
133. *İslâm Ansiklopedisi* (Istanbul: 1940-), Vol. 10, pp. 497-498.
134. *WI* 3 (1915), p. 4.
135. From a proclamation of *ʿulamāʾ*, issued 20 - 11 1914 on the instigation of the *Shaykh al-Islām*. Germ. transl. in: *WI* 3 (1915), pp. 10-18; Engl. transl. in: *IQ* 19 (1975), pp. 159-163; a similar but more elaborate treatise was promulgated by the Committee of National Defence by the end of 1914. Dutch transl. in: C. Snouck Hurgronje, 'Een belangrijk document betreffende den heiligen oorlog van den Islam (1914) en eene officiëele correctie', *Verspreide Geschriften*, Vol. 3, pp. 327-355.
136. In the allied countries this matter aroused considerable indignation, which was not entirely free from hypocrisy. Since the word jihad evoked images of religious fanaticism and ruthless slaughter of infidels, Germany, who was suspected of having suggested this move to Turkey, was reproached for resorting to mediaeval intellectual weapons. At the same time this indignation betrayed a certain anxiety as to the loyalty of the colonized Moslems. The colonial powers used to see everywhere the spectre of Pan-Islamism. They overrated its impact and therefore feared this open and undisguised appeal to religious loyalties. Illustrative is the polemical discussion between the Dutch orientalist Snouck Hurgronje and his German colleague Becker. Cf. C. Snouck Hurgronje, 'The Holy War made in Germany', *Verspreide Geschriften*, Vol. 3, pp. 285-293; Id. 'Deutschland und der heilige Krieg', *Verspreide Geschriften*, Vol. 3, pp. 285-293; C. H. Becker, 'Die Kriegsdiskussion über den Heiligen

Krieg', *Vom Wesen und Werden der islamischen Welt. Islamstudien* (2 vols. Leipzig: 1932), Vol. 2, pp. 281-310; see also: Friedrich Schwally, 'Der heilige Krieg des Islam in religionsgeschichtlicher und staatsrechtlicher Bedeutung', *Internationale Monatsschrift für Wissenschaft, Kunst und Technik* (1916), pp. 678-714.

137. Djamāl al-Dīn al-Afghānī, *Al-Aʿmāl al-kāmilah. Maʿ dirāsah ʿan al-Afghānī. Al-ḥaqīqah al-kulliyyah* (Ed. and intr. by Muḥammad ʿAmmārah. Cairo: Dār al-Kitāb al-ʿArabī, n.d.), p. 368.

138. E.g. Muḥammad Adīb al-Djarrāḥ (who was a judge in the Court of Appeal in Mosul), *Risālat al-djihād ʿalā fatwā khalīfatinā al-aʿẓam al-Sulṭān al-Ghāzī Muḥammad Rashād* (Mosul: Maṭbaʿat Nīnawā, 1333), 88 p.; Aḥmad Fakhr al-Dīn ʿAbd Allāh al-Fayḍī, *Irshād al-ʿibād ilā l-ghazw wa-l-djihād* (Istanbul: Al-maṭbaʿah al-ʿĀmirah, 1336/*c.* 1917), 250 + 6 pp. This work was written in the first half of 1912 on the occasion of the Balkan-war and the Italian conquest of Libya and dedicated to Enver Paşa. It was, however, not printed until 1917-18. Y. I. Sarkīs (*Muʿdjam al-maṭbūʿāt al-ʿArabiyyah wa-l-Muʿarrabah*, Cairo: 1346/1928) mentions a few more treatises on jihad published in this period; these, however, I was not able to find. Proclamations and *fatwās* of Shīʿite *ʿulamā'* of Najaf, Germ. transl. in: *WI* 3 (1915), pp. 51-56, 131-133, 205-213, *WI* 4 (1916), pp. 217-225; Proclamation of the Society of Islamic *ʿulamā'*, Germ. transl. in: *WI* 3 (1915), pp. 121-125. The *fatwās* of the Shīʿite *ʿulamā'* of Irak do mention the word jihad, although, according to the strict doctrine of the Shīʿite *fiqh*, jihad is only possible when there is an *Imām*. Probably, this was a display of Ottoman loyalty on their part.

139. George Antonius, *The Arab Awakening* (5th ed., New York: Capricorn Book, 1965), pp. 139-148.

140. For a specimen, see: Scheich Salih Ascharif Attunisi, *Haqiqat al-dschihad. Die Wahrheit über dem Glaubenskriege* (Transl. from the Ar. by Karl E. Schabinger; Intr. by Martin Hartmann. Berlin: Deutsche Gesellschaft für Islamkunde, 1915).

141. Ageron (1968), Vol. 2, pp. 1177-1182.

142. Faruqi (1969), p. 61.

143. Ageron (1968), Vol. 2, p. 1176.

144. Niemeijer (1972), p. 63; *WI* 3 (1915), p. 58.

145. E.g. in Khartoum, where Muḥammad Māḍī Abū l-ʿAzā'im, teacher of *fiqh* at Gordon College and *shaykh* of the ʿAzamiyyah *ṭarīqah*, held a series of lectures and sermons on the subject. Cf. Muḥammad Māḍī Abū l-ʿAzā'im, *Al-djihād* (Publ. by ʿIzz al-Dīn Māḍī Abū l-ʿAzā'im. Cairo: Dār Mashyakhat al-Ṭarīqah al-ʿAzamiyyah, 1970), 120 pp.

146. Niemeijer (1972), pp. 38, 63, 72, 102; Ageron (1968), Vol. 2, p. 1175.

147. Smith (1946), p. 197; Ageron (1968), Vol. 2, pp. 1182-1183.

148. Amal Vinogradof, 'The 1920 revolt in Iraq reconsidered. The role of the tribes

in national politics', *IJMES* 3 (1972), pp. 135-136. The declarations and *fatwās* of the Shiʿite *ʿulamā'* during the revolt did not mention the word jihad. Cf. Fariq al-Muzhir Āl Firʿawn, *Al-ḥaqā'iq al-nāṣiʿah fī l-thawrah al-ʿIrāqiyyah sanat 1920 wa-natā'idjihā* (2 vols. Baghdad, 1371/1952), Vol. 1, pp. 149-152, 192-195. On the occasion of the 1941 coup d'état the Iraqi *ʿulamā'* played a similar role. Cf. *OM* 16 (1941), pp. 293 and 368.

149. David Waines, 'The failure of nationalist resistance'. In: Ibrahim Abu Lughod (ed.), *The Transformation of Palestine* (Evanstone: North West University Press, 1971), p. 228.
150. In order to make the boycott of the elections for a legislative council, in which the Arabs would occupy only a minority of the seats, succeed, the nationalist leaders, with the help of the local *imāms*, proclaimed that Moslems that would participate in the elections, were apostates who could not be buried in Moslem cemeteries. Cf. Y. Porath, *The Emergence of the Palestinian Arab National Movement, 1918-1929* (London: Frank Cass, 1974), pp. 149, 153-154.
151. John Hope Simpson, *Palestine. Report on Immigration, Land Settlement and Development* (London: H.M. Stationery Office, 1930), Cmd. 3686; Government of Palestine, *Report of a Committee on the Economic Condition of Agriculturists in Palestine and Fiscal Measures of the Government in Relation Thereto* (Johnson-Crosbie report), Jerusalem, 1930; summary in: *OM* 11 (1931), pp. 25-27.
152. ʿAbd al-Wahhāb al-Kayyālī, *Tārīkh Filasṭīn al-ḥadīth* (Beirut: Al-Mu'assasat al-ʿArabiyyah li-l-dirāsāt wa-l-nashr, 1970), pp. 252-254; Kāmil Maḥmūd Khillah, *Filasṭīn wa-l-intidāb al-Barīṭānī, 1922-1939* (Beirut: Markaz al-Abḥāth, 1974), pp. 306-307, 352-353; Y. Porath, *The Palestinian Arab National Movement, 1929-1939. From Riots to Rebellion* (London: Frank Cass, 1977), p. 131.
153. On Qassām and his movement, see: Porath (1977), pp. 134-139; ʿĀdil Ḥasan Ghunaym, 'Thawrat ʿIzz al-Dīn al-Qassām', *Shu'ūn Filasṭīniyyah* 6 (Jan. 1972), pp. 181-193; Kayyālī (1970), pp. 291-297; Ibrāhīm al-Shaykh Khalīl, 'Risālah min mudjāhid qadīm: dhikrayāt ʿan al-Qassām', *Shu'ūn Filasṭīniyyah* 7 (March 1972), pp. 267-269; Khillah (1974), pp. 375-383; Ṣubḥī Yāsīn, *Al-thawrah al-ʿArabiyyah al-kubrā fī Filasṭīn* (Cairo: Dār al-Kitāb al-ʿArabī, 1959), pp. 30-42.
154. *Annual Report on the Administration of Palestine*, PRO-CO 814-10, pp. 39-40; *OM* 15 (1935), pp. 640-643; Porath (1977), p. 142.
155. Porath (1977), p. 263; *OM* 18 (1938), pp. 236-237.
156. ʿAbd al-Wahhāb al-Kayyālī, *Wathā'iq al-muqāwamah al-Filasṭīniyyah ḍidd al-iḥtilāl al-Barīṭānī wa-l-Ṣahyūniyyah, 1918-1939* (Beirut: Mu'assasat al-Dirāsāt al-Filasṭīniyyah, 1968), pp. 615-616.
157. Porath (1977), p. 248; *OM* 18 (1938), pp. 557-558.
158. Porath (1977), pp. 264-265.
159. Khillah (1974), pp. 148, 290; *The Report of the Palestine Enquiry Committee*

on the Palestine Disturbances of August 1929 (Shaw Report) (London: H.M. Stationery Office, 1930), Cmd. 3530, p. 54.

160. *Report on the Political Situation in Palestine, March 1922*, PRO-CO 733-23; *Report on the Political Situation in Palestine, June 1923*, PRO-CO 733-50; *OM* 2 (1922-23), p. 107; Porath (1974), pp. 205-206.
161. Emmanuel Sivan, *Islam et Croisade. Idéologie et propagande dans les réactions musulmanes aux Croisades* (Paris: Maisonneuve, 1968), *passim*.
162. Kayyāli (1968), p. 429; *OM* 16 (1936), p. 511.
163. *OM* 8 (1928), pp. 470-471, 526.
164. Khillah (1974), p. 283; *Shaw Report*, pp. 48-49.
165. Porath (1974), pp. 267-269.
166. Kayyāli (1970), p. 244; Khillah (1974), p. 291.
167. *OM* 9 (1929), pp. 428-430, 526.
168. On the Jerusalem Conference of 1931, see: *OM* 11 (1931), pp. 526-530; ʿĀdil Ḥasan Ghunaym, 'Al-Mu'tamar al-Islāmi al-ʿĀmm (1931)', *Shu'ūn Filasṭiniyyah* 25 (Sept. 1973), pp. 119-136; H. A. R. Gibb, 'The Islamic Congress of Jerusalem in December, 1931'. In: A. J. Toynbee, *Survey of International Affairs 1934* (London: Oxford University Press, 1935), pp. 94-105; Khillah (1974), pp. 326-328.
169. *OM* 13 (1933), p. 619.
170. Toynbee (1935), p. 282.
171. *OM* 13 (1933), p. 618.
172. *OM* 17 (1937), pp. 438, 461-462, 501, 540.
173. Government of India to High Commissioner of Palestine, 17 November, 1937, PRO-CO 733-333 (75156/32).
174. *OM* 17 (1937), p. 540; *OM* 18 (1938), pp. 422, 548.
175. *Al-Yahūd wa-l-Islām qadīm^{an} wa-ḥadīth^{an}. Al-Yahūd wa-Filasṭin wa-āyāt al-djihād wa-l-aḥādīth ʿanhu. Risālat Maktab al-Istiʿlāmāt al-Filasṭini al-ʿArabi bi-l-Qāhirah ilā l-ʿālam al-Islāmi* (Cairo: 1937), 31 pp. Cf. *OM* 18 (1938), p. 688.
176. H.M. Consul in Beirut to High Commissioner of Palestine, 11 April, 1938, PRO-CO 733-367 (75156/14).
177. Texts in: Muḥammad al-Ḥusayn Kāshif al-Ghiṭā', *Qaḍiyyat Filasṭin al-kubrā fi khuṭub al-Imām al-rāḥil Muḥammad al-Ḥusayn Kāshif al-Ghiṭā'* (Nadjaf: Maṭbaʿat al-Nuʿmān, 1969); *al-Taqwā* 15 (1938), pp. 500 ff; Engl. transl. of both *fatwās* in PRO-CO 733-367 (75156/3).
178. *OM* 18 (1938), p. 553.
179. H.M. Ambassador in Cairo to Colonial Secretary, 26 August, 1938, PRO-CO 733-368 (75156/16); *OM* 18 (1938), pp. 520-521.
180. Muḥammad Ṣabri ʿĀbidin, *Al-djihād fi sabil Allāh bi-munāsabat ahl Filasṭin wa-difāʿihim ʿan al-Masdjid al-Aqṣā wa-l-diyār al-muqaddasah* (Cairo: Maṭbaʿat al-Qāhirah, 1357), pp. 3-4. Similar pamphlets and articles published

in this period: Al-Hay'ah al-ʿArabiyya al-ʿUlyā li-Filasṭin, *Al-djihād fī sabil Allāh* (Cairo: 1357), 23 pp.; pamphlet distributed in Cairo in October, 1938, Engl. transl. in *The Egyptian Gazette*, 29 Oct. 1938; pamphlet distributed in Mecca and signed: *Ikhwānukum ahl Filasṭin* (your brethren, the people of Palestine), copy to be found in PRO-CO 733-367 (75156/6).

181. Olivier Carré, *L'Idéologie palestinienne de résistance* (Paris: Colin, 1972), p. 107.
182. In 1969, after the arson in the al-Aqṣā Mosque, King Fayṣal proclaimed jihad against Israel. Cf. *Rābiṭat al-ʿĀlam al-Islāmī* 7 (1969), nr. 5, p. 71.
183. I owe this comparison to Prof. Dr. J. Brugman. Cf. J. Brugman, 'Voeren de Palestijnen een heilige oorlog?', *Palestijnse Drukken en Herdrukken* 6 (Oct. 1972), p. 10.

NOTES TO CHAPTER 4: THE DOCTRINE OF JIHAD IN MODERN ISLAM

1. *Kitāb al-djihād* (ed. by Nazīh al-Ḥammād. Beyrut: Dār al-Nūr, 1391/1971), 122 pp.
2. Cf. Sivan (1968); Hadia Dajani-Shakeel, 'Jihad in twelfth-century Arabic poetry: a moral and religious force to counter the Crusades', *MW* 66 (1976), pp. 96-113. For more details, v. the title-indices of GAL and GAS s.v. *djihād*, *kitāb al-djihād*, *risālat al-djihād*, *faḍl al-djihād*, *faḍā'il al-jihād* e.t.q. Some of these works have been printed, e.g.: ʿImād al-Dīn Ismāʿīl ibn ʿUmar *al-maʿrūf bi-*Ibn Kathīr (d. 774/1372-73), *Al-idjtihād fī ṭalab al-djihād* (Cairo: Djamʿiyyat al-nashr wa-l-ta'līf al-Azhariyyah, 1347/1928-29), 24 pp. (GAL, Vol. II, p. 49); Shams al-Dīn Aḥmad ibn Ibrāhīm ibn Muḥammad ibn al-Naḥḥās al-Dimashqī al-Dumyāṭī,*Mashāriʿ al-ashwāq ilā maṣāriʿ al-ʿushshāq wa-muthīr al-gharām ilā dār al-Islām*. Publ. in an abridged version by Maḥmūd al-ʿĀlim (d. 1311/1893) under the title: *Fukāhat al-adhwāq min mashāriʿ al-ashwāq*, 1st ed. (Cairo: al-Maṭbaʿah al-Saniyyah al-Kubrā, 1290 H.) 76 pp.; 2nd ed. (Cairo: Maktabat al-Qāhirah, 1390/1970), 144 pp. (GAL S, Vol. II, p. 83).
3. *Al-djihād fī l-Islām* (Cairo: Djāmiʿat al-Azhar/al-Hay'ah al-ʿĀmmah li-Shu'ūn al-Maṭābiʿ al-Amīriyyah, 1967), 82 pp.
4. *Fatāwā khaṭirah fī wudjūb al-djihād al-dīnī al-muqaddas li-inqādh Filasṭīn wa-ṣiyānat al-Masdjid al-Aqṣā wa-sā'ir al-muqaddasāt* (Cairo: al-Maṭbaʿah al-Salafiyyah [1948]), p. 8.
5. *Kitāb al-Mu'tamar al-Rābiʿ li-Madjmaʿ al-Buḥūth al-Islāmiyyah* (Cairo: 1388/1968), p. 301.
6. *Le Monde*, 24-11-1977.
7. E.g. the *fatwā* issued by the *muftī* of Egypt in June 1948, publ. in: *Fatāwā khaṭirah*, pp. 29-31.
8. For India and Algeria during the nineteenth century, cf. Rudolph Peters,

'Dār al-Ḥarb, Dār al-Islām und der Kolonialismus'. In: *XIX. Deutscher Orientalistentag (Freiburg, Sept.-Okt. 1975). Vorträge* (Wiesbaden: 1977), pp. 579-587 and the literature quoted there. For the Arab-Israeli conflict, cf. ʿAbdallāh al-Qalqīlī, *Al-fatāwā l-Urdunniyyah. Qism al-taʿāmul maʿ al-ʿaduww wa-aḥkām al-djihād* ([Beyrut:] al-Maktab al-Islāmī, 1389/1969), 110 pp.

9. Hunter (1974), pp. 185-186; Ahmad Khan (1872), pp. i-ii; C. Snouck Hurgronje (1894), Vol. II, pp. 387-388; al-Djazā'irī (1964), pp. 316; Mercier (1939), pp. 76-83; Depont & Coppolani (1897), pp. 33-37.
10. Faradj Muḥammad Ghayth, *Ghāyat al-irshād ilā aḥkām al-djihād* (Cairo: Muṣṭafā l-Bābī al-Ḥalabī, 1955), p. 27.
11. Maḥmūd Shīt Khaṭṭāb, *Irādat al-qitāl fī l-djihād al-Islāmī* (Beyrut: Dār al-Irshād, 1968), p. 34.
12. Khaṭṭāb (1968), p. 39; ʿUthmān al-Saʿīd al-Sharqāwī, *Sharīʿat al-qitāl fī l-Islām* (Cairo: Maktabat al-Azhar, 1392/1972), pp. 244-248.
13. Abū l-Aʿlā l-Mawdūdī, *Al-djihad fī sabīl Allāh* (Beyrut: Dār al-Fikr, n.d.), pp. 27-29; in the same strain: Sayyid Quṭb in: Abū l-Aʿlā l-Mawdūdī, Ḥasan al-Bannā and Sayyid Quṭb, *Al-djihād fī sabīl Allāh* (Beyrut: Al-Ittiḥād al-Islāmī al-ʿĀlamī li-l-munaẓẓamāt al-ṭullābiyyah, 1969), pp. 105-109; and ʿAbd al-Ḥāfiẓ ʿAbd Rabbih, *Falsafat al-djihād fī l-Islām* (Beyrut: Dār al-Kitāb al-Rusnānī, 1972), pp. 56-57.
14. Kāmil Salāmah al-Daqs, *Āyāt al-djihād fī l-qur'ān al-karīm* (Kuwait: Dār al-Yayān, 1392/1972), pp. 98-99.
15. Zuḥaylī (1965), pp. 18-19. To the same effect: ʿAbd Rabbih (1972), p. 15; Daqs (1972), p. 6; Muḥammad ʿIzzat Darwazah, *Al-djihād fī sabīl Allāh fī l-Qur'ān wa-l-hadīth* (Dimashq: Dār al-Yaqaẓah al-ʿArabiyyah, 1395/1975), p. 64; Muḥammad Ismāʿīl Ibrāhīm, *Al-djihād rukn al-Islām al-sādis* (Cairo: Dār al-Fikr al-ʿArabī, 1970), p. 136; Muḥammad Faradj, *Al-madrasah al-ʿaskariyyah al-Islāmiyyah* (Cairo: Dār al-Fikr al-ʿArabī, n.d. [*c.* 1969]), pp. 71-89; ʿAlī ʿAlī Manṣūr, *Al-sharīʿah al-Islāmiyyah wa-l-qānūn al-dawlī al-ʿāmm* (Cairo: al-Madjlis al-Aʿlā li-l-Shu'ūn al-Islāmiyyah, 1390/1971), p. 237; al-Sharqāwī (1972), pp. 19-20.
16. Djamāl al-Dīn ʿAyyād, *Nuẓum al-ḥarb fī l-Islām* (Cairo: Maktabat al-Khāndjī, 1370 [*c.* 1951]), pp. 26-28; ʿAbd Rabbih (1972), p. 341; Muḥammad ʿAbdallāh Darāz, 'Mabādi' al-qānūn al-dawlī al-ʿāmm li-l-Islām', *Risālat al-Islām* 2 (1950), pp. 148-164; p. 159; Muḥammad ʿAbdallāh al-Sammān, *Al-Islām wa-l-amn al-dawlī* (Cairo: Dār al-Kitāb al-ʿArabī), 1952, p. 7; Manṣūr (1971), p. 319.
17. The classical authors held either that these verses had been abrogated by the Verses of Fighting that give a general command to fight the unbelievers, or they interpreted these verses in accordance with classical theory. Thus, the word *'peace-greeting'* (*al-salām*) in K 4:90 is understood as *'conversion to Islam'* (*al-Islām*), whereas the command of K 8:61 is taken to be restricted by K 47:35

(*'So do not grow faint and call for peace, seeing you have the upper hand . . . .'*), so that the order obtains only when the Moslems are weak and it is in their interest to conclude peace. Cf. Ibn ʿArabī, Vol. I, p. 481, Vol. II, p. 864; Djaṣṣāṣ, Vol. IV, pp. 254-255.

18. Maḥmūd Shaltūt, *Al-qur'ān wa-l-qitāl* (Cairo: Maṭbaʿat al-Naṣr wa-Maktab al-Ittiḥād al-Sharqī, 1367/1948), pp. 60-61.
19. E.g. Maḥmūd Shīt Khaṭṭāb, *Al-rasūl al-qā'id* (2nd rev. ed., Cairo: Dār al-Qalam, 1964), 499 pp.; Faradj (*c.* 1969).
20. ʿAbdallāh Muṣṭafā l-Marāghī, *Al-djihād* (Cairo: Maṭbaʿat al-Sunnah al-Muḥammadiyyah, 1369/1950), p. 14.
21. Faradj (*c.* 1969), p. 231.
22. For the opinion of classical authors on this topic, cf. Morabia (1975), p. 343.
23. J. J. G. Jansen, *The Interpretation of the Koran in Modern Egypt.* (Leyden: E. J. Brill, 1974), pp. 35-54.
24. Shaltūt (1948), p. 39.
25. ʿAbdallāh Ghawshah, 'Al-djihād ṭarīq al-naṣr'. In: *Kitāb al-Mu'tamar al-Rābiʿ li-Madjmaʿ al-Buḥūth al-Islāmiyyah* ([Cairo:] 1388/1968), p. 263. Evidently, this part of the interpretation of K 8:60 indirectly criticizes the Egyptian government for its heavy reliance on Soviet military and technological aid.
26. Djamāl al-Dīn al-Afghānī, 'Al-Ḥarb al-ʿādilah wa-l-ḥarb ghayr al-ʿādilah'. In: *Al-Aʿmāl al-Kāmilah* (ed. by Muḥammad al-ʿAmmārah. Cairo: Dār al-Kātib al-ʿArabī, n.d.), p. 439; Muḥammad ʿAbduh & Muḥammad Rashīd Riḍa, *Tafsīr al-Manār* (2nd ed., Cairo: Dār al-Manār), Vol. 10, pp. 69-72, 168; Daqs (1972), pp. 113-114; Ghawshah (1968), pp. 261-263; Shaltūt (1948), pp. 44-45; Khaṭṭāb (1964), p. 29.
27. Shaltūt (1948), p. 53; Mohammad Talaat Al Ghunaimi, *The Muslim Conception of International Law and the Western Approach* (The Hague: Martinus Nijhoff, 1968), pp. 177-178; Zuḥaylī (1965), p. 119.
28. Rashīd Riḍā (1912), p. 36.
29. Mawdūdī (n.d.), p. 10; Aḥmad Muḥammad Djamāl, *Muftarayāt ʿalā l-Islām* (Beyrut: Dār al-Fikr, 1392/1972), pp. 268-269.
30. Morābia (1975), pp. 480-563.
31. Ibrāhīm (1964), p. 56.
32. Muḥammad Shadīd, *Al-djihād fī l-Islām* (Cairo: Mu'assasat al-Maṭbūʿāt al-Ḥadīthah, n.d.), pp. 7, 90; Niʿmat Ṣidqī, *Al-djihād fī sabīl Allāh* (Cairo: Dār al-Iʿtiṣām, 1975), pp. 22-31.
33. *Al-bayān al-usbūʿī li-l-ra'īs al-Ḥabīb Būrqībah*, 5-2-1960 (Tūnus: Kitābat al-Dawlah li-l-akhbār wa-l-irshād).
34. For the ensuing discussion, cf. Rudolph Peters, 'Recente discussies rond de Islamitische vastenmaand, Ramadan', *Internationale Spectator* (The Hague), 23 (1969), pp. 1812-1825.
35. Muḥammad al-Ḥabīb ibn al-Khūdjah, 'Al-djihād fī l-Islām'. In: *Min Waḥy*

Laylat al-Qadr. Dirāsāt Islāmiyyah (Tūnus: al-Dār al-Tūnusiyyah li-l-Nashr, 1971), p. 130.

36. Sobhi Mahmassani, 'The principles of international law in the light of the Islamic doctrine'. In: *Académie de droit international. Recueil des cours* 117 (1966), Vol. I, p. 321; Darwazah (1975), p. 7; Shadīd (n.d.), p. 153.
37. A. Sanhoury, *Le califat. Son évolution vers une Société des Nations orientale* (Paris: Geuthner, 1926), pp. 148-150.
38. Muḥammad Abū Zahrah, 'Al-djihād'. In: *Kitāb al-Mu'tamar al-Rābiʿ li-Madjmaʿ al-Buḥūth al-Islāmiyyah* ([Cairo:] 1388/1968), p. 67.
39. Ḥasan al-Bannā, 'Risālat al-djihād'. In: *Madjmūʿat rasā'il al-Imām al-shahīd Ḥasan al-Bannā* (Beyrut: Dār al-Nūr, n.d.), p. 58; Mawdūdi (n.d.), p. 29.
40. *Tafsīr al-Manār*, Vol. 2, p. 254.
41. Ibid., p. 460.
42. Muḥammad Radjā' Ḥanafī ʿAbd al-Mutadjallī, *Ramaḍān shahr al-djihād* (Cairo: al-Madjlis al-Aʿlā li-l-Shu'ūn al-Islāmiyyah, 1973), p. 23.
43. ʿAbd al-Ḥalīm Maḥmūd, 'Al-djihād'. In: *Kitāb al-Mu'tamar al-Rābiʿ li-Madjmaʿ al-Buḥūth al-Islāmiyyah* ([Cairo:] 1388/1968), p. 43; ʿAbd al-Fattāḥ Ḥasan, *Mīthāq al-umam wa-l-shuʿūb fī l-Islām* (Cairo: al-Idārah al-ʿAmmah li-l-Thaqāfah al-Islāmiyyah bi-l-Djāmiʿ al-Azhar, 1959), p. 1.
44. E.g. Manṣūr (1971), p. 216; Mahmassani (1966), p. 282; Khadduri (1955), pp. 70-71.
45. ʿAbd al-Raḥmān ibn Muḥammad ibn Khaldūn, *Muqaddimah* (ed. by ʿAlī ʿAbd al-Wāḥid Wāfī. 2nd ed., Cairo: Ladjnat al-Bayān al-ʿArabī, 1384/1965), Vol. 2, p. 823.
46. In accordance with his theory that state and religion are to be separated in Islam, ʿAlī ʿAbd al-Rāziq maintained that jihad in Islam only served state interests and had nothing to do with religion: 'At first sight it is clear that the aim of jihad is not only missionary and that it does not serve the purpose of bringing people to believe in Allah and His Prophet. Its aim is only the corroboration of power and the expansion of authority.' (ʿAlī ʿAbd al-Rāziq, *Al-Islām wa-uṣūl al-ḥukm*. Ed. and ann. by Muḥammad ʿAmmārah. Beyrut: Al-Mu'assasah al-ʿArabiyyah li-l-Dirāsāt wa-l-Nashr, 1972, pp. 147-148.) Elsewhere in his book, however, he contradicts this statement by saying: 'No wonder that jihad is one of these means [i.e. means of corroborating religion and supporting the mission]. It is a violent and harsh means, but how can one know, maybe something evil is sometimes required to attain something good and destruction may be necessary to achieve civilization.' (Ibid., p. 166.) For criticisms on this point, raised by the orthodox *ʿulamā'*, see: ʿAbdelhamid Muhammad Ahmad, *Die Auseinandersetzung zwischen al-Azhar und der modernistischen Bewegung in Ägypten* (Hamburg, 1963), pp. 88-89, 96-99.
47. By freedom of religion Moslem authors refer to the freedom of *dhimmīs* to exercise their religion under certain conditions, the freedom of Moslems to

exercise their religion outside the Territory of Islam and the freedom of non-Moslems to be converted to Islam. This freedom does not include the right of Moslems to abandon their religion. Cf. Rudolph Peters & Gert J. J. de Vries, 'Apostasy in Islam'. *WI*, n.s. 17 (1976-77), pp. 1-25.

48. In classical Islam, there existed various interpretations of this verse. According to some, it has been abrogated by the unconditional command to fight the unbelievers. Others hold that it refers to a certain custom amongst the women of the *Anṣār*, according to which these women, when a baby died, would vow that the next one, if it remained alive, would be converted to Judaism. In general, however, this verse was taken as a prohibition to force those who could become *dhimmīs* to embrace Islam. This implies that it was allowed to compel pagan Arabs and apostates to conversion. Being aware of the impossibility of forcing a conviction upon somebody, they professed that outward behaviour in conformity with Islamic prescriptions was sufficient. In most cases conviction would follow automatically. Others saw this not as a compulsion to be converted but rather as a punishment for obstinacy: By the time Mohammed began to fight, he had adduced so much evidence and so many arguments for the truth of his mission, that not believing in it ought to be regarded as sheer obstinacy. Ibn al-ʿArabī, Vol. 1, pp. 232-234; Abū ʿAbd Allāh Muḥammad b. Aḥmad al-Anṣārī al-Qurṭubī, *Al-djāmiʿ li-aḥkām al-qur'ān* (Cairo: Dār al-Kutub al-Miṣriyyah, 1354/1935), Vol. 3, pp. 279-281; Ibn Ḥazm, Vol. 7, p. 346.
49. Shaltūt (1948), p. 13. This opinion is similar to Paret's interpretation of K 2:256, according to which *'there is no compulsion in religion'* means *'there* can *be no compulsion in religion'* and not *'there* should *be no compulsion in religion'*. Cf. R. Paret, 'Lā ikrāha fi-d-dīn. Toleranz oder Resignation', *Der Islam* 45 (1969), pp. 299-301.
50. *Tafsīr al-Manār*, Vol. 2, p. 211.
51. Ghayth (1955), p. 62; to the same effect, Zuḥaylī (1965), p. 99.
52. Although the exclusively defensive character of jihad was only recently put forward by the modernists, there are indications that this concept is much older. The classical rule that the *Imām* is obliged to raid enemy territory once a year in order to keep the idea of jihad alive must have been a dead letter during long periods of Islamic history. Morabia (1975, pp. 480-563) describes the effects of the stagnation of the Islamic expansion on the doctrine of jihad, and calls it the 'internalizing' (*intériorisation*) of the jihad-doctrine. In his view this consists of three elements: the application of the concept of jihad to the struggle for the protection of Islam against internal dangers like rebellions and heresies, the development of the notion of jihad as moral struggle (*al-amr bi-l-maʿrūf wa-l-nahy ʿan al-munkar*) and, finally, the development of the notion of jihad as a spiritual struggle against one's own evil inclinations. To these elements a fourth one might be added: the conviction amongst the common people that jihad is

only a defensive war, obligatory in case the enemy attacks Islamic territory. The collection of *Thousand and One Nights* contains the didactic story of Tawaddud, a slave girl that astonishes the *ʿulamā'* by her extensive knowledge of Islam. With regard to jihad, we read: 'He said: "What is the jihad and what are its essential elements (*arkān*)?" She answered: "As for its essential elements, they are: an attack on us by the unbelievers, the presence of an *Imām*, preparedness and constance when one meets the enemy".' (*Alf laylah wa-laylah*, 4 vols. Cairo: Maṭbaʿat Muḥammad ʿAlī Ṣubayḥ wa-Awlādih, n.d., Vol. 2, p. 309.) These phrases cannot be traced back to the works on *fiqh*. My assumption is that they reflect popular ideas on jihad. Admittedly, this assumption is based upon scant evidence and the topic deserves, therefore, further research.

53. Ahmad Khan (1872), pp. xviii-xix. The original article had appeared in *The Pioneer* of the 23rd November, 1871.
54. Cf. Moulavi Cheragh Ali, *A Critical Exposition of the Popular 'jihād', showing that all the Wars of Mohammad were Defensive; and that Aggressive War, or Compulsory Conversion, is not allowed in the Koran* (Calcutta: Thacker, Spink and Co., 1885), civ + 249 pp.; Moulvi Abu Said Mohammed Husain, *A Treatise on Jihad* [*Iqtisad fi masail il-jihad*] (Lahore: Victoria Press, 1887), 32 pp.; Syed Ameer Ali, *A Critical Examination of the Life and Teachings of Mohammed* (London, etc.: Williams & Norgate, 1873), pp. 147-216; J. M. S. Baljon, *The Reforms and Religious Ideas of Sir Sayyid Ahmad Khan* (Leyden: Brill, 1949), pp. 30-31; Smith (1946), pp. 14-47; Aziz Ahmad & G. E. von Grunebaum, *Muslim Self-statement in India and Pakistan, 1857-1968* (Wiesbaden: Harrassowitz, 1970), pp. 3-5.
55. Husain (1887), p. 2.
56. Muḥammad ʿAbduh, *Al-Islām wa-l-Naṣrāniyyah maʿ al-ʿilm wa-l-madaniyyah* (8th ed., Cairo: Dār al-Manār, 1373 [*c. 1954*]), pp. 62-67; *Tafsīr al-Manār*, Vol. 2, pp. 103-104, 208-213, 312-318, Vol. 3, p. 39, Vol. 10, pp. 167-173, 360-377, Vol. 11, pp. 123-126; J. Jomier, *Le Commentaire coranique du Manar.* (Paris: Maisonneuve, 1954), pp. 251-281; Rashīd Riḍā (1912); Id. *Al-waḥy al-Muḥammadī* (5th ed., Cairo: *Dār al-Manār*, 1375 [*c.* 1955]), pp. 126-136; Id. *Fatāwā* (ed. by Ṣalāḥ al-Dīn al-Munadjdjid & Yūsuf Q. Khūrī. Beyrut: Dār al-Kitāb al-Djadīd, 1390/1970), Vol. 2, pp. 575-576, Vol. 3, pp. 1152-1157.
57. Olivier Carré, *Enseignement islamique et idéal socialiste* (Beyrut: Dar el-Machreq, 1974), pp. 206-211.
58. Rashīd Riḍā (1912), p. 35.
59. Shaltūt (1948), p. 30.
60. Fundamentalist literature on jihad: Mawdūdī (n.d.); Abū 'l-Aʿlā l-Mawdūdī, Ḥasan al-Bannā & Sayyid Quṭb, *Al-djihād fī sabīl Allāh* (Beyrut: Al-Ittiḥād al-Islāmī al-ʿĀlamī li-Munaẓẓamāt Ṭullābiyyah, 1969), 135 pp.; Ḥasan al-Bannā

(n.d.); Sayyid Quṭb, *Fi ẓilāl al-qur'ān* (5th ed., Beyrut: Dār al-turāth al-ʿArabī, 1386/1967), Vol. 1, part 2, pp. 159-167, Vol. 3, part 9, pp. 174-201, Vol. 4, part 10, pp. 9-11, 103-110, 218-220, Vol. 5, part 17, pp. 17, 94-100; Id. *Ṭarīq al-daʿwah fī ẓilāl al-qur'ān* (ed. by Aḥmad Fā'iz. 2nd ed., Beyrut: Dār al-Arqam, 1394/1974), 386 pp.; Id. *Al-salām al-ʿālamī wa-l-Islām* (5th ed., Cairo: Maktabat Wahbah, 1386/1966), 199 pp.; Aḥmad Nār, *Al-qitāl fī l-Islām* (Djuddah: Al-Dār al-Suʿūdiyyah li-l-nashr wa-l-tawzīʿ, 1389/1969), 264 pp.; Daqs (1972).

61. Mawdūdī (n.d.), pp. 12-13.
62. Quṭb (1974), pp. 310-311.
63. Quṭb (1967), Vol. 3, part 9, pp. 166-167; id. in: Mawdūdī, a.o. (1969), p. 101; Nār (1969), pp. 18-21.
64. *Tafsīr al-Manār*, Vol. 2, p. 211; Darwazah (1975), p. 47; Shaltūt (1948), pp. 27-28; Abū Zahrah (1968), p. 92.
65. Mawdūdī (n.d.), pp. 30-31; Quṭb in: Mawdūdī, a.o. (1969), p. 110; Daqs (1972), p. 87.
66. Daqs (1972), p. 105. To the same effect and with attacks especially directed against Ahmad Khān and the Ahmadiyyah-movement: Muḥammad al-Bahī, *Al-fikr al-Islāmī al-ḥadīth wa-ṣilatuh bi-l-istiʿmār al-gharbī* (6th ed., Beyrut: Dār al-Fikr, 1973), pp. 44, 47-49; Zuḥaylī (1965), pp. 94-95.
67. Quṭb (1967), Vol. 3, part 9, p. 174.
68. Nār (1969), p. 42.
69. In classical Islam, some held that this verse had been abrogated by the sword-verses, whereas others were of the opinion that the Moslems only had to accept such a peace-offer if they had an interest in doing so. Ibn al-ʿArabī, Vol. 2, pp. 864-865.
70. Shadīd (n.d.), p. 127.
71. Ibrāhīm (1964), pp. 56, 87, 139-140; Aḥmad Mūsā Sālim, *Al-Islām wa-qaḍāyānā l-muʿāṣirah (Cairo: Maktabat al-Qāhirah al-Ḥadīthah, n.d.* [c. 1970]), p. 260; Aḥmad Muḥammad al-Ḥawfī, *Al-djihād* (Cairo: Al-Madjlis al-Aʿlā li-l-Shu'ūn al-Islāmiyyah, 1970), pp. 10-11; see also the discussion between a number of leading *ʿulamā'* on the duty of Moslems to defend their fatherland in *Liwā' al-Islām* 10 (1956), nr. 6, pp. 378-384.
72. To the best of my knowledge the word *waṭan* was first used in combination with jihad during the ʿUrābī revolt. Many preachers that backed ʿUrābī's cause, coupled the concept of defence of the fatherland with that of defence of religion. Cf. Naqqāsh (1884), Vol. 5, p. 150, 196.
73. *Al-Muṣawwar* (Cairo), 12-10-1973. Dr. U. Haarmann of Freiburg (FRG) kindly sent me a copy of this text. See also U. Haarmann, 'Die Pflichten des Muslims – Dogma und geschichtliche Wirklichkeit', *Saeculum* 26 (1975), p. 109.
74. Cf. Shameem Akhtar, 'An inquiry into the nature, origin and source of Islamic

law of nations', *IS*, 10 (1971), pp. 23-37; Najib Armanazi, *L'Islam et le droit international* (thèse) (Paris: Librairie Picart, 1929) 162 pp. (Ar. transl.: *Al-shar' al-dawlī fī l-Islām.* Damascus: Maṭbaʿat Ibn Zaydūn, 1930, 184 pp.); Muḥammad ʿAbd Allāh Darāz, 'Mabādi' al-qānūn al-dawlī al-ʿāmm li-l-Islām', *Risālat al-Islām* 2 (1950), pp. 148-164; M. A. Draz, 'Le droit international public et l'Islam', *Revue Égyptienne de Droit International Public* (1947), pp. 17-27; Al Ghunaimi (1968); Hamidullah (1953); Ḥasan (1378/1959); Zafrullah Khan, 'Islam and international relations', *Internationale Spectator* (The Hague), 10 (1956), 11, pp. 308-323; Mahmassani (1966); Manṣūr (1390/1971); Ahmed Rechid, 'L'Islam et le droit des gens'. In: *Académie de Droit International. Recueil des Cours* 60 (1937), II, pp. 375-504; Ḥāmid Sulṭān, *Aḥkām al-qānūn al-dawlī fī l-sharīʿah al-Islāmiyyah* (Cairo: Dār al-Nahḍah al-ʿArabiyyah, 1970), 269 pp.; Muḥammad Kāmil Yāqūt, *Al-shakhṣiyyah al-dawliyyah fī l-qānūn al-dawlī al-ʿamm wa-l-sharīʿah al-Islāmiyyah* (Cairo: ʿĀlam al-Kutub, 1970-71), 785 + 14 pp.; There are also a few Arabic authors on international law that mention in passing some of the Islamic prescriptions. E.g.: ʿAbd al-ʿAzīz ʿAlī Djāmiʿ, ʿAbd al-Fattāḥ ʿAbd al-ʿAzīz and Ḥasan Darwīsh, *Qānūn al-ḥarb* (Cairo: Maktabat al-Anglo-Miṣriyyah, 1952), pp. 37-39; Khālid Farrādj and Ḥasan Darwīsh, *Al-mūdjaz fī l-qānūn al-dawlī al-ʿāmm* (Cairo: Maktabat al-Anglo-Miṣriyyah, 1967), pp. 119-123; Sumūḥī Fawq al-ʿĀdah, *Al-qānūn al-dawlī al-ʿāmm* (Damascus: Maṭbaʿat al-Inshā', 1960), 1073 pp., *passim*; Muḥammad Ḥāfiẓ Ghānim, *Al-uṣūl al-djadīdah li-l-qānūn al-dawlī al-ʿāmm* (Cairo: Maṭbaʿat Nahḍat Miṣr, 1952), pp. 423-424; Id. *Mabādi' al-qānūn al-dawlī al-ʿāmm* (Cairo: Dār al-Nahḍah al-Miṣriyyah, 1967), pp. 714-715; Muḥammad Ṭalʿat al-Ghunaymī, *Al-Aḥkām al-ʿāmmah fī qānūn al-umam. Dirāsah fī kull min al-fikr al-gharbī wa-l-ishtirākī wa-l-Islāmī. Qānūn al-salām* (Alexandria: Munsha'at al-Maʿārif, 1970), 1237 pp., *passim*; Muḥammad Saʿd al-Dīn Zakī, *Al-ḥarb wa-l-salām* (Cairo: 1965), pp. 25-28, 179-218.

75. E.g.: K.Th. Pütter, *Beiträge zur Völkerrechts-Geschichte und Wissenschaft* (Leipzig: Adolph Wienbrack, 1843), 219 pp.; E. Nys, 'Le droit des gens dans les rapports des Arabes et des Byzantins'. In: E. Nys. *Études de droit international public et droit politique* (Brussels: Alfred Castaigne, 1896), pp. 46-74.
76. Only according to Shafiʿite opinion can the relatives of an unbeliever, killed by Moslems in defiance of the rules that forbid to kill certain categories of unbelievers, like women, children, etc., or to wage war without previous warning, claim *diyah* (bloodmoney).
77. 'Law of nations or international law is the name for the body of customary or treaty rules which are considered legally binding by States in their intercourse with each other.' L. Oppenheim, *International Law. A Treatise* (ed. by H. Lauterpacht. London, etc.: Longman, Green & Co., 1955), Vol. I, pp. 4-5.
78. Kruse (1953), p. 5.

79. Hermann Janson, *Die rechtlichen und ideologischen Beziehungen des islamischen Staatenkreises zum Abendländischen Völkerrecht* (Diss.) (Bern, 1955), p. 35.
80. Armanazi (1929), p. 40.
81. Hamidullah (1953), pp. 3-4.
82. Al Ghunaimi (1968), p. 96.
83. Al Ghunaimi (1968), p. 195; Yāqūt (1970-71), p. 486.
84. Hamidullah (1953), p. 3.
85. Ibid., p. 38.
86. Ibid., p. 62.
87. Ibid., pp. 231-232.
88. One author works the other way round as he tries 'to show that the main principles of international law are in conformity with the basic doctrine or philosophy of Islam and perhaps may even be said to be part of that doctrine or philosophy'. Mahmassani (1966), p. 205.
89. Art. 38 – not 30 – of the Statute of the International Court of Justice says: 'The Court, whose function is to decide in accordance with international law such disputes as are submitted to it, shall apply: (a) . . .; (b) . . .; (c) . . .; (d) Subject to the provisions of Article 59, judicial decisions and the teachings of the most highly qualified publicists of the various nations, as subsidiary means for the determination of rules of law'.
90. Akhtar (1971), p. 33.
91. Al Ghunaimi (1968), p. 223.
92. Ezzeldin Foda, *The Protected Arab Court of Justice. A Study in Regional Jurisdiction with Specific Reference to the Muslim Law of Nations* (The Hague: Martinus Nijhoff, 1957), pp. 124-139.
93. This attitude can also be observed in writings on other branches of Islamic law. Often, the same arguments are used. Cf. J. Brugman, *De betekenis van het Mohammedaanse recht in het hedendaagse Egypte* (Diss. Leiden) (The Hague: 1960), pp. 131-150.
94. E. Nys *Les Origines de droit international* (Brussels, 1894).
95. M. de Taube, 'Le monde de l'Islam et son influence sur l'Europe orientale'. In: *Académie de Droit International. Recueil des Cours* (1926), I, pp. 380-397.
96. Armanazi (1929), pp. 50-52; Hamidullah (1953), pp. 66-68; Manṣūr (1971), pp. 28-30; Al Ghunaimi (1968), pp. 82-86; Daqs (1972), p. 88.
97. J. Brugman (1960), p. 140.
98. Cf. Hamidullah (1953), pp. 43-44; Ḥasan (1959), p. 7; Mahmassani (1966), pp. 242-244; Sulṭān (1970), pp. 72-73, 157; Darāz (1950), p. 149; Muḥammad Abū Zahrah, *Al-ʿalāqāt al-dawliyyah fī l-Islām* (Cairo: al-Dār al-Qawmiyyah li-l-Ṭibāʿah wa-l-Nashr, 1384/1964), pp. 20-25.
99. Al Ghunaimi (1968), pp. 196-197.
100. Ibid., p. 198.
101. Ibid., p. 129.

102. To this category belong: Al Ghunaimi (1968), Sulṭān (1970), Manṣūr (1971) and Yāqūt (1970-71).
103. Descriptions of this kind are to be found in: Armanazi (1929), Rechid (1937), Darāz (1947), Hamidullah (1953), and Mahmassani (1966).
104. contrary to Bell's translation which reads: '*and*'.
105. Al Ghunaimi (1968), pp. 69-70, 124-128; Sulṭān (1970), pp. 18-19, 178-185; Akhtar (1971), p. 28.
106. Yāqūt (1970-71), pp. 481-490.
107. Darāz (1950), p. 161; Mahmassani (1966), pp. 234-235; Al Ghunaimi (1968), pp. 91, 96-103; Sulṭān (1970), pp. 46, 201-207; Yāqūt (1970-71), pp. 746-747, note 1. One must doubt, however, whether these Moslem authors have really found the philosophers' stone in connection with this problem. The crux of international law is the absence of an authority that can enforce the observance of international legal rules by *all* legal subjects. Even if we assume that religious sanction can to a certain extent replace a law enforcing authority, then this would still affect only the Moslem legal subjects.
108. Brugman (1960), p. 137.
109. Armanazi (1929), pp. 38-42; Rechid (1937), pp. 421-433; Abū Zahrah (1964), pp. 72-73; Mahmassani (1966), pp. 264-267; Zuḥaylī (1965), pp. 328-345; Sulṭān (1970), pp. 199-201; Manṣūr (1971), pp. 327-329.
110. Whether this treaty, mentioned by Wāqidī and Ibn Isḥāq, has really existed is open to doubt. Cf. W. Montgomery Watt, *Muhammad in Medina* (London, etc.: Oxford University Press, 1956), pp. 196-197.
111. Cf. Chapter 2, par. 14.
112. Al Ghunaimi (1968), p. 211; Sulṭān (1970), p. 209.
113. Abū Zahrah (1964), pp. 74-83; Zuḥaylī (1965), pp. 362-367; Al Ghunaimi (1968), pp. 184-185; Sulṭān (1970), p. 210.
114. Cf. Wensinck (1936-69), Vol. III, p. 98.
115. Muḥammad al-Bishbīshī, *Al-ʿalāqāt al-dawliyyah al-islāmiyyah* (Cairo: Al-Madjlis al-Aʿlā li-l-Shu'ūn al-Islāmiyyah, 1965), pp. 53-54; Aḥmad Shalabī, *Al-djihād fī l-tafkīr al-Islāmī* (Cairo: Maktabat al-Nahḍah al-Miṣriyyah, 1968), p. 114; Sulṭān (1970), pp. 208-209.
116. Cf. Chapter 2, par. 5.
117. Armanazi (1929), pp. 73-75; Rechid (1937), pp. 464-466; Ḥasan (1950), pp. 20-21; Hamidullah (1953), pp. 190-194; Abū Zahrah (1964), pp. 94-95; Zuḥaylī (1965), pp. 150-161; Mahmassani (1966), p. 289; Sulṭān (1970), p. 248; Manṣūr (1971), pp. 296-303; Daqs (1972), p. 91.
118. Cf. Chapter 2, par. 6, 7 and 8.
119. Manṣūr (1971), p. 320.
120. ʿAbd al-Mutaʿālī al-Ṣaʿīdī, *Fī maydān al-idjtihād* (Helwan: Djamʿiyyat al-thaqāfah al-Islāmiyyah, n.d.), pp. 133-139.
121. Hamidullah (1953), pp. 231-232.

122. Amīn al-Khawlī, *Al-djundiyyah wa-l-silm. Wāqiʿ wa-mithāl* (Cairo: Dār al-Maʿārif, 1960), p. 106; Zakī (1965), p. 203; Hamidullah (1953), p. 283.
123. Cf. Chapter 2, par, 12.
124. The most detailed statement of the modernist position is to be found in Zuḥaylī (1965), pp. 403-474, and Daqs (1972), pp. 550-569.
125. Hamidullah (1953), pp. 269-271; Zuḥaylī (1965), p. 637; Mahmassani (1966), pp. 295-297.
126. Cf. Chapter 2, par. 14.
127. Rechid (1937), pp. 500-502; Ḥasan (1950), pp. 22-23; Zuḥayli (1965), pp. 356-357; Bishbīshī (1965), pp. 53-58; Mahmassani (1966), pp. 53-58.
128. Abū Zahrah (1964), pp. 78-79; Al Ghunaimi (1968), pp. 184-185; Manṣūr (1971), pp. 281-286, 370-379; Sharqāwī (1972), p. 40.

NOTES TO CHAPTER 5: CONCLUSIONS

1. Only after independence did the Pakistan government call for jihad in its conflict with India over Kashmir. Cf. L. Binder, *Religion and Politics in Pakistan* (Berkeley: University of California Press, 1961), pp. 136, 193.
2. R. Mitchell, *The Society of the Muslim Brothers* (London: Oxford University Press, 1969), pp. 193-194.
3. This has also been observed by father Jomier in Egypt during the October war of 1973. J. Jomier, 'Le Coran et la guerre du 6 octobre 1973 (10 ramadan 1393)', *Bulletin d'Études Orientales. Institut Français de Damas* 29 (1977), p. 262.
4. Cf. p. 134.
5. Hunter (1974), p. 186; Dupont & Coppolani (1897), p. 37; Naqqāsh (1884), Vol. 5, p. 186.

Bibliography

Abbreviations used

BSOAS	*Bulletin of the School of Oriental and African Studies*
IC	*Islamic Culture* (1927 seq.)
IJMES	*International Journal of Middle East Studies* (1970 seq.)
IQ	*Islamic Quarterly* (1954 seq.)
IR	*Islamic Review* (1913 seq.)
IS	*Islamic Studies* (1965 seq.)
MEJ	*The Middle East Journal* (1977 seq.)
MW	*The Moslem World*
REI	*Revue des Études Islamiques*
SI	*Studia Islamica*
WI	*Die Welt des Islam*
ZDMG	*Zeitschrift den deutschen Morgenländischen Gesellschaft*

1. ARABIC LITERATURE ON JIHAD

(In this and the next section I have only listed literature that deals exclusively with jihad.)

ʿAbd al-Mutadjallī, Muḥammad Radjāʾ Ḥanafī, *Ramaḍān shahr al-djihād*. Cairo: Al-Madjlis al-Aʿlā li-l-Shuʾūn al-Islāmiyyah, 1973, 135 pp.

ʿAbd Rabbih, ʿAbd al-Ḥāfiẓ, *Falsafat al-djihād fī l-Islām*. Beyrut: Dār al-Kitāb al-Lubnānī, 1972, 595 pp.

ʿĀbidīn, Muḥammad Ṣabrī, *Al-djihād fī sabīl Allāh, bi-munāsabat djihād ahl Filasṭīn al-Muslimīn wa-difāʿihim ʿan al-Masdjid al-Aqṣā wa-l-diyār al-muqaddasah*. Cairo: Maṭbaʿat al-Qāhirah, 1357/1939.

Abū ʿAzāʾim, Muḥammad Māḍī, *Al-djihād*. [Cairo:] Dār Mashyakhat al-Ṭarīqah al-ʿAzamiyyah, 1390/1970, 120 pp.

Abū Zahrah, Muḥammad, 'Qānūn al-ḥarb fī l-Islām', *Liwāʾ al-Islām* 2 (1948-49), No. 8, pp. 39-44; No. 9, pp. 39-44; No. 10, pp. 40-44.

Abū Zahrah, Muḥammad, 'ʿAlāqat al-Muslimīn bi-ghayrihim fī l-ḥarb wa-l-silm', *Risālat al-Islām* 8 (1956), pp. 357-365.

Abū Zahrah, Muḥammad, *Naẓariyyat al-ḥarb fī l-Islām*. Cairo: Al-Madjlis al-Aʿlā li-l-Shuʾūn al-Islāmiyyah, 1961, 80 pp. (Dirāsāt fī l-Islām, 5).

Abū Zahrah, Muḥammad, *Al-ʿalāqāt al-dawliyyah fī l-Islām*. Cairo: Al-Maktabat al-ʿArabiyyah, 1384/1964, 119 pp.

Abū Zahrah, Muḥammad, 'Al-djihād'. In: *Kitāb al-Mu'tamar al-Rābiʿ li-Madjmaʿ al-Buḥūth al-Islāmiyyah,* Vol. 1. [Cairo:] 1388/1968, pp. 67-121.

Abū Zahrah, Muḥammad, 'Al-ʿalāqāt al-dawliyyah fī l-Islām'. In: *Al-Tawdjīh al-idjtimāʿi fī l-Islām. Min buḥūth mu'tamarāt Madjmaʿ al-Buḥūth al-Islāmiyyah,* Vol. 1. Cairo: 1391/1971, pp. 93-153.

Afghānī, Djamāl al-Dīn, 'Al-ḥarb al-ʿādilah wa-l-ḥarb ghayr al-ʿādilah'. In: Djamāl al-Dīn al-Afghānī, *Al-aʿmāl al-kāmilah*. Ed. by Muhammad ʿAmmārah. Cairo: Dār al-Kitāb al-ʿArabī, n.d., pp. 436-442.

ʿAlī, ʿAbd al-Ḥafīẓ Faraghlī, *Al-ishāʿāt al-Islāmiyyah fī maʿrakat al-ʿāshir min Ramaḍān*. [Cairo:] Al-Madjlis al-Aʿlā li-l-sh'ūn al-Islāmiyya, 1394/1974, 140 pp. (Dirasat fī l-Islām, 155).

al-ʿAlim, Maḥmūd, *Fukahat al-adhwāq min mashāriʿ al-ashwāq fī faḍl al-djihād wa-l-targhīb fīh wa-l-ḥathth ʿalayh*. 2nd ed., Cairo: Maktabat al-Qāhirah, 1390/1970, 144 pp. [1st impr. Būlāq: al-Maṭbaʿah al-Saniyyah al-Kubrā, 1290 H.].

Al Saʿdī, ʿAbd al-Raḥmān ibn Nāṣir, *Wudjūb al-taʿāwun bayn al-Muslimīn wa-mawḍūʿ al-djihād al-dīnī wa-bayān kulliyyāt min barāhīn al-dīn*. [Cairo:] Al-Maṭbaʿah al-Salafiyyah, 1368 [*c*. 1949], 78 pp.

ʿAllūsh, Ḥasan Kaẓim al-Hillī, *Al-khuṭbah al-nāriyya fī tanfīdh al-aḥkām al-Islamiyyah wa-stirdjāʿ arḍ Filasṭīn al-ʿArabiyyah*. Nadjaf: Maṭbaʿat al-Qaḍā', 1388/1967, 28 pp.

al-Armanāzī, Nadjīb, *Al-sharʿ al-dawlī fī l-Islām*. Damascus: Maṭbaʿat Ibn Zaydūn, 1930, 184 pp. [Arr. transl. of Armanazi (1929)].

ʿAwn, ʿAbd al-Ra'uf, *Al-fann al-ḥarbī fī ṣadr al-Islām*. Cairo: Dār al-Maʿārif, 1961, 352 pp.

ʿAyyad, Djamal al-Dīn, *Nuẓum al-ḥarb fī l-Islām*. Cairo: Maktabat al-Khāndjī, 1370 [*c*. 1951], 132 pp.

ʿAyyad, Djamal al-Dīn, *Al-ḥurub al-Islāmiyyah wa-l-mabādi' al-insāniyyah*. Cairo: Dar al-Thaqafah al-ʿArabiyyah li-l-nashr, 1970, 4 pp.

ʿAzzam, ʿAbd al-ʿAzīz, *Al-ʿudwān al-ṣahyūnī wa-wādjib al-shuʿūb al-Islāmiyyah wa-l-ʿArabiyyah*. Beyrut: Maṭbaʿat Dār al-Kutub, 1391/1971, 183 pp.

ʿAzzam, Ṣalah, *Al-djihad fī khuṭub wa-aḥādith sayyidinā rasūl Allāh*. Cairo: Al-Madjlis al-Aʿla li-l-Shu'un al-Islāmiyyah, 1970, 37 pp. (Kutub Islāmiyyah, 111)

Bakhit, ʿAbd al-Ḥamid, *Ṣalat al-ḥarb*. Cairo: Al Maktabah al-Anglo al-Miṣriyyah, 1376/1956.

al-Banna, Ḥasan, 'Risālat al-djihad'. In: Hasan al-Bannā, *Madjmūʿat rasā'il al-Imam*
al-Shahīd ——. Rev. and enl. ed. Beyrut: Dār al-Nūr, n.d., pp. 23-61

al-Banna, Muḥammad, 'Athr ikhtilāf al-ʿulamā' fī l-djihad', *Liwā' al-Islām* 1 (1947-48), No. 9, pp. 34-39.

al-Bannā, Muḥammad, 'Al-iṣrāḥ al-ḥarbī fī l-Islām', *Liwā' al-Islām* 7 (1953-54), No. 4, pp. 219-223; No. 6, pp. 349-355, No. 8, pp. 477-483; No. 12, pp. 726-733.

al-Bishbīshī, Muḥammad, *Al-ʿalāqāt al-dawliyyah al-Islāmiyyah*. Cairo: Al-Madjlis al-Aʿlā li-l-Shu'ūn al-Islāmiyyah, 1965, 80 pp. (Kutub Islāmiyyah, 49).

al-Daqs, Kāmil Salāmah, *Āyāt al-djihād fī l-qur'ān al-karīm*. Kuwait: Dār al-Bayān, 13; 3?2; 841 574 cv.

Darāz, Muḥammad ʿAbd Allāh, 'Al-qānūn al-dawlī al-ʿāmm wa-l-Islām', *Al-Madjallah al-Miṣriyyah li-l-Qānūn al-Dawlī* 5 (1949), pp. 4 sqq.

Darāz, Muḥammad ʿAbd Allāh, 'Mabādi' al-qānūn al-dawlī al-ʿāmm li-l-Islām', *Risālat al-Islām* 2 (1950), pp. 146-164. [Also publ. separately: Cairo: Maṭbaʿat al-Azhar, 1371/1952.]

Darwazah, Muḥammad ʿIzzah, *Al-djihād fī sabīl Allāh fī l-qur'ān wa-l-ḥadīth*. Damascus: Dār al-Yaqaẓah al-ʿArabiyya, 1395/1975, 383 pp.

Djamāl, Aḥmad Muḥammad, 'Taʿqīb ʿalā aḥkām al-ʿalāqāt al-dawliyyah fī l-Islām', *Rābiṭat al-ʿĀlam al-Islāmī* 195 (1967-68), No. 1, pp. 33-37; No. 2, pp. 27-33; No. 3, pp. 13-18; No. 4, pp. 12-17; No. 5, pp. 28-31; No. 6, pp. 21-25. [Also publ. in Djamāl (1392/1972), pp. 259-295.]

al-Djarrāḥ, Muḥammad Adīb, *Risālat al-djihād ʿalā fatwā khalīfatinā l-aʿẓam al-Sulṭān al-Ghāzī Muḥammad Rashād*. Mosul: Maṭbaʿat Ninawā, 1333 [1914-15], 88 pp.

al-Djihād fī sabīl Allāh, bi-munāsabat ahl Filasṭīn al-Muslimīn wa-difāʿihim ʿan al-Masdjid al-Aqṣā wa-diyār al-muqaddasah. Cairo: Al-Hay'ah al-ʿArabiyyah al-ʿUlyā li-Filasṭīn, 1357 [1938-39], 22 pp. [Same text as ʿĀbidīn (1357), without, however, the author's name.]

al-Djihād fī l-Islām. Cairo: Djāmiʿat al-Azhar/Al Hay'ah al-ʿĀmmah li-l-Shu'ūn al-Maṭābiʿ al-Amīriyyah, 1967, 82 pp.

al-Djihād. Cairo: Al-Madjlis al-Aʿlā li-l-Shu'ūn al-Islāmiyyah, 1967, 78 pp.

al-Djihād. Kuwait: Djamʿiyyat al-Iṣlāḥ al-Idjtimāʿī, 1389/1979, 30 pp. (Min Rasā'il al-Djamʿiyyah, 20.)

al-Djihād fī l-Islām. [Cairo:] Djumhūriyyat Miṣr al-ʿArabiyyah, Al-Madjlis al-Aʿlā li-l-Shu'ūn al-Islāmiyyah, 1973, 87 pp. [Same text as *Al-Djihād fī l-Islām* (1967).]

Faradj, Muḥammad, *Al-salām wa-l-ḥarb fī l-Islām*. Cairo: Dār al-Fikr al-ʿArabī, 1379/1960, 197 + 2 pp.

Faradj, Muḥammad, *Al-salām fī l-Islām*. Cairo: Al-Madjlis al-Aʿlā li-l-Shu'ūn al-Islāmiyyah, 1963, 80 pp. (Dirāsāt fī l-Islām, 25).

Faradj, Muḥammad, *Aḥādīth fī l-ḥarb*. Cairo: Dār al-Qawmiyyah, 1963, 43 pp. (Ikhtarnā li-l-djundī, 15).

Faradj, Muḥammad, *Al-madrasah al-ʿaskariyyah al-Islāmiyyah*. Cairo: Dār al-Fikr al-ʿArabī, n.d. [*c.* 1969], 430 pp.

Faradj, Muḥammad, *Al-istrātīdjiyyah al-ʿaskariyyah al-Islāmiyyah. Al-naẓariyyah wa-l-taṭbīq*. Cairo: Al-Hay'ah al-ʿĀmmah li-l-Shu'ūn al-Maṭābiʿ al-Amīriyyah,

1395/1975, 371 pp. (Buḥūth Islāmiyyah, 79).
Fatāwā khaṭirah fī wudjūb al-djihād al-dīnī al-muqaddas li-inqādh Filasṭīn wa-ṣiy ānat al-Masdjid al-Aqṣā wa-sā'ir al-muqaddasāt. Cairo: Al-Maṭbaᶜah al-Salafiyyah, [1948], 32 pp.
al-Fayḍī, Aḥmad Fakhr al-Dīn ibn ᶜAbd Allāh, *Irshād al-ᶜibād ilā l-ghazw wa-l-djihād*. Istanbul: Al-Maṭbaᶜah al-ᶜĀmirah, 1336 [*c*. 1917-18], 250 + 6 pp.
Ghawshah, ᶜAbd Allāh, 'Al-djihād ṭarīq al-naṣr'. In: *Kitāb al-Mu'tamar al-Rābiᶜ li-Madjmaᶜ al-Buḥūth al-Islāmiyyah*, Vol. 1 [Cairo:] 1388/1968, pp. 183-277.
Ghayth, Faradj Muḥammad, *Ghāyat al-irshād fī aḥkām al-djihād*. Cairo: Muṣṭafā l-Bābī al-Ḥalabī, 1374/1955, 158 pp.
Ḥadjdjādj, Maḥmūd Muṣṭafā, 'Al- muᶜāhadah fī l-Islām', *Liwā' al-Islām* 4 (1950-51), No. 8, pp. 614-621.
Ḥammādah, ᶜAbd al-Munᶜim, *Alwān min al-djihād*. Cairo: Al-Madjlis al-Aᶜlā li-l-Shu'ūn al-Islāmiyyah, 1967, 132 pp. (Dirāsāt fī l-Islām, 73).
Ḥasan, ᶜAbd al-Fattāḥ, *Mīthāq al-umam wa-l-shuᶜūb fī l-Islām*. Cairo: Al-Idārah al-ᶜĀmmah li-l-Thaqāfah al-Islāmiyyah bi-l-Djāmiᶜ al-Azhar, 1378 [1958-59], 24 pp.
Ḥaṭṭah, Muḥammad Kāmil, *Siyāsat al-ḥarb fī l-Islām*. Cairo: n.d. [*c*. 1970], 36 pp.
Ḥaṭṭah, Muḥammad Kāmil, *Al-ṣawm wa-l-djihād*. Cairo: Mu'assasat Dār al-Taᶜāwun li-l-Ṭabᶜ wa-l-Nashr, 1970, 48 pp. (Kitāb al-Taᶜāwun, 404).
al-Ḥawfī, Aḥmad Muḥammad, *Al-djihād*. Cairo: Al-Madjlis al-Aᶜlā ṅ-l-Shu'ūn al-Islamiyyah, 1970, 287 pp. (Al-Taᶜrīf bi-l-Islām, 57).
Ḥukm al-Islām fī qaḍiyyat Filasṭīn. Fatāwā sharᶜiyyah khaṭirah. Cairo: Al-Hay'ah al-ᶜArabiyyah al-ᶜUlyā li-Filasṭīn, 1375/1956, 43 cp.
Ḥusayn, Muḥammad al-Khiḍr, *Ādāb al-ḥarb fī l-Islām*. Cairo: Dār al-Iᶜtiṣām, 1974, 37 pp.
Ibn Kathīr, Ismāᶜīl ibn ᶜUmar (d. 774 H), *Al-idjtihād fī ṭalab al-djihād*. Cairo: Djamᶜiyyat al-Nashr wa-l-Ta'līf al-Azhariyyah, 1347 [1928-29], 24 pp.
Ibn al-Khūdjah, Muḥammad al-Ḥabīb, 'Al-djihād fī l-Islām'. In: *Min waḥy Laylat al-Qadr. Dirāsāt Islāmiyyah*. [Tunis:] Al-Dār al-Tūnusiyyah li-l-nashr, 1971, pp. 97-133.
Ibn al-Mubārak, ᶜAbd Allāh (d. 181 H), *Kitāb al-djihād*. Ed. by Nazīh Ḥammād. Beyrut: Dār al-Nūr, 1391/1971, 192 pp.
Ibrahīm, Muḥammad Ismāᶜīl, *Al-djihād rukn al-Islām al-sādis*. Cairo: Dār al-Fikr al-ᶜArabī, 1964, 176 pp. [repr. in 1970 and 1974.]
Islam, Al — — wa-l-djihād. Mukhtārāt al-idhāᶜah. Cairo: Wizārat al-Irshād al-Qawmī, Murāqabat al-Shu'ūn al-Thaqāfiyyah, n.d., 144 pp.
ᶜIzz, Muṣṭafā, *Kitāb ṭarīq al-rashād fī l-ḥathth ᶜalā l-djihād*. Cairo: Maṭbaᶜat Djarīdat al-Hidāyah, 1317 [1899-1900], 16 pp.
Kāshif al-Ghiṭā', Muḥammad al-Ḥusayn, *Qaḍiyyat Filasṭīn al-kubrā fī khuṭub al-Imām al-rāḥil — —*. Nadjaf: Maṭbaᶜat al-Nuᶜmān, 1969, 183 pp.
Khālid, Ḥasan, 'Al-djihād fī sabīl Allāh'. In: *Kitāb al-Mu'tamar al-Rābiᶜ li-*

Madjmaʿ al-Buḥūth al-Islāmiyyah, Vol. 1. [Cairo:] 1388/1968, pp. 163-183.

Khālid, Ḥasan, *Al-shahīd fī l-Islām*. Beyrut: Dār al-ʿIlm li-l-Malāyīn, 1971, 144 pp.

Khallāf, ʿAbd al-Wahhāb, 'Al-djihād fī sabīl Allāh'. *Liwā' al-Islām* 5 (1951-52), No. 7, pp. 408-412.

Khaṭṭāb, Maḥmūd Shīt, *Al-rasūl al-qā'id*. 2nd ed., Cairo: Dār al-Qalam, 1964, 499 pp.

Khaṭṭāb, Maḥmūd Shīt, 'Irādat al-qitāl fī l-djihād'. In: *Kitāb al-Mu'tamar al-Rābiʿ li-Madjmaʿ al-Buḥūth al-Islāmiyyah*, Vol. 1 [Cairo:] 1388/1968, pp. 123-162. [Also publ. separately under the title: *Irādat al-qitāl fī l-djihād al-Islāmī*. Beyrut: Dār al-Irshād, 1968, 47 pp.]

Khaṭṭāb, Maḥmūd Shīt, ʿAbd al-Ḥalīm Maḥmūd and Muḥammad Abū Zahrah, *Irādat al-qitāl wa-l-djihād fī sabīl Allāh*. Cairo: Dār al-Djumhūriyyah, 1969, 111 pp. (Kitāb al-Djumhūriyyah al-Dīnī). [Contains three articles on jihad by Khaṭṭāb, Maḥmūd and Abū Zahrah, previously publ. in *Kitāb al-Mu'tamar al-Rābiʿ li-Madjmaʿ al-Buḥūth al-Islāmiyyah*, Vol. 1. [Cairo:] 1388/1968, pp. 35-162.]

Khaṭṭāb, Maḥmūd Shīt, *Al-Islām wa-l-naṣr. Al-iʿdād al-maʿnawī li-l-djihād*. Beyrut: Dār al-AiTr0 1593¨ 1*f*72, 263 pp.

al-Khawlī, Amīn, *Al-djundiyyah wa-l-silm. Wāqiʿ wa-mithāl*. Cairo: Dār al-Maʿrifah, 1960, 182 pp.

Kishk, Muḥammad Djalāl, *Al-jihād . . . thawratunā l-dā'imah*. Beyrut: Dār al-Irshād, 1389/1970, 62 pp.

Kitāb al-Mu'tamar al-Rābiʿ li-Madjmaʿ al-Buḥūth al-Islāmiyyah. (1388/1968), 3 vols. [Cairo:] Al-Azhar, Madjmaʿ al-Buḥūth al-Islāmiyyah, 1970. Vol. 1: *Al-djihād*; Vol. 2: *Al-Muslimūn wa-l-ʿudwān al-Isrā'īlī*; Vol. 3: *Buḥūth fī l-fiqh wa-l-tarbiyah wa-l-mudjtamaʿ* [Vols. 1 and 2 have also been published in Engl. under the title: *The Fourth Conference of the Academy of Islamic Research*.]

al-Maḥmaṣānī, Ṣubḥī, 'Al-djihād wa-musawwighātuh al-sharʿiyyah', *Madjallat Madjmaʿ al-Lughah al-ʿArabiyyah bi-Dimashq* 44 (1969), pp. 309-322.

Maḥmūd, ʿAbd al-Ḥalīm, 'Al-djihād'. In: *Kitāb al-Mu'tamar al-Rābiʿ li-Madjmaʿ al-Buḥūth al-Islāmiyya*, Vol. 1 [Cairo:] 1388/1968, pp. 35-67.

Maḥmūd, ʿAbd al-Ḥalīm, *Al-djihād wa-l-naṣr*. Cairo: Dār al-Kātib al-ʿArabī, 1968, 180 pp.

Manṣūr, ʿAlī ʿAlī, 'Muqāranāt bayn al-sharīʿah al-Islāmiyyah wa-l-qānūn al-dawlī al-ʿāmm', *Risālat al-Islām*, 14 (1963), pp. 75-96.

Manṣūr, ʿAlī ʿAlī, *Al-sharīʿah al-Islāmiyyah wa-l-qānūn al-dawlī al-ʿāmm*. Cairo: Al-Madjlis al-Aʿlā li-l-Shu'ūn al-Islāmiyyah, 1384/1963, 409 pp. [Repr. 1390/1971.]

al-Marāghī, ʿAbd Allāh Muṣṭafā, *Al-djihād*. Cairo: Maṭbaʿat al-Sunnah al-Muḥammadiyyah, 1369/1950, 122 pp.

al-Mawdūdī, Abū l-Aʿlā, *Al-djihād fī sabīl Allāh*. Transl. from the Urdu. Beyrut:

Dār al-Fikr, n.d., 53 pp.

al-Mawdūdī, Abū l-Aʿlā, Ḥasan al-Bannā and Sayyid Quṭb, *Al-djihad fī sabīl Allāh*. Beyrut: Al-Ittiḥād al-Islāmī al-ʿĀlamī li-Munaẓẓamāt Ṭullābiyyah, 1969, 135 pp. [Contains Bannā's *Risālah fī l-djihād*, a summary of Mawdūdī's *Al-djihād fī sabīl Allāh* and a treatise by Quṭb on the same subject.]

Muṣṭafā, Ḥāmid, *Al-djihād fī l-Islām. Māḍih wa-ḥāḍiruh*. Baghdad: Maktabat al-Muthannā, 1948, 81 pp.

Nār, Aḥmad, *Al-qitāl fī l-Islām*. 2nd ed., Djedda: Al-Dār al-Saʿūdiyyah li-l-Nashr wa-l-Tawzīʿ, 1389/1969, 264 pp. [1st impr. Cairo, 1952.]

al-Nawawī, ʿAbd al-Raḥmān Ḥusayn, *Risālat al-djihād ʿizzah wa-karāmah*. Cairo: Maṭbaʿat Amīn ʿAbd al-Raḥmān, 1966, 46 pp.

al-Qalqīlī, ʿAbd Allāh, *Al-fatāwā l-Urdunniyyah. Qism al-taʿāmul maʿ al-ʿadūw wa-aḥkām al-djihād*. [Beirut:] 1389/1968, 110 pp. (Manshūrāt al-Maktab al-Islāmī).

Qurāʿah, ʿAlī, *Al-ʿalāqāt al-dawliyyah fī l-ḥurūb al-Islāmiyyah*. Cairo: Dār Miṣr li-l-Ṭibāʿah wa-l-Nashr, 1374/1955, 172 pp.

Quṭb, Sayyid, *Al-salām al-ʿālamī wa-l-Islām*. 5th ed., Cairo: Maktabat Wahbah, 1386/1966, 199 pp.

al-Rāwī, Ibrāhīm, 'Al-wādjib ʿalā kull Muslim al-djihād immā bi-nafsih aw bi-mālih fī sabīl inqādh Filasṭīn. Fatwā', *Al-Taqwā* 15 (1938), pp. 500 sqq.

Rashīd Riḍā, Muḥammad, 'Al-djihād fī l-Islām', *Al-Manār* 15 (1912), pp. 33-40.

Sabʿ, Tawfīq Muḥammad, *Al-mudjāhidūn fī Allāh*. Cairo: Madjmaʿ al-Buḥūth al-Islāmiyyah, 1390/1971, 175 pp. (Al-Buḥūth al-Islāmiyyah, 26).

al-Ṣaʿīdī, ʿAbd al-Mutaʿālī, 'Ra'y fī āyah min āyāt al-qitāl', *Risālat al-Islām* 9 (1959), pp. 189-197.

al-Sammān, Muḥammad ʿAbd Allāh, *Al-Islām wa-l-amn al-dawlī*. Cairo: Dār al-Kitāb al-ʿArabī, 1952, 200 pp. [2nd impr. Cairo: Dār al-Kutub al-Ḥadīthah, 1960, 269 pp.]

al-Sanūsī, Muḥammad al-Mahdī Aḥmad – al-Khaṭṭābī al-Ḥusaynī al-Idrīsī, *Bughyat al-musāʿid fī aḥkām al-mudjāhid. Risālah bi-qalam – fī l-ḥathth ʿalā l-djihād*. Cairo: Maṭbaʿat Djarīdat al-Shaʿb, 1332 [1913-14], 58 pp.

al-Sarakhsī, Muḥammad ibn Aḥmad (d. 483 H), *Sharḥ kitāb al-Siyar al-Kabīr li-Muḥammad ibn al-Ḥasan al-Shaybānī*, 5 vols. Ed. by Ṣalāḥ al-Dīn al-Munadjdjid. Cairo: Maʿhad al-Makhṭūṭāt bi-Djāmiʿat al-Duwal al-ʿArabiyyah, 1971.

Shaʿbān, Ghaṭfat, *Al-djihād*. Tripolis: Al-Maṭbaʿah al-Ḥadīthah, 1948, 102 pp.

Shadīd, Muḥammad, *Al-djihād fī l-Islām*. Cairo: Mu'assasat al-Maṭbūʿāt al-Ḥadīthah, n.d., 157 pp. (Maʿ al-Islām, 8).

Shalabī, Aḥmad, *Al-djihād fī l-tafkīr al-Islāmī*. Cairo: Maktabat al-Nahḍah al-Miṣriyyah, 1968, 120 pp. (Dirāsāt fī l-Ḥaḍārah al-Islāmiyyah, 6). [2nd rev. and enl. impr. under the title *Al-djihād wa-l-nuẓum al-ʿaskariyyah fī l-tafkīr al-Islāmī*. Cairo: Dār al-Nahḍah al-Miṣriyyah, 1974, 132 pp.]

Shaltūt, Maḥmūd, *Al-Daʿwah al-Muḥammadiyyah wa-l-qitāl fī l-Islām*. Cairo: Al-Maktabah al-Salafiyyah, 1352 [1933-34], 41 pp.
Shaltūt, Maḥmūd, *Al-qur'ān wa-l-qitāl*. Cairo: Maṭbaʿat al-Naṣr, 1367/1948, 65 pp. [2nd impr. Cairo: Dār al-Kitāb al-ʿArabī, 1951, 67 pp.; also publ. under the title *Al-Islām wa-l-ʿalāqāt al-dawliyyah fi l-silm wa-l-ḥarb*. Cairo: Maṭbaʿat al-Azhar, 1370/1951; Engl. transl. in R. Peters, *Jihad in Mediaeval and Modern Islam*. Leiden, 1977.]
Sharaf al-Dīn, Aḥmad al-Shahāwī Saʿd, *Al-djihād fī sabīl Allāh*. Cairo: Dār Rasā'il al-Djib al-Islāmiyyah, n.d. [*c*. 1968], 59 pp.
al-Sharabāṣī, Aḥmad, *Aḥādīth al-djihād wa-l-furūsiyyah*. Cairo: Dār al-Qawmiyyah li-l-Ṭibāʿah wa-l-Nashr, n.d., 66 pp. (Ikhtarnā li-l-djundī, 19).
al-Sharqāwī, ʿUthmān al-Saʿīd, *Sharīʿat al-qitāl fī l-Islām*. Cairo: Maktabat al-Azhar, 1392/1972, 248 pp.
al-Shaybānī, Muḥammad ibn al-Ḥasan, *see under* Sarakhsī.
al-Shīrāzī, Muḥammad al-Mahdī al-Ḥusaynī, *Kayf nudjāhid al-aʿdā'*. Beyrut: Dār al-Ṣādiq, 1388 [1968-69], 20 pp. (Al-Farā'id al-Islāmiyyah, 6).
Sīdābī, Muḥammad ʿAlī Aḥmad, ʿAbd al-Qādir al-Shaykh Idrīs and Muḥammad Hadjdjāz Muddathir, *Al-jihād fī l-Islām wafq muqarrar al-shahādah al-thanawiyyah al-ʿulyā*. 4th ed., Damascus: Al-Dār al-Sūdāniyyah, 1974, 106 pp.
Ṣidqī, Niʿmat, *Al-djihād fī sabīl Allāh*. Cairo: Dār al-Iʿtiṣām, 1395/1975, 46 pp.
al-Subkī, Muḥammad ʿAbd al-Laṭīf, 'Al-djihād fī l-Islām'. In: *Kitāb al-Mu'tamar al-Rābiʿ li-Madjmaʿ al-Buḥūth al-Islāmiyyah*, Vol. 1. [Cairo:], 1388/1968, pp. 277-301.
Sulṭān, Ḥāmid, *Aḥkām al-qānūn al-dawlī fī l-sharīʿah al-Islāmiyyah*. Cairo: Dār al-Nahḍah al-ʿArabiyyah, 1979, 269 pp.
al-Ẓālimī, Muḥammad Ṣāliḥ Djaʿfar, *Min al fiqh al siyāsī fī l Islām*. Beyrut: Dār Maktabat al-Ḥayāh, 1971, 183 pp.
al-Zuḥaylī, Wahbah, *Āthār al-ḥarb fī l-fiqh al-Islāmī. Dirāsah muqārinah*. Beyrut: Dār al-Fikr al-ʿArabī, 1965, 890 pp.

2. LITERATURE ON JIHAD IN OTHER LANGUAGES

Abbott, Freeland, 'The jihad of Sayyid Ahmad Shahid', *MW* 52 (1962), pp. 216-222.
Abbott, Freeland, 'The transformation of the Jihad movement', *MW* 52 (1962), pp. 288-296.
Abd al-Hakim, Khalifa, 'War and peace'. In: Aziz Ahmad and G. E. von Grunebaum (eds.), *Muslim Self-statement in India and Pakistan, 1858-1968*. Wiesbaden: 1970, pp. 182-189.
Abu Zahra, Mohamed [= Muḥammad Abū Zahrah], *Concepta de la guerra en el Islam*. Transl. from the Ar. by Rudolfo Gil Benumeya, rev. by Ateya Haykal.

Cairo: Consejo Superior de Asuntos Islamicos, 1964. [Spanish transl. of Abū Zahrah (1961).]

Abu Zahra, Muhammad [= Muḥammad Abū Zahrah], *Begriff des Krieges im Islam*. Transl. from the Ar. by Omar Amin von Leers, rev. by Ezz El-Din Ismail. [Cairo:] Der Oberste Rat für Islamische Angelegenheiten, n.d., 73 pp. [Germ. transl. of Abū Zahrah (1961).]

Abu-Zahra, Mohamed [= Muḥammad Abū Zahrah], 'International relations in Islam'. In: *The First Conference of the Academy of Islamic Research*. [Cairo:] S.O.P. Press, 1383/1964, pp. 187-236.

Ahmad, Aziz, 'Le mouvement des Mujahidin dans l'Inde au XIXe siècle'. *Orient* 15 (1960), pp. 106-116.

Ahmad Khan Bahadur, *Review on Dr. Hunter's Indian Musalmans: Are they bound in conscience to rebel against the Queen*. Benares: Medical Hall Press, 1872, 53 + xxvi pp.

Akhtar, Shameem, 'An inquiry to the nature, origin and source of Islamic Law of Nations', *IS* 10 (1971), pp. 23-37.

Al Ghunaimi, Mohammad Talaat [= Muḥammad Ṭalʿat al-Ghunaymī], *The Muslim conception of International Law and the Western approach*. The Hague: Martinus Nijhoff, 1968, 228 pp.

Ameen, Abdul Rahman, 'The martyr in Islam'. In: *The Sixth Conference of Islamic Research*. [Cairo:] 1391/1971, pp. 301-321.

Armanazi, Najib [= Nadjib al-Armanāzī], *L'Islam et le droit international*. Paris: 1929, 162 pp.

el-Andalusy, ʿAly Ben ʿAbderrahman Ben Hoḏeïl, *see under* L. Mercier.

Arnaldez, R., 'La Guerre Sainte selon Ibn Ḥazm de Cordoue'. In: *Études d'Orientalisme, Dédiées à la Mémoire de Lévi-Provençal*, 2 vols. Paris: Maisonneuve, 1962, Vol. 2, pp. 445-459.

Attunisi, Salih Ascharif [= Ṣaliḥ al-Sharīf al-Tūnusī], *Haqiqat aldschihād. Die Wahrheit über den Glaubenskrieg*. Transl. from the Ar. by Karl E. Schabinger. Berlin: Deutsche Gesellschaft für Islamkunde, 1915.

Basillie, N. B. E., 'Jihad in Mohammedan Law and its application to British India', *Journal of the Royal Asiatic Society of Bengal* 5 (1871), pp. 401-408.

Bechebichy, Mohamed Aly [= Muḥammad al-Bishbīshī], *Les relations internationales islamiques*. Transl. from the Ar. by Ibrahim El-Mouelhy, rev. by Ahmed Rachad. Cairo: Conseil Supérieur des Affaires Islamiques, 1966, 56 pp. (Études sur l'Islam, 2). [Fr. transl. of Bishbīshī (1965).]

Becker, C. H., 'Die Kriegsdiskussion über den Heiligen Krieg (1915)'. In: C. H. Becker, *Vom Wesen und Werden der islamischen Welt. Islamstudien*, 2 vols. Leipzig: Verlag Quelle und Meyer, 1924, 1932. Vol. 2, pp. 281-310.

Bercher, L., 'Le livre de la guerre sainte', *Revue Tunisienne de Droit* 2 (1954), pp. 123-149. [Fr. transl. of the chapter on jihad from Qudūrī's *Mukhtaṣar*.]

Brugman, J., 'Voeren de Palestijnen een heilige oorlog?' *Palestijnse Drukken en*

Herdrukken 6 (Oct. 1972), pp. 3-10.
Cheragh Ali, *A Critical Exposition of the Popular 'jihád', Showing that all the Wars of Mohammed were Defensive; and that Aggressive War, or Compulsory Conversion, is not allowed in the Koran.* Calcutta: Thacker, Spink, 1885, civ + 249 pp.
Conference, The Fourth – of the Academy of Islamic Research (1388/1968). Cairo: El Azhar, The Academy of Islamic Research, 1970, x + 935 pp. [Engl. transl. of Vols. 1 and 2 of *Kitāb al-Mu'tamar al-Rābiʿ li-Madjmaʿ al-Buḥūth al-Islāmiyyah.*]
Dajani-Shakeel, Hadia, 'Jihad in twelfth-century Arabic poetry: a moral and religious force to counter the Crusades', *MW* 66 (1976), pp. 96-113.
Draz, M. A. [= Muḥammad ʿAbd Allāh Darāz], 'Le droit international publique et l'Islam', *Revue Égyptienne de Droit International Publique*, 1947, pp. 17-27.
Fagnan, E., *Le Djihad ou Guerre Sainte selon l'école Malékite.* Algiers: Jourdan, 1908, 20 pp.
Gardner, W. R. W., 'Jihād', *MW* 2 (1912), pp. 347-357.
Ghalib, Qasim, 'The martyr in Islam'. In: *The Sixth Conference of the Academy of Islamic Research.* [Cairo:] 1391/1971, pp. 251-301.
Ghunaimi, *see under* Al Ghunaimi.
Gräf, Erwin, 'Religiöse und rechtliche Vorstellungen über Kriegsgefangenen im Islam und Christentum', *WI*, n.s. 8 (1962-63), pp. 89-139.
Graefe, Erich, 'Der Aufruf des Scheichs der Senūsija zum Heiligen Kriege', *Der Islam* 3 (1912), pp. 141-150.
Hamidullah, Muhammad, *Die Neutralität im islamischen Völkerrecht.* Bonn: 1936, 25 pp. [Also publ. in *ZDMG* 89 (1935), pp. 68-88.]
Hamidullah, Muhammad, *Muslim Conduct of State. Being a treatise on siyar, that is the Islamic notion of public international law, consisting of the laws of peace, war and neutrality, together with precedents from orthodox practice and preceded by a historical and general introduction.* 3rd ed., Lahore: Sh. Muhammad Ashraf, 1953, 389 pp.
Haneberg, B., 'Das muslimische Kriegsrecht', *Abh. d. bayer. Akad. d. Wissensch.*, Philos.-philol. Cl., Bd. 12. Munich: 1871, 2. Abth., pp. 219-295.
Hatschek, Julius, *De Musta'min. Ein Beitrag zum internationalen Privat- und Völkerrecht des islamischen Gesetzes.* Berlin: Walter de Gruyter, 1920, 108 pp.
Heffening, W., *Das islamische Fremdenrecht bis zu den islamisch-fränkischen Staatsverträgen.* Hannover: 1925, xx + 219 pp.
Huart, C., 'Le Khalifat et la guerre sainte', *Revue de l'Histoire des Religions* 72 (1915), pp. 228-302.
Huart, C., 'Le droit de la guerre', *Revue du Monde Musulman* 2 (1907), pp. 331-346.
Hunter, W. W., *Our Indian Musalmans: Are they bound in conscience to Rebel against the Queen?.* 2nd ed., Lahore: Premier Book House, 1974, 187 pp. [1st impr. London: Trübner and Co., 1871, 215 pp.]

Husain, Abu Said Mohammad, *A Treatise on Jihad (Iqtisad fi masail-il-Jihad).* Transl. from the Urdu. Lahore: Victoria Press, 1887, 32 pp.

Jäschke, G., 'Mustafa Kemal und der Glaubenskrieg', *WI,* n.s., 10 (1965-67), pp. 174-181.

Janson, Hermann, *Die rechtlichen und ideologischen Beziehungen des islamischen Staatenkreises zum abendländischen Völkerrecht.* Göttingen: Martin Sasz und Co., 1955, 78 pp.

Jomier, J., 'Le Coran et la guerre du 6 octobre 1973 (10 ramadan 1393)', *Bulletin d'Études Orientales. Institut Français de Damas* 29 (1977), pp. 261-267.

Jurji, Edward J., 'The Islamic theory of war', *MW* 30 (1940), pp. 332-342.

Khadduri, Majid, *The Law of War and Peace in Islam.* London: Luzac, 1940, 132 pp.

Khadduri, Majid, *War and Peace in the Law of Islam.* Baltimore: The Johns Hopkins Press, 1955, 321 pp.

Khadduri, Majid, 'The Islamic system: its competition and coexistence with Western systems'. In: R. H. Nolte (ed.), *The Modern Middle East.* New York: Atherton Press, 1963, pp. 150-155.

Khadduri, Majid, 'Islam and the modern law of nations', *American Journal of International Law* 50 (1956), pp. 358-372.

Khadduri, Majid, 'The Islamic theory of international relations and its contemporary relevance'. In: J. H. Proctor (ed.), *Islam and International Relations.* London: Pall Mall Press, 1965, pp. 24-39.

Khadduri, Majid, *The Islamic Law of Nations. Shaybānī's Siyar.* Transl. with an intr., notes and app. by ———. Baltimore: The Johns Hopkins Press, 1966, 311 pp.

Khadduri, Majid, 'The greater war (A modern interpretation of Jihad)', *Aramco World Magazine* 19 (1968), No. 4, pp. 24-28.

Khadduri, Majid, 'The impact of international law upon the Islamic world order', *American Journal of International Law* 66 (1972), pp. 46-49.

Khan, Zafrullah, 'Islam and international relations', *Internationale Spectator* (The Hague), 10 (1956), pp. 308-322.

Kohlberg, Etan, 'The development of the Imāmī Shīʿī doctrine of jihād', *ZDMG* 126 (1976), pp. 64-86.

Kruse, Hans, *Islamische Völkerrechtslehre. Der Staatsvertrag bei den Hanafiten des 5./6. Jahrhunderts d.H. (11./12. Jahrh. n. Chr.).* Göttingen: 1953, xi + 174 + 39 pp.

Kruse, Hans, 'Al Shaybani on international instruments', *Journal of the Pakistan Historical Society* 1 (1953), pp. 90-100.

Kruse, Hans, 'Die Begründung der islamischen Völkerrechtslehre', *Saeculum* 5 (1954), pp. 221-241.

Kruse, Hans, 'The Islamic doctrine of international treaties', *IQ* (1954), pp. 152-158.

Lambton, A. K. S., 'A nineteenth century view of Jihād', *SI* 32 (1970), pp. 181-192.

Lamonte, J. L., 'Crusade and jihad'. In: N. A. Faris (ed.), *The Arab Heritage.* Princeton: Princeton University Press, 1944, pp. 159-199.

Lewis, Bernard, 'Politics and war'. In: Joseph Schacht and C. E. Bosworth (eds.), *The Legacy of Islam.* 2nd ed., London, etc.: Oxford University Press, 1974, pp. 156-210.

Lewis, Geoffrey, 'The Ottoman proclamation of Jihād in 1914', *IQ* 19 (1975), pp. 157-163.

Lüling, Günter, 'Der Göttinger Handschrift Arab. 49 'Risāla fī l-gihād'. Ihr Verfasser und die Umstände ihrer Abfassung'. In: *Festgabe für Hans Wehr.* Ed. by Wolfdietrich Fischer. Wiesbaden: 1969, pp. 86-93.

Mahmassani, Sobhi [= Ṣubḥī al-Maḥmaṣānī], 'Principles of international law in the light of the Islamic doctrine', *Académie de Droit International. Recueil des Cours* 117 (1966), No. 1, pp. 205-328.

Mercier, Louis, *ʿAly ben ʿAbderrahman ben Hodeïl el Andalusy. L'Ornement des âmes et la devise des habitants d'el Andalus. Traité de guerre sainte.* Transl. from the Ar. with intro. by ———. Paris: Geuthner, 1939, 349 pp.

Morabia, Alfred, *La notion de gihâd dans l'Islâm médiéval des origines à al-Ǧazâlî* (Thèse Univ. Paris IV, 1974). Lille: Service de réproduction des thèses, Université Lille III, 1975, 638 pp.

Nallino, C. A., 'Appunti sulla natura del "Califfato" in genere e sul presunto "Califfato ottomano"'. In: C. A. Nallino, *Raccolta di scritti editi e inediti,* Vol 3. Rome: 1941, pp. 234-259.

al-Azharī, Ṣāliḥ ʿAbd al-Samīʿ al-Ābī, *Al-thamr al-dānī fī taqrīb al-maʿānī sharḥ risālat Abī Zayd al-Qayrawānī.* Cairo: Muṣṭafā l-Bābī al-Ḥalabī, 1363/1944, 531 pp.

Noth, Albrecht, *Heiliger Krieg und heiliger Kampf in Islam und Christentum. Beiträge zur Vorgeschichte und Geschichte der Kreuzzüge.* Bonn: Ludwig Röhrscheid Verlag, 1966, 160 pp. (Bonner Historische Forschungen, 28).

Obbink, H.Th., *De heilige oorlog volgens den Koran.* Leiden: E. J. Brill, 1901, 123 pp.

Paret, R., 'Sure 9,122 und der Ǧihâd', *WI,* n.s., 2 (1953), p. 232.

Peters, Rudolph, 'Djihad: war of aggression or defense?'. In: *Akten des VII. Kongresses für Arabistik und Islamwissenschaft (Göttingen, 15-22 August 1974).* Göttingen: 1976, pp. 282-289.

Peters, Rudolph, *Jihad in mediaeval and modern Islam. The chapter on jihad from Averroes' legal handbook 'Bidāyat al-Mudjtahid' and the treatise 'Koran and fighting' by the late Shaykh al-Azhar, Maḥmūd Shaltūt.* Transl. and ann. by ———. Leiden: E. J. Brill, 1977, 90 pp. (Nisaba, 5).

Peters, Rudolph, 'Dār al-Ḥarb, Dār al-Islām und der Kolonialismus'. In: *XIX. Deutscher Orientalistentag (Freiburg, Sept.-Okt. 1975). Vorträge.* Wiesbaden: 1977, pp. 579-587.

Rechid, Ahmed, 'L'Islam et le droit des gens', *Académie de Droit International.*

Recueil des Cours 60 (1937), No. 2, pp. 375-504.
Reland, Adriaan, *Verhandeling van de godsdienst der Mahometaanen alsmede van het krygs-regt by haar ten tyde van oorlog tegens de Christenen gebruykelyk. Uyt het Latyn vertaalt.* Utrecht: Willem Broedelet, 1718, 299 + 21 pp. [Originally publ. in Latin.]
Rossi, Oliviero, 'La posizione giuridica degli infideli nella respublica Christiana e nell' Islam'. In: *Atti del Primo Convegno Nazionale di Studi Giuridico-comparativi.* Rome: 1953, pp. 625-655.
al-Sayyid, ʿAbdul-Sattar, 'The martyr in Islam'. In: *The Sixth Conference of the Academy of Islamic Research.* [Cairo:] 1391/1971, pp. 231-251.
Schwally, F., 'Der heilige Krieg des Islam in religionsgeschichtlicher und staatsrechtlicher Bedeutung', *Internationale Monatsschrift* (1916), pp. 678-714.
al-Shaybāni, Muḥammad ibn al-Ḥasan, *see under* M. Khadduri.
Siddiqi, Abdul Hamid, 'Jihad in Islam. Its nature and significance', *The Criterion* 3 (1968), No. 6, pp. 26-43.
Siddiqi, Aslam, 'Jihad, an instrument of Islamic revolution', *IS* 2 (1963), pp. 383-398.
Sivan, Emmanuel, *L'Islam et la Croisade. Idéologie et propagande dans les réactions musulmanes aux Croisades.* Paris: Maisonneuve, 1968, 222 pp.
Smith, M. C., 'The Jihad of Shehu dan Fodio: some problems'. In: I. M. Lewis (ed.), *Islam in Tropical Africa.* London, etc.: Oxford University Press, 1966, pp. 408-420.
Snouck Hurgronje, C., 'The holy war, made in Germany (1915)'. In: C. Snouck Hurgronje, *Verspreide Geschriften.* Bonn, etc.: 1923-27, Vol. 3, pp. 257-285.
Snouck Hurgronje, C., 'Deutschland und der Heilige Krieg (1915)'. In: C. Snouck Hurgronje, *Verspreide Geschriften.* Bonn, etc.: 1923-27, Vol. 3, pp. 287-292.
Snouck Hurgronje, C., 'De Heilige Oorlog en de zending (1915)'. In: C. Snouck Hurgronje, *Verspreide Geschriften.* Bonn, etc.: 1923-27, Vol. 3, pp. 295-297.
Snouck Hurgronje, C., 'Een belangrijk document betreffende den heiligen oorlog van den Islam (1914) en eene officiëele correctie (1917)'. In: C. Snouck Hurgronje, *Verspreide Geschriften.* Bonn, etc.: 1923-27, Vol. 3, pp. 327-355.
Trowbridge, Stephen van Rensselaer, 'Mohammed's view of religious war', *MW* 3 (1913), pp. 290-305.
Tschudi, R., 'Die fetwa's des Schejch-ül-Islām über die Erklärung des heiligen Krieges, nach dem Ṭanin, Nummer 2119 vom 15. November 1914'. *Der Islam* 5 (1914), pp. 391-393.
Urvoy, D., 'Sur l'évolution de la notion de Ǧihâd dans l'Espagne musulmane', *Mélanges de la Casa Velazquez*, 9 (1973), pp. 335-371.
Veth, P. J., 'De Heilige Oorlog in den Indischen Archipel', *Tijdschrift voor Nederlandsch Indië* (1870), pp. 168-176.
Wansbrough, John, 'The safe-conduct in Muslim chancery practice', *BSOAS* 34

(1971), pp. 20-35.
Waterman, Peter, 'The Jihad in Haussaland', *Kroniek van Afrika* 5 (1975), No. 2, pp. 141-153.
Watt, W. Montgomery, 'The significance of the theory of Jihād', In: *Akten des VII. Kongresses für Arabistik und Islamwissenschaft (Göttingen, 15-22 August 1974).* Göttingen: 1976, pp. 390-394.
Wechsel, Ruth, *Das Buch Qidwat al-Ġāzī. Ein Beitrag zur Geschichte der Ǧihād-Literatur* (Diss. Rheinische Friedrich-Wilhelm-Universität). Bonn: 1970, 165 pp.
Willis, J. H., 'Jihād fī sabīl Allāh, its doctrinal basis in Islam and some aspects of its evolution in 19th century West Africa', *Journal of African History* 8 (1967), pp. 395-417.
Zafrullah Khan, *see under* Khan, Zafrullah.

3. OTHER REFERENCES IN ARABIC

ʿAbd al-Rāziq, ʿAlī, *Al-Islām wa-uṣūl al-ḥukm.* Ed. and ann. by Muḥammad ʿAmmārah. Beyrut: Al-Mu'assasah al-ʿArabiyyah li-l-Dirāsāt wa-l-Nashr, 1972, 192 pp.
ʿAbduh, Muḥammad, *Al-Islām wa-l-Naṣrāniyyah maʿ al-ʿilm wa-l-madaniyyah.* 8th ed., Cairo: Dār al-Manār, 1373 [1953-54], 182 pp.
ʿAbduh, Muḥammad and Muḥammad Rashīd Riḍā, *Tafsīr al-qur'ān al-karīm al-shahīr bi-Tafsīr al-Manār,* 12 vols. Cairo: Dār al-Manār, 1367-1372 [1948-53].
Abū Khalīl, Shawqī, *Al-Islām fī qafaṣ al-ittihām.* N.p.: Dār al-Rashīd, 1971, 386 pp.
Abū Salīm, Muḥammad Ibrāhīm, *Al-ḥarakah al-fikriyyah al-Mahdiyyah.* Khartoum: Djāmiʿat al-Kharṭūm, 1979, 209 pp.
al-Afghānī, Djamāl al-Dīn, *Al-aʿmāl al-kāmilah. Maʿ dirāsah ʿan al-Afghānī. Al-ḥaqīqah al-kulliyyah.* Ed. and intr. by Muḥammad ʿAmmārah. Cairo: Dār al-Kātib al-ʿArabī, n.d. [*c.* 1968], 547 pp.
Aḥmad, Ibrāhīm Khalīl, *Al-istishrāq wa-l-tabshīr wa-ṣilatuhumā bi-l-imbariyāliyyah al-ʿālamiyyah.* Cairo: Maktabat al-Waʿy al-ʿArabī, 1973, 193 pp.
Al Firʿawn, Farīq al-Muzhir, *Al-ḥaqā'iq al-nāṣiʿah fī l-thawrah al-ʿIrāqiyyah sanat 1920 wa-natā'idjihā,* 2 vols. Baghdad: Maṭbaʿat al-Nadjāḥ, 1371/1952.
Alf laylah wa-laylah, 4 vols. Cairo: Maṭbaʿat Muḥammad ʿAlī Ṣubayḥ wa-anlādih, n.d.
ʿAllūsh, Nādjī, *Al-ḥarakah al-waṭaniyyah al-Filasṭīniyyah amām al-Yahūd wa-l-Ṣahyūniyyah, 1882-1948.* Beyrut: Markaz al-Abḥāth, 1974, 293 pp.
al-ʿAqqād, ʿAbbās Maḥmūd, *Mā yuqāl ʿan al-Islām.* Cairo: Dār al-ʿUrūbah, n.d., 358 pp.

al-ʿAqqād, ʿAbbās Maḥmūd, *Haqā'iq al-Islām wa-abāṭil khuṣūmih*. Cairo: Maṭbaʿat Miṣr, 1957, 304 pp.

al-Azharī, Ṣāliḥ ʿAbd al-Samīʿ al-Ābī, *Al-thamr al-dānī fī taqrīb al-maʿānī sharḥ risālat Abī Zayd al-Qayrawānī*. Cairo: Muṣṭafā l-Bābī al-Ḥalabī, 1363/1944, 531 pp.

ʿAzzām, ʿAbd al-Raḥmān, *Al-risālah al-khālidah*. 4th ed., Beyrut: Dār al-Shurūq/Dār al-Fikr, 1969, 341 pp. [Engl. transl. under the title *The Eternal Message of Muhammad*. New York, 1965.]

al-Bādjūrī, Ibrāhīm, *Ḥāshiyat al-Bādjūrī*, 2 vols. Cairo: ʿIsā l-Bābī al-Ḥalabī, 1340/1922.

al-Bahī, Muḥammad, *Al-fikr al-Islāmī al-ḥadīth wa-ṣilatuh bi-l-istiʿmār al-gharbī*. 6th ed., Beyrut: Dār al-Fikr, 1973, 616 pp.

Bayt al-Maqdis, Ḥawl ——. [Cairo:] Al-Madjlis al-Aʿlā li-l-Shu'ūn al-Islāmiyyah, 1389/1969, 205 pp. (Al-Taʿrīf bi-l-Islām, 55).

al-Dasūqī, Muḥammad ibn ʿArafah, *Ḥāshiyat al-Dasūqī ʿalā al-Sharḥ al-Kabīr*, 4 vols. Cairo: Dār Iḥyā' al-Kutub al-ʿArabiyyah, n.d.

Djamāl, Aḥmad Muḥammad, *Muftarayāt ʿalā l-Islām*. Beyrut: Dār al-Fikr, 1392/1972. 339 pp.

Djāmiʿ, ʿAbd al-ʿAzīz ʿAlī, ʿAbd al-Fattāḥ ʿAbd al-ʿAzīz and Ḥasan Darwīsh, *Qānūn al-ḥarb*. Cairo: Al-Maktabah al-Anglo al-Miṣriyyah, 1952, 300 pp.

al-Djaṣṣāṣ, Abū Bakr ibn ʿAlī al-Rāzī, *Aḥkām al-qur'ān*, 5 vols. Ed. by Muḥammad al-Ṣādiq al-Qamḥāwī. 2nd ed., Cairo: Dār al-Muṣḥaf, n.d.

al-Djazā'irī, Muḥammad ibn ʿAbd al-Qādir, *Tuḥfat al-zā'ir fī tārīkh al-Djazā'ir wa-l-Amīr ʿAbd al-Qādir*, 2 vols. Ed. Mamdūḥ Ḥaqqī. 2nd ed., Beyrut: Dār al-Yaqaẓah al-ʿArabiyyah, 1384/1964.

Faḍl Allāh, Muḥammad Ḥusayn, *Uslūb al-daʿwah fī l-qur'ān*. Beyrut: Dār al-Zahrā', 1392/1972, 173 pp.
1392/1972, 173 pp.
al-Faḥḥām, Muḥammad, *Al-Muslimūn wa-stirdād al-Quds*. Cairo: Madjmaʿ al-Buḥūth al-Islāmiyyah, 1390/1970, 98 pp.

Farrādj, Khālid and Ḥasan Darwīsh, *Al-mūdjaz fī l-qānūn al-dawlī al-ʿāmm*. Cairo: Al-Maktabah al-Anglo al-Miṣriyyah, 1967, 191 pp.

Fawq al-ʿĀdah, Sumūḥī, *Al-qānūn al-dawlī al-ʿāmm*. Damascus: Maṭbaʿat al-Inshā', 1960, 1073 pp.

Ghānim, Muḥammad Ḥāfiẓ, *Al-uṣūl al-djadīdah li-l-qānūn al-dawlī al-ʿāmm. Dirāsah li-ṣiyāghatih al-ḥāliyyah wa-li-aḥkām al-qaḍā' al-dawlī*. Cairo: Maṭbaʿat Nahḍat Miṣr, 1952, 555 pp.

Ghānim, Muḥammad Ḥāfiẓ, *Mabādi' al-qānūn al-dawlī al-ʿāmm*. Cairo: Dār al-Nahḍah al-Miṣriyyah, 1967, 800 pp.

al-Ghazālī, Abū Ḥāmid Muḥammad, *Iḥyā' ʿulūm al-dīn*, 4 vols. Cairo: Dār Iḥyā' al-Kutub al-ʿArabiyyah/ʿĪsā l-Bābī al-Ḥalabī, n.d.

Ghunaym, ʿĀdil Ḥasan, 'Al-Mu'tamar al-Islāmī al-ʿĀmm (1931)', *Shu'ūn Filas-*

ṭiniyyah 25 (Sept. 1973), pp. 119-136.
Ghunaym, ʿĀdil Ḥasan, 'Thawrat ʿIzz al-Dīn al-Qassām', *Shu'ūn Filasṭiniyyah* 6 (Jan. 1972), pp. 181-193.
al-Ghunaymī, Muḥammad Ṭalʿat, *Al-aḥkām al-ʿāmmah fī qānūn al-umam. Dirāsah fī kull min al-fikr al-gharbī wa-l-ishtirākī wa-l-Islāmī. Qānūn al-salām.* Alexandria: Munsha'at al-Maʿārif, 1970, 1237 pp.
Ḥadīdī, ʿAlī, *ʿAbd Allāh al-Nadīm, khaṭīb al-waṭaniyyah.* Cairo: Al-Mu'assasah al-Miṣriyyah al-ʿĀmmah, n.d., 399 pp.
al-Ḥaṭṭāb, Abū ʿAbd Allāh Muḥammad ibn Muḥammad al-Ṭarābulusī al-Maghribī, *Mawāhib al-djalīl li-sharḥ Mukhtaṣar Khalīl*, 6 vols. Tripoli: Maktabat al-Nadjāḥ, n.d.
al-Ḥawfī, Aḥmad Muḥammad, *Samāḥat al-Islām.* Cairo: Al-Madjlis al-Aʿlā li-l-Shu'ūn al-Islāmiyyah, 1383/1963, 248 pp. (Al-Taʿrīf bi-l-Islām, 6).
al-Ḥillī, Djaʿfar ibn al-Ḥasan – al-Muḥaqqiq al-Awwal, *Sharā'iʿ al-Islām fī masā'il al-ḥalāl wa-l-ḥarām*, 4 vols. Ed. by Abū l-Ḥusayn Muḥammad ʿAlī. Nadjaf: Maṭbaʿat al-Ādāb, 1389/1969.
Ḥusayn, Ṭāhā, *Ḥadīth al-Arbiʿā'*, 3 vols. Cairo: Dār al-Maʿārif, n.d.
Ḥusaynī, Isḥāq Mūsā, Ḥasan ʿAbd al-Ḥalīm and ʿAbd al-Ḥamīd al-Sā'iḥ, *Bayt al-Maqdis fī l-Islām.* Cairo: Madjmaʿ al-Buḥūth al-Islāmiyyah, 1379/1969, 128 pp. (Al-Buḥūth al-Islāmiyyah, 5).
Ibn ʿĀbidīn, Muḥammad Amīn, *Radd al-muḥtār ʿalā l-durr al-mukhtār sharḥ tanwīr al-abṣār*, 5 vols. Bulaq: Dār al-Ṭibāʿah al-Amīriyyah, 1299 [1882].
Ibn al-ʿArabī, Abū Bakr Muḥammad ibn ʿAbd Allāh, *Aḥkām al-qur'ān.* 4 vols. Cairo: ʿĪsā l-Bābī al-Ḥalabī, 1387/1967.
Ibn Djamāʿah, Badr al-Dīn Abū ʿAbd Allāh Muḥammad ibn Burhān al-Dīn Abī Isḥāq Ībrāhīm —, *Taḥrīr al-aḥkām fī tadbīr millat al-Islām.* Ed. by Hans Kofler. *Islamica* 6 (1934), pp. 349-411; 7 (1935), pp. 1-34. [Germ. transl. by Hans Kofler, *Islamica*, 7 (1935), pp. 35-64, Schlussheft (1938), pp. 18-130.]
Ibn Djuzayy, Abū l-Qāsim Muḥammad ibn Aḥmad —— al-Gharnāṭī al-Kalbī, *Al-qawānīn al-fiqhiyyah.* New and rev. impr., n.p., n.d., 350 pp.
Ibn Ḥazm, Abū Muḥammad ʿAlī ibn Aḥmad ibn Ṣaʿīd ——, *Kitāb al-fiṣal fī l-milal wa-ahwā' al-niḥal*, 5 vols. Cairo: Al-Maṭbaʿah al-Adabiyyah, 1318-20 [1900-03].
Ibn Ḥazm, Abū Muḥammad ʿAlī ibn Aḥmad ibn Ṣaʿīd ——, *Al-Muḥallā*, 11 vols. Beyrut: Al-Maktab al-Tidjārī, n.d.
Ibn Khaldūn, ʿAbd al-Raḥmān ibn Muḥammad ——, *Muqaddimah*, 4 vols. Ed. by ʿAlī ʿAbd al-Wāḥid Wāfī. 2nd ed., Cairo: Ladjnat al-Bayān al-ʿArabī, 1384/1965.
Ibn Manẓūr, Abū l-Faḍl Djamāl al-Dīn Muḥammad ibn Makram ——, *Lisān al-ʿArab*, 15 vols. Beyrut: Dār Ṣādir/Dār Beyrut, 1373/1955.
Ibn Qudāmah, Abū Muḥammad ʿAbd Allāh ibn Aḥmad ibn Muḥammad, *Al-mughnī ʿalā Mukhtaṣar al-Khiraqī*, 9 vols. Ed. by Ṭāhā Muḥammad al-Zaynī. Cairo: Maktabat al-Qāhirah, 1388/1968.

Ibn Rushd, Abū l-Walīd Muḥammad, *Kitāb al-muqaddamāt*, 2 vols. Cairo: Maṭbaʿat al-Saʿādah, 1325/1907.

Ibn Rushd, Abū l-Walīd Muḥammad al-Hafīd, *Bidāyat al-mudjtahid wa-nihāyat al-muqtaṣid*, 2 vols. 3rd ed., Cairo: Muṣṭafā l-Bābī al-Ḥalabī, 1379/1960.

Ibn Taymiyyah, Abū ʿAbbās Aḥmad, *Al-siyāsah al-sharʿiyyah fī iṣlāḥ al-rāʿī wa-l-raʿiyyah*. Ed. by Muḥammad Ibrāhīm al-Bannā and Muḥammad Aḥmad ʿĀshūr. Cairo: Dār al-Shaʿb, 1971, 191 pp.

Ibrāhīm, ʿAbd Allān ʿAlī, *Al-ṣirāʿ bayn al-Mahdī wa-l-ʿulamā'*. Khartoum: Shuʿbat Abḥāth al-Sūdān, Kulliyyat al-Ādāb, Djāmiʿat al-Kharṭūm, 1968, 64 pp.

ʿIllaysh, Abū ʿAbd Allāh Muḥammad, *Fatḥ al-ʿalī al-mālik fī l-fatwā ʿalā madhhab al-imām Mālik*, 2 vols. Cairo: Maṭbaʿat al-Taqaddum al-ʿIlmiyyah, 1319 [1901-02].

Kanafānī, Ghassān, 'Thawrat 1936-39 fī Filasṭīn. Khalfiyyat wa-tafāṣīl wa-taḥlīl'. *Shu'ūn Filasṭīniyyah* 6 (Jan. 1972), pp. 45-78.

al-Kayyālī, ʿAbd al-Wahhāb, *Wathā'iq al-muqāwamah al-Filasṭīniyyah ḍidd al-iḥtilāl al-Bariṭānī wa-l-Ṣahyūniyyah*. Beyrut: Mu'assasat al-Dirāsāt al-Filasṭīniyyah, 1968, 688 pp.

al-Kayyālī, ʿAbd al-Wahhāb, *Tārīkh Filasṭīn al-ḥadīth*. Beyrut: Al-Mu'assasah al-ʿArabiyyah li-l-Dirāsāt wa-l-Nashr, 1970, 472 pp.

Khalīl, Ibrāhīm al-Shaykh, 'Risālah min mudjāhid qadīm. Dhikrayāt ʿan al-Qassām', *Shu'ūn Filasṭīniyyah* 7 (March 1972), pp. 267-269.

Khallāf, ʿAbd al-Wahhāb, *Al-siyāsah al-sharʿiyyah aw niẓām al-dawlah al-Islāmiyyah fī l-shu'ūn al-dustūriyyah wa-l-khāridjiyyah wa-l-māliyyah*. Cairo: 1350 [1931-32], 148 pp.

al-Khaṭīb, ʿAbd al-Karīm, *Qaḍiyyat Filasṭīn. Ra'y al-Islām fīhā wa-mawqif al-Muslimīn minhā*. Cairo: Dār al-Fikr al-ʿArabī, 1967, 157 pp.

Khillah, Kāmil Maḥmūd, *Filasṭīn wa-l-intidāb al-Bariṭānī, 1922-1939*. Beyrut: Markaz al-Abḥāth, 1974, 566 pp.

al-Mahdī, Muḥammad al-ʿAbbāsī, *Al-fatāwā al-Mahdiyyah fī l-waqā'iʿ al-Miṣriyyah*, 7 vols. Cairo: Al-Maṭbaʿah al-Azhariyyah, 1301 [1883-84].

Maḥmūd ʿAbd al-Ḥalīm, *Al-ʿibādah. Aḥkām wa-asrār*, 2 vols. Cairo: Dār al-Kutub al-Ḥadīthah, 1388-89/1968-69.

Makhlūf, Ḥasanayn Muḥammad, *Fatāwā sharʿiyyah wa-buḥūth Islāmiyyah*, 2 vols. 2nd ed., Cairo: Muṣṭafā l-Bābī al-Ḥalabī, 1385/1965.

al-Marghīnānī, Abū l-Ḥasan ʿAlī ibn Abī Bakr ibn ʿAbd al-Djalīl, *Al-hidāyah sharḥ bidāyat al-mubtadi'*, 4 vols. Cairo: Muṣṭafā l-Bābī al-Ḥalabī, 1384/1965.

Maṭāmiʿ —— al-yahūd fī l-amākin al-muqaddasah bi-Filasṭīn. Cairo: Al-Hay'ah al-ʿArabiyyah al-ʿUlyā ri-Firaytin, n.d., 53 pp.

al-Māwardī, Abū l-Ḥasan ʿAlī ibn Muḥammad ibn Ḥabīb al-Baṣrī al-Baghdādī, *Al-aḥkām al-sulṭāniyyah wa-l-wilāyāt al-dīniyyah*. 2nd ed., Cairo: Muṣṭafā l-Bābī al-Ḥalabī, 1386/1966, 264 pp.

al-Mawwāq, Abū ʿAbd Allāh Muḥammad ibn Yūsuf al-Abdarī, *Al-tādj wa-l-iklīl li-Mukhtaṣar Khalīl*, 6 vols. Tripoli: Maktabat al-Nadjāḥ, n.d. [printed in the margin of al-Ḥaṭṭāb's *Mawāhib al-djalīl.*]

al-Muqaddasāt al-Islāmiyyah fī Filasṭīn. Al-āyāt al-qur'āniyyah wa-l-aḥādīth al-nabawiyyah fī bayān makānat Filasṭīn al-dīniyyah wa-qudsiyyatihā. Daʿwat al-Muslimīn kāffat[an] *ilā ḥimāyat muqaddasātihā wa-ṣadd al-ʿudwān al-yahūdī ʿanhā.* Cairo: Al-Hay'ah al-ʿArabiyyah al-ʿUlyā li-Filasṭīn/Al-Maṭbaʿah al-Salafiyya, 1370 [1950-51], 64 pp.

al-Naqqāsh, Salīm Khalīl, *Miṣr li-l-Miṣriyyīn*, 8 vols. Alexandria: Maṭbaʿat al-Djarīdah al-Maḥrūsah, 1302/1884.

al-Nawawī, Abū Zakariyā' Yaḥyā ibn Sharaf, *Minhādj al-ṭālibīn.* Ed. and transl. by L. W. C. van den Berg with Fr. title *Le guide des zélés croyants. Manuel de jurisprudence musulmane selon le rite de Châfiʿî*, 3 vols. Batavia: Imprimerie du Gouvernement, 1882-84.

al-Nuʿmān —— ibn Muḥammad al-Tamīmī *al-maʿrūf bi-*Qāḍī Nuʿmān, *Daʿā'im al-Islām wa-dhikr al-ḥalāl wa-l-ḥarām wa-l-qaḍāyā wa-l-aḥkām ʿan ahl bayt rasūl Allāh ʿalayh wa-ʿalayhim afḍal al-salām*, 2 vols. Ed. by Āṣāf ibn ʿAlī Aṣghar Fayḍī [= A. A. A. Fyzee] Cairo: Dār al-Maʿārif, 1370-79/1951-60.

Qāḍī Nuʿmān, *see under* al-Nuʿmān.

al-Qurṭubī, Abū ʿAbd Allāh Muḥammad ibn Aḥmad al-Anṣārī, *Al-djāmiʿ li-aḥkām al-qur'ān*, 20 vols. Cairo: Dār al-Kutub al-Miṣriyyah, 1354/1935.

Quṭb, Sayyid, *Ṭarīq al-daʿwah fī ẓilāl al-qur'ān.* Coll. and prep. by Aḥmad Fā'iz. 2nd ed., Beyrut: Dār al-Arqam, 1394/1974, 386 pp. [Contains a collection of treatises on the propagation of Islam, taken from Quṭb's Koran commentary *Fī ẓilāl al-qur'ān.*]

Quṭb, Sayyid, *Fī ẓilāl al-qur'ān*, 30 vols. 5th ed., Beyrut: Dār Iḥyā' al-Turāth al-ʿArabī, 1386/1967.

al-Rāfiʿī, ʿAbd al-Raḥmān, *Al-thawrah al-ʿUrābiyyah wa-l-iḥtilāl al-Inglīzi0* Cairo: Maṭbaʿat al-Nahḍah, 1355/1937, 583 pp.

Rashīd Riḍā, Muḥammad, *Tārīkh al-ustādh al-imām, al-shaykh Muḥammad ʿAbduh*, 3 vols. Cairo: Maṭbaʿat al-Manār, 1351/1931.

Rashīd Riḍā, Muḥammad, *Al-waḥy al-Muḥammadī.* 5th ed., Cairo: Dār al-Manār, 1375/1955, 270 pp.

Rashīd Riḍā, Muḥammad, *Fatāwā*, 6 vols. Coll. and ed. by Ṣalāḥ al-Dīn al-Munadjdjid and Yūsuf Q. Khūrī. Beyrut: Dār al-Kitāb al-Djadīd, 1390/1970.

Sābiq, al-Sayyid, *ʿAnāṣir al-quwwah fī l-Islām.* Cairo: Maktabat Wahbah, 1963, 240 pp.

Saḥnūn ibn Saʿīd al-Tanūkhī, *Al-mudawwanah al-kubrā*, 16 vols. Cairo: Maṭbaʿat al-Saʿādah, 1323 [1905-06].

al-Saʿīd, Rifʿat, *Al-asās al-idjtimāʿī li-l-thawrah al-ʿUrābiyyah.* Cairo: Dār al-Kūtus al-ʿArabī, 1387/1967, 258 pp.

al-Ṣaʿīdī, ʿAbd al-Mutaʿālī, *Fī maydān al-idjtihād. Tawdjīh djadīd li-l-idjtihād fī l-Islām.* Helwan: Djamʿiyyat al-Thaqāfah al-Islāmiyyah, n.d., 164 pp.

al-Ṣāliḥ, Ṣubḥī, *Al-nuẓum al-Islāmiyyah. Nash'atuhā wa-taṭawwuruhā.* Beyrut: Dār al-ʿIlm li-l-Malāyīn, 1375/1965, 608 pp.

Salīm, Aḥmad Mūsā, *Al-Islām wa-qaḍāyānā l-muʿāṣirah.* Cairo: Maktabat al-Qāhirah al-Ḥadīthah, n.d. [*c.* 1970], 293 pp.

Sarkīs, Yūsuf Ilyān, *Muʿdjam al-maṭbūʿāt al-ʿArabiyyah wa-l-muʿarrabah. Wa-huwa shāmil li-asmā' al-kutub al-maṭbūʿah fī l-aqṭār al-sharqiyyah wa-l-gharbiyyah. Wa-dhālika min yawm ẓuhūr al-ṭibāʿ ah ilā nihāyat al-sanah al-hidjriyyah 1399 al-muwāfiqah li-sanat 1919 M.* Cairo: 1346/1929, 2024 cols.

al-Shāfiʿī, Abū ʿAbd Allāh Muḥammad ibn Idrīs, *Kitāb al-umm fī furūʿ al-fiqh*, 7 vols. Bulaq: Al-Maṭbaʿah al-Kubrā al-Amīriyyah, 1321-25 [1903-08].

Shaltūt, Maḥmūd, *Min tawdjīhāt al-Islām.* Cairo: Dār al-Qalam, 1964, 581 pp.

Shaltūt, Maḥmūd, *Al-Islām ʿaqīdah wa-sharīʿah.* Cairo: Dār al-Fikr, n.d., 574 pp.

Shaykhzādeh, ʿAbd al-Raḥmān ibn Muḥammad, *Madjmaʿ al-abḥur sharḥ multaqā l-anhur li-Muḥammad Ibrāhīm al-Ḥalabī*, 2 vols. Istanbul: Dār al-ʿĀmirah li-l-Ṭibāʿah, 1301 [1883-84].

al-Shirwānī, ʿAbd al-Ḥamīd, *Ḥāshiyah ʿalā tuḥfat al-muḥtādj sharḥ al-minhādj li-Abī Zakariyā' Yaḥyā l-Nawawī*, 8 vols. Mecca: Al-Maṭbaʿah al-Mīriyyah, 1304-05 [1886-88].

Shuqayr, Naʿūm, *Tārīkh al-Sūdān al-qadīm wa-l-ḥadīth wa-djughrāfiyyatuh*, 3 vols. Cairo: Maṭbaʿat al-Maʿārif, n.d. [1903].

al-Ṭabarī, Muḥammad ibn Djarīr, *Kitāb ikhtilāf al-fuqahā'.* Ed. by Joseph Schacht. Leiden: E. J. Brill, 1933, xvi + 274 pp.

al-Tahānawī, Muḥammad Aʿlā ibn ʿAlī, *Kitāb kashshāf iṣṭilāḥāt al-funūn*, 2 vols. Ed. by Muḥammad Wadjīh, ʿAbd al-Ḥaqq and Ghulām Qādir. Calcutta: The Asiatic Society of Bengal, 1862.

al-Yahūd wa-l-Islām qadīm^{an} wa-ḥādīth^{an}. Al-Yahūd wa-Filasṭīn wa-āyāt al-djihād wa-l-aḥādth ʿanhu. Cairo: Maktab al-Istiʿlāmāt al-Filasṭīnī al-ʿArabī, 1937, 31 pp.

Yāqūt, Muḥammad Kāmil, *Al-shakhṣiyyah al-dawliyyah fī l-qānūn al-dawlī al-ʿāmm wa-l-sharīʿah al-Islāmiyyah.* Cairo: ʿĀlam al-Kutub, 1970-71, 785 + 14 pp.

Yāsīn, ʿAbd al-Qādir, *Kifāḥ al-shaʿb al-Filasṭīnī qabl al-ʿām 1948.* Beyrut: Markaz al-Abḥāth, 1975, 214 pp.

Yāsīn, Ṣubḥī, *Al-thawrah al-ʿArabiyyah al-kubrā fī Filasṭīn.* Cairo: Dār al-Kitāb al-ʿArabī, 1959, 240 pp.

Zakī, Muḥammad Saʿd al-Dīn, *Al-ḥarb wa-l-salām.* Cairo: 1965, 571 pp.

al-Zamakhsharī, Djār Allāh Maḥmūd ibn ʿUmar, *Al-kashshāf ʿan ḥaqā'iq al-tanzīl wa-ʿuyūn al-aqāwīl*, 4 vols. Cairo: Muṣṭafā l-Bābī al-Ḥalabī, 1966.

4. REFERENCES IN OTHER LANGUAGES

ʿAbd al-ʿAzīz, Shāh, *Fatāwā-yi ʿAzīzī*, 2 vols. Deoband, n.d.

Abu Lughod, Ibrahim, 'The transformation of the Egyptian elite. Preludes to the ʿUrabi revolt', *MEJ* 21 (1967), pp. 325-345.

Abun-Nasr, Jamil, *A History of the Maghreb*. Cambridge: Cambridge University Press, 1971, 416 pp.

Ageron, Charles-Robert, 'L'émigration des Musulmans algériens et l'exode de Tlemcen', *Annales. Économies, sociétés, civilisation* 22 (1967), pp. 1047-1068.

Ageron, Charles-Robert, *Les Algériens musulmans et la France*, 2 vols. Paris: Presses Universitaires de France, 1968.

Ahmad, Abdelhamid Muhammad, *Die Auseinandersetzung zwischen al-Azhar und der modernistischen Bewegung in Agypten*. Hamburg, 1963.

Ahmad, Aziz, *Studies in Islamic Culture in the Indian Environment*. London, etc.: Oxford University Press, 1964, 311 pp.

Ahmad, Aziz, 'Mawdudi and orthodox fundamentalism in Pakistan', *MEJ* 21 (1967), pp. 369-380.

Ahmad, Aziz, *Islamic Modernism in India and Pakistan, 1857-1964*. London, etc.: Oxford University Press, 1967, 294 pp.

Ahmad, Aziz and G. E. von Grunebaum, *Muslim Self-statement in India and Pakistan, 1857-1968*. Wiesbaden: Harrassowitz, 1970, 240 pp.

Ahmad, Qeyamuddin, *The Wahabi Movement in India*. Calcutta, Mukhopadhyay, 1966, 391 pp.

Ali, Ameer, *A Critical Exposition of the Life and the Teachings of Mohammed*. London, etc.: Williams and Norgate, 1873, 346 pp.

Antonius, George, *The Arab Awakening*. 5th ed., New York, Capricorn Books, 1965, 471 pp.

Arnold, T. W., *The Caliphate*. 2nd ed., London: Routledge and Kegan Paul, 1965, 267 pp.

ʿAzzam, ʿAbd-al-Rahman, *The Eternal Message of Muhammad*. Transl. from the Ar. by Caesar E. Farah. New York: A Mentor Book, 1965, 254 pp. [Engl. transl. of ʿAbd al-Raḥmān ʿAzzām *Al-risālah al-khālidah*.]

Baer, Gabriel, *Studies in the Social History of Modern Egypt*. Chicago, etc.: The University of Chicago Press, 1969, 259 pp.

Baljon, J. M. S., *The Reforms and Religious Ideas of Sir Sayyid Ahmad Khan*. Leiden: Brill, 1949, 101 pp.

Bari, Abdul, 'The Farā'iḍī Movement.' In: *Proceedings of the Pakistan History Conference* (5th session). Karachi: 1955, pp. 197-208.

Bari, Muhammad Abdul, 'The politics of Sayyid Ahmad Barelwi', *IC* 31 (1957), pp. 156-164.

Bell, R., *The Qur'ān translated with a critical rearrangement of the Sūrah's*, 2 vols. Edinburgh, 1939.

Berg, L. W. C. van den, *see under* al-Nawawī, *Minhādj al-Ṭālibīn*.
Berque, Jacques, *L'Égypte. Impérialisme et révolution*. Paris: Gallimard, 1967, 746 pp.
Bilmen, Ömer Nasuhi, *Hukuki Islamiyye ve Istılahatı fıkhiyye kamusu*, 6 vols. Istanbul: Istanbul Üniversitesi Hukuk Fakültesi, 1949-52.
Binder, Leonard, *Religion and Politics in Pakistan*. Berkeley, etc.: University of California Press, 1961, 440 pp.
Borthwick, Bruce Mayard, *The Islamic Sermon as a Channel of Political Communication in Syria, Jordan and Egypt*. University of Michigan, 1965, 209 pp. (Ph.D. thesis, typewritten).
Briggs, F. S., 'The Indian Hijrat of 1920', *MW* 20 (1930), pp. 164-168.
Brown, Leon Carl, 'The Sudanese Mahdiya'. In: Robert I. Rotberg and Ali A. Mazrui (eds.), *Protest and Power in Black Africa*. New York: Oxford University Press, 1970, pp. 145-168.
Brugman, Jan, *De betekenis van het Mohammedaanse recht in het hedendaagse Egypte*. The Hague: 1960, 215 pp.
Brunschvig, R., 'Averroes juriste'. In: *Études d'orientalisme dédiées à la mémoire de Lévi-Provençal*, 2 vols. Paris: Maisonneuve, 1962, Vol. 1, pp. 35-68.
Carré, Olivier, *L'idéologie Palestinienne de résistance*. Analyse de textes, 1964-1970. Paris: Colin, 1972, 164 pp. (Travaux et recherches de science politique, 20.)
Carré, Olivier, 'Le contenu socio-économico-politique des manuels d'enseignement religieux musulman dans l'Égypte actuelle', *REI*, 38 (1970), pp. 87-126.
Carré, Olivier, *Enseignement islamique et idéal socialiste. Analyse conceptuelle des manuels d'instruction musulmane en Égypte*. Beyrut: Dar al-Machreq, 1974, 330 pp. (Publ. du Centre Culturel Universitaire. Hommes et Sociétés du Proche-Orient, 6).
Churchill, Charles Henry, *La vie d'Abd el-Kader*. Transl. from the Engl. by Michel Hobart. 2nd ed., Algiers: SNED, 1974, 353 pp.
Dekmejian, Richard H. and Margaret J. Wyszomirski, 'Charismatic leadership in Islam: The Mahdi of the Sudan', *Comparative Studies in Society and History* 14 (1972), pp. 193-214.
Depont, Octave and Xavier Coppolani, *Les confréries religieuses musulmanes*. Algiers: Jourdan, 1897.
Dietrich, E. L., 'Der Mahdi Mohammed Ahmed vom Sudan nach arabischen Quellen', *Der Islam* 14 (1925), pp. 199-288.
Edwardes, M., *British India 1772-1947. A Survey of the Nature and Effects of Alien Rule*. London: Sidgwick and Jackson, 1967, 396 pp.
Elsschot, Willem, 'Lijmen'. In: *Verzameld Werk*. 6th ed., Amsterdam: P. N. van Kampen en Zn, 1963, pp. 251-362.
Émerit, Marcel, 'L'Algérie à l'époque d'Abd el-Kader', *Revue de l'Histoire Moderne et Contemporaine*, 1 (1954), pp. 199-213.
Émerit, Marcel, 'L'état d'esprit des musulmans d'Algérie de 1847 à 1870', *Revue*

de l'Histoire Moderne et Contemporaine 8 (1961), pp. 265-276.
Estailleur-Chanteraine, P. d', *L'Émir magnanime Abd el-Kader le Croyant*. Paris: 1959, 220 pp.
Faruqi, Ziya-ul-Hasan, *The Deoband School and the Demand for Pakistan*. London: Asia Publishing House, 1963, 148 pp.
Fattal, Antoine, *Le statut légal des non-musulmans en pays d'Islam*. Beyrut: Imprimerie Catholique, 1958, 394 pp. (Recherches publ. sous la direction de l'Institut des Lettres Orientales de Beyrouth, 10).
Foda, Ezzeldin, *The Projected Arab Court of Justice. A Study in Regional Jurisdiction with Specific Reference to the Muslim Law of Nations*. The Hague: Martinus Nijhoff, 1957, 258 pp.
Gallissot, René, 'Abd el-Kader et la nationalité algérienne', *Revue Historique*, 233 (1965), pp. 233-268.
Gallissot, René, 'La guerre d'Abd el-Kader ou la ruine de la nationalité algérienne', *Hespéris-Thamuda* 5 (1964), pp. 119-141.
Gallissot, René, 'L'Algérie pré-coloniale'. In: *Sur le féodalisme*. Paris: Centre d'Études et de Recherches Marxistes, 1974, pp. 147-179.
Galwash, Ahmad A., *The Religion of Islam*, 2 vols. Cairo: The Supreme Council of Islamic Affairs, n.d. (Studies in Islam.)
Gibb. H. A. R., 'The Islamic Congress of Jerusalem in December 1931'. In: A. J. Toynbee, *Survey of International Affairs 1934*. London, etc.: Oxford University Press, 1935, pp. 94-105.
Gopal, Ram, *Indian Muslims. A Political History (1858-1947)*. London: Asian Publishing House, 1959, 351 pp.
Haarmann, Ulrich, 'Die Pflichten des Muslims. Dogma und geschichtliche Wirklichkeit', *Saeculum* 26 (1975), pp. 95-110.
Hardy, P., *The Muslims of British India*. Cambridge: Cambridge University Press, 1972, 306 pp.
Hill, Richard, *Egypt in the Sudan, 1820-1881*. London, etc.: Oxford University Press, 1959, 188 pp.
History, The Cambridge —— of Islam, 2 vols. Ed. by P. M. Holt, Ann K. S. Lambton and Bernard Lewis. Cambridge: Cambridge University Press, 1970.
Holt, P. M., 'Modernization and reaction in nineteenth century Sudan'. In: P. M. Holt, *Studies in the History of the Near East*. London: Frank Cass, 1973, pp. 135-148.
Holt, P. M., *The Mahdist State in the Sudan, 1881-1898. A Study of its Origins and Overthrow*. 2nd ed., London, etc.: Oxford University Press, 1970, 225 pp.
Hopwood, Derek, 'A pattern of revival movements in Islam', *IQ* 15 (1971), pp. 149-158.
Islâm —— Ansiklopedisi. Istanbul: Millî Egitim Basımevi, 1940 seq.
[Ismāʿil, Shāh], *Ṣirāṭ-i mustaqim*. N.p., n.d., 180 pp.
Jansen, J. J. C., *The Interpretation of the Koran in Modern Egypt*. Leiden: E. J.

Brill, 1974, 114 pp.

Jomier, J., *Le commentaire coranique du Manār*. Paris: Maisonneuve, 1954, 357 pp.

Julien, Ch.-A., *Histoire de l'Algérie contemporaine. La conquête et les debuts de la colonisation (1827-1871)*. Paris: Presses Universitaires de France, 1964, 632 pp.

Karim, M. Nurul, 'Part played by Haji Sharīᶜatullah and his son in the socio-political history of East Bengal'. In: *Proceedings of the Pakistan History Conference* (5th session). Karachi: 1955, pp. 175-182.

Khadduri, Majid and Herbert J. Liebesny, *Law in the Middle East*. Vol. 1: *Origin and Development of Islamic Law*. Washington: The Middle East Institute, 1955, 395 pp.

Khaled, Leila, *Mein Volk soll leben. Autobiographie einer Revolutionärin*. Ed. by George Hajjar. Munich: Trikont Verlag, 1974, 184 pp.

Khan, Muᶜin-ud-Din Ahmad, *History of the Farā'iḍī Movement in Bengal (1818-1906)*. Karachi: Pakistan Historical Society, 1965, cxviii + 169 pp.

Kofler, Hans, *see under* Ibn Djamāᶜah.

Lacoste, Y., A. Nouschi and A. Prenant, *L'Algérie, passé et présent. Le cadre et les étapes de la constitution de l'Algérie actuelle*. Paris: Éds Sociales, 1960, 462 pp.

Laffin, John, *The Arab Mind*. London: Cassell and Collier Macmillan, 1975.

Lesch, A. M., 'The Palestine Arab nationalist movement under the Mandate'. In: William B. Quandt, a.o., —— *The Politics of Palestinian Nationalism*. Berkeley, etc.: University of California Press, 1973, pp. 5-43.

Løkkegaard, F., *Islamic Taxation in the Classic Period with Special Reference to the Circumstances in Iraq*. Copenhagen: Branner og Korch, 1950, 213 pp.

Maddison, Angus, *Class Structure and Economic Growth in India and Pakistan since the Moghuls*. London: Allen and Unwin, 1971, 181 pp.

Majumdar, R. C., *The Sepoy Mutiny and the Revolt of 1857*. 2nd ed., Calcutta: Mukhopadhyay, 1963, 503 pp.

May, Lini S., *The Evolution of Indian-Muslim Thought after 1857*. Lahore: Sh. Muhammad Ashraf, 1970, 488 pp.

Michaux-Bellaire, E., 'Traduction de la Fetoua du Faqih ᶜAly Et Tsouli contenant le "Souāl" de Hādj Abdelqāder ben Mahi ed Dīn et la response', *Archives Marocaines* 11 (1907), pp. 116-128, 395-454; 15 (1909), pp. 158-184.

Mitchell, R. P., *The Society of Muslim Brothers*. London, etc.: Oxford University Press, 1969, 347 pp.

Mujeeb, M., *The Indian Muslims*. 2nd ed., London: Allen and Unwin, 1969, 590 pp.

Nadir, Ahmed, 'Les ordres religieuses et la conquête française (1830-1851)', *Revue Algérienne des Sciences Juridiques, Économiques et Politiques*, 9 (1972), pp. 819-873.

Niemeijer, A. C., *The Khilafat Movement in India, 1919-1924*. The Hague: Martinus Nijhoff, 1972, 263 pp. (Verh. KITLV, 62).

Nizami, K. A., 'Muslim political thought and activity in India during the first half of the 19th century', *Studies in Islam* 4 (1967), pp. 97-113, 139-162.

Nys, E., *Les origines de droit international.* Brussels, 1894.

Nys, E., 'Le droit des gens dans les rapports des Arabes et des Byzantins'. In: E. Nys, *Études de droit international public et droit politique.* Brussels: Alfred Castaigne, 1896, pp. 46-74.

Ochsenwald, William L., 'Arab Muslims and the Palestine problem', *MW* 66 (1976), pp. 287-296.

Oppenheim, L., 'International Law. A Treatise', 2 vols. Ed. by H. Lauterpacht. London, etc.: Longman, Green, 1955.

Owen, Roger, 'Egypt and Europe: From French expedition to British Occupation'. In: Roger Owen and Bob Sutcliffe (eds.), *Studies in the Theory of Imperialism.* London: Longman, 1972, pp. 195-208.

Palestine. —— A Study of Jewish, Arab and British Policies, 2 vols. Publ. for the ESCO Foundation for Palestine, Inc. New Haven, etc.: Yale University Press, 1947.

Pareja, F. M., A. Bausani and L. Hertling, *Islamologia.* Rome: Orbis Catholicus, 1951, xv + 842 pp.

Paret, R., 'Lā ikrāha fī-d-dīn. Toleranz oder Resignation', *Der Islam* 45 (1969), pp. 299-301.

Peters, Rudolph, 'Recente discussies rond de Islamitische vastenmaand, Ramadan', *Internationale Spectator* (The Hague) 23 (1969), pp. 1812-1825.

Peters, Rudolph and Gert J. J. de Vries, 'Apostasy in Islam', *WI*, n.s. 17 (1976-77), pp. 1-25.

Porath, Yehoshua, *The Emergence of the Palestinian-Arab National Movement, 1918-1929.* London: Frank Cass and Co., 1974, 406 pp.

Porath, Yehoshua, *The Palestinian Arab National Movement, 1929-1939. From Riots to Rebellion.* London: Frank Cass and Co., 1977, 414 pp.

Pritchard, E. E. Evans, *The Sanusi of Cyrenaica.* London, etc.: Oxford University Press, 1949, 240 pp.

Pütter, K. Th., *Beiträge zur Völkerrechts Geschichte und Wissenschaft.* Leipzig: Adolph Wienbrack, 1843, 219 pp.

Qureshi, Ishtiaq Husain, *The Muslim Community of the Indo-Pakistan Subcontinent, 610-1947. A Brief Historical Analysis.* The Hague: Mouton, 1962, 334 pp.

Rehatsek, E., 'The history of the Wahhabys in Arabia and India', *Journal of the Bombay Branch of the Royal Asiatic Society* 14 (1878-80), pp. 274-401.

Report, The —— of the Palestine Inquiry Commission on the Palestine Disturbances of August, 1929 (Shaw-report). London: H.M. Stationery Office, 1930, Cmd 3530.

Rodinson, Maxime, *Islam and Capitalism.* Transl. from the French by Brian Pearce. London: Allen Lane, 1974, 296 pp.

Sanhoury, A., *Le califat. Son évolution vers une Société des Nations Orientale.* Paris: Paul Geuthner, 1926, 627 pp. (Travaux du Séminaire Oriental d'Études

Juridiques et Sociales, 4).
Schacht, Joseph, *An Introduction to Islamic Law.* London, etc.: Oxford University Press, 1964, 304 pp.
Schölch, Alexander, Ägypten den Ägyptern! Die politische und gesellschaftliche Krise der Jahre 1878-1882 in Ägypten. Zürich, etc.: Atlantis Verlag [1972], 396 pp.
Sen, Surendra Nath, *Eighteen Fifty Seven.* Calcutta: Government of India Press, 1957, 468 pp.
Shaw-Report, *see under* Report of the Palestine Inquiry Commission.
Shinar, Pessah, "ʿAbd al-Qādir and ʿAbd al-Krīm. Religious influences on their thought and action', *Asian and African Studies* 1 (1965), pp. 139-174.
Simpson, John Hope, *Palestine. Report on Immigration, Land Settlement and Development.* London: H.M. Stationery Office, 1930, Cmd 3686.
Sivers, Peter von, 'The Realm of Justice. Apocalyptic revolts in Algeria (1849-1879)', *Humaniora Islamica* (The Hague) 1 (1973), pp. 47-60.
Smith, Wilfred Cantwell, *Modern Islam in India. A Social Analysis.* 2nd ed., London: Gollancz, 1946, 344 pp.
Smith, Wilfred Cantwell, *Islam in Modern History.* New York, etc.: A Mentor Book, 1959, 319 pp.
Snouck Hurgronje, C., *Verspreide Geschriften*, 7 vols. Bonn/Leiden: Kurt Schroeder Verlag/E. J. Brill, 1923-27.
Snouck Hurgronje, C., *De Atjehers*, 2 vols. Batavia/Leiden: Landsdrukkerij/ E. J. Brill, 1894.
Spear, Percival, *India. A Modern History.* Rev. and enl. ed. Ann Arbor: The University of Michigan Press, 1970, 511 + xix pp.
Steppat, Fritz, 'Kalifat, Dar al-Islam und die Loyalität der Araber bei Hanafitischen Juristen des 19. Jahrhunderts'. In: *Actes du Vᵉ Congrès de l'Union Européenne d'Arabisants et d'Islamisants (Brussels, 1970).* Brussels: Centre pour l'Étude des Problèmes du Monde Musulman Contemporain, 1971, pp. 456-460.
Taube, Baron Michel de, 'Le monde de l'Islam et son influence sur l'Europe orientale', *Académie de Droit International. Recueil des Cours* 11 (1926), No. 1, pp. 380-397.
Trimingham, J. Spencer, *Islam in the Sudan.* London, etc.: Oxford University Press, 1949, 280 pp.
Vinogradof, Amal, 'The 1920 revolt in Iraq reconsidered. The role of the tribes in national politics', *IJMES* 3 (1972), pp. 123-139.
Waines, David, 'The failure of nationalist resistance.' In: Ibrahim Abu Lughod (ed.), *The Transformation of Palestine.* Evanstone: North West University Press, 1971, pp. 207-237.
Watt, W. Montgomery, *Muhammad in Medina.* London, etc.: Oxford University Press, 1956, 418 pp.

Wensinck, A. J., a.o., *Concordance et indices de la tradition musulmane*, 7 vols. Leiden: E. J. Brill, 1936-69.

Williams, John Alden (ed.), *Themes of Islamic Civilization*. Berkeley, etc.: University of California Press, 1971, 382 pp.

Wingate, F. R., *Mahdiism and the Egyptian Sudan. Being an Account of the Rise and Progress of Mahdiism and the Subsequent Events in the Sudan in the Present Time*. 2nd ed., London: Frank Cass and Co., 1968, 617 pp.

Ziadeh, Nicola A., *Sanūsiya. A study of a Revivalist Movement in Islam*. Leiden: E. J. Brill, 1958, 148 pp.

Index of Names and Subjects

Index of Koranic Verses

Religion and Society

1. *Ibn Taimīya's Struggle against Popular Religion.*
With an Annotated Translation of his
Kitāb iqtiḍā' aṣ-ṣirāṭ al-mustaqīm mukhālafat aṣḥāb al-jaḥīm
by Muhammad Umar Memon
(*University of Wisconsin*)

2. *Tibetan Religious Dances.*
Tibetan Text and Annotated Translation of the 'chams yig
by René de Nebesky-Wojkowitz
With an Appendix by Walter Graf
Edited by Christoph von Fürer-Haimendorf

3. *Johann Christian Edelmann.*
From Orthodoxy to Enlightenment,
by Walter Grossmann
(*University of Massachusetts*)

4. *Sharastānī on the Indian Religions,*
by Bruce B. Lawrence
(*Duke University*)
With a Preface by Franz Rosenthal

5. *The Precarious Organisation.*
Sociological Explorations of the Church's Mission and Structure
by Mady A. Thung
With a Foreword by C. J. Lammers

6. *The Many Faces of Murukan.*
The History and Meaning of a South Indian God
by Fred W. Clothey
(*Boston University*)

7. *Divine Word and Prophetic Word in Early Islam.*
A Reconsideration of the Sources, with Special Reference to the Divine Saying or Hadîth Qudsî
by William A. Graham
(*Harvard University*)

9. *Danseurs dans le désert.*
Une étude de dynamique sociale
par Johan van Kessel
With a summary in English

10. *Redemptive Suffering in Islām.*
A Study of the Devotional Aspects of 'Āshūrā' in Twelver Shī'ism
by Mahmoud Ayoub
(*University of Toronto*)

11. *American Catholic Leadership. A Decade of Turmoil 1966–1976.*
A Sociological Analysis of the National Federation of Priests' Councils
by James H. Stewart
(*St. Olaf College, Northfield, Minnesota*)

12. *Korean Shamanistic Rituals*
by Jung Young Lee
(*University of North Dakota*)

13. *Symbols of Ancient Egypt in the Late Period (21st Dynastie)*
by Beatrice L. Goff
(*Yale University*)

14. *Orthodoxie religieuse et sciences humaines*
    by Jean-Pierre Deconchy
    (*Université Paris VII*)

15. *From Lordship to Stewardship. Religion and Social Change in Malta*
    by Mario Vassallo
    (*University of Malta*)

16. *From Temple to Meeting House*
    by Harold W. Turner
    (*University of Aberdeen*)

17. *Self and Non-Self in Early Buddhism*
    by Joaquín Pérez-Remón
    (*Universidad de Deusto, Bilbao*)

18. *The Alternative Tradition. A Study of Unbelief in the Ancient World*
    by James Thrower
    (*University of Aberdeen*)

19. *Official and Popular Religion. Analysis of a Theme for Religious Studies*
    ed. by P. H. Vrijhof and J. Waardenburg
    (*University of Utrecht*)

MOUTON PUBLISHERS · THE HAGUE · PARIS · NEW YORK

mouton paperpack religion

*Jihad (in the sense of 'Holy War', lit. 'exerting oneself to th
utmost') has always been considered a salient feature of Islam b
Western observers. The present book scrutinizes the role of the do
trine of jihad in the confrontation between Islam and Wester
colonialism in the Arab world during the 19th and 20th centurie
Anti-colonial resistance, especially during the first stages of Euro
pean expansion into the Islamic world, was often inspired by reli
gion and armed struggle was waged under the banner of jiha
Later, however, when secular nationalist ideologies began t
dominate anti-colonial struggle, proclamations of jihad becam
more part of ordinary war propaganda.*
*Modernist Muslim intellectuals have reinterpreted the doctrine o
jihad, in the sense of Holy War, arguing that it concerns essen
tially defensive warface. The classical notions of jihad, howeve
have not disappeared entirely and occupy a significant place in th
ideology of religiously motivated militant groups.*

ISBN 3 11 0100223

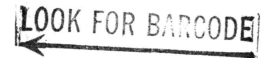